lonely planet

COSTA RICA

Mara Vorhees, Robert Isenberg,
Elizabeth Lavis, Janna Zinzi

Ride the waves and relax in the sand. Make sense of the present by learning about the pre-Columbian and colonial past. Pump that adrenaline with hiking, rafting or ziplining adventures. Energize your taste buds with coffee and chocolate. Be amazed by awesome volcanoes. Soak up the markets and museums of the bustling capital. Retreat to the family *fincas* (farms) in the countryside. Immerse yourself in wildlife and wilder landscapes. Refresh your body and mind at gushing cascades.

This is Costa Rica.

TURN THE PAGE AND START PLANNING
YOUR NEXT BEST TRIP →

Northern Highlands & Lowlands 112
San José & the Central Valley 42
Caribbean Coast 82
Peninsula de Nicoya 136
Central Pacific Coast 182
Southern Costa Rica & Peninsula de Osa 208

Experience Costa Rica online

Meet our writers

Mara Vorhees
@mara_vorhees

Mara is always amazed at how tiny Costa Rica packs in so much adventure, wildlife and *pura vida*. On this visit, her favorite experience was taking a night hike with her 12-year-old twins and spotting the endangered Baird's tapir (p146). Follow their adventures at *havetwinswilltravel.com*.

Robert Isenberg

Robert Isenberg is a writer and multimedia producer who lives in Rhode Island with his family. Find more of his work at *robertisenberg.net*.

Elizabeth Lavis

Elizabeth Lavis has lived and worked all over Costa Rica, Thailand and Georgia, and traveled extensively in Southeast Asia, South America and Europe. You can find her trekking through the Andes mountains or chilling out on Costa Rica's Pacific coast. Read her work in *American Way* magazine, *Huffington Post*, *Canadian Traveller* and Lonely Planet.

Janna Zinzi
wanderwomxntravels

Janna A. Zinzi (jaz) is a travel and culture writer, and co-founder of WanderWomxn, which centers the travel adventures of women and femmes of color.

Puma (p212)

PREVIOUS SPREAD: WORLDTRAVELER_1/SHUTTERSTOCK

Contents

JURATEBUIVIENE/SHUTTERSTOCK

Playa Cocles (p99)

ESSAYS

VISUAL GUIDES

Costa Rica has about 212km of coastline on the Caribbean and more than 1000km on the Pacific.

The first 50m of shoreline (above the high-tide mark) are public property. Consequently, Costa Rica has no private beaches; all are accessible to the public.

SAND & **SURF**

With nearly 1300km of tropical coastline, Costa Rica attracts wave riders of all abilities to its warm waters and big surf. Some famous spots are for experts only, while more benign surf is better for beginners. Of course, surfing isn't the only attraction on these shores: many beaches offer placid waters and soft sand that are perfect for swimming and leisurely lounging.

JORGE A. RUSSELL/SHUTTERSTOCK

Left Playa Carrillo (p175)
Right Surfer Merary Jiménez
Below Isla Tortuga (p167)

→ SURF SEASONS

Find the biggest waves on the Pacific Coast from May to October, while the Caribbean side is great for surfing from November to May.

LEARN TO SURF

Surf camps are plentiful on Península de Nicoya and are an immersive way to learn to surf. Beginners and pros can level up their skills in seven to 10 days.

▶ Learn to ride the waves (p169)

RIGHT: NICOLA STRONA/ALAMY
LEFT: JONATHAN GREGSON/LONELY PLANET

↑ BABY TURTLES BONANZA

The Península de Nicoya is one of the few places you can see an *arribada* (a mass turtle hatching). Thousands of sea turtles are born and swim out to sea.

▶ Witness an *arribada* and learn how you can help protect sea turtles (p161)

Best Beach Experiences

- **Ride the Caribbean waves like a local at Playa Cocles in Puerto Viejo.** (p98)
- **Sunbathe under swaying palm trees at Playa Carrillo.** (p175)
- **Cheer for the country's best at a sunset surf competition on Playa Hermosa.** (p202)
- **Visit Costa Rica's most popular surf destination, Tamarindo.** (p170)

TAKE A TRIP **BACK IN TIME**

Historical sights many not be high on the list of things to do in Costa Rica. But history buffs will be surprised and delighted by the country's rich and diverse past – from pre-Columbian archaeology to colonial-era architecture to battles to protect and preserve an independent Costa Rica.

→ ANCIENT ARCHAEOLOGY

Diquís spheres are perfectly symmetrical yet mysterious stones created by Costa Rica's pre-Columbian societies. They have become a symbol of indigenous culture and history.

▶ Learn about Costa Rica's pre-Columbian history at Sitio Arqueológico Finca 6 (p219).

MARCO DIAZ SEGURA/SHUTTERSTOCK

Left Museo Nacional (p51), San José
Right Diquís spheres (p219)
Below Bellavista Military Barracks (p51)

WHO WAS JUAN SANTAMARÍA?

Juan Santamaría was a drummer in the Costa Rican army, who heroically burned down the enemy stronghold, leading to victory in the Fillibuster War against US mercenaries.

▶ Get to know Costa Rica's war hero Juan Santamaría (p59)

RIGHT: ADVENTURE-MAX/ALAMY
LEFT: MABELIN SANTOS/ALAMY

↑ FROM BARRACKS TO MUSEUM

Once the national army headquarters, the Bellavista Military Barracks became a house of culture and learning after the military was abolished. It now houses the Museo Nacional.

▶ Wander the exhibits of the Museo Nacional (p51)

Best History Experiences

▶ **Engage with Costa Rica's past through archaeological artifacts and pre-Columbian art at Museo del Jade and the Museo del Oro Precolombino.** (p49)

▶ **View mystical pre-Columbian stone spheres at the Finca 6 UNESCO World Heritage Site.** (p219)

▶ **Connect with the Boruca tribe's powerful history and culture at Museo Comunitario Indígena de Boruca.** (p217)

▶ **Learn about Costa Rica's most beloved war hero at Museo Histórico Cultural Juan Santamaría.** (p59)

EXTREME EXCURSIONS

Costa Rica is a small country but the landscape is varied, offering every sort of outdoor adventure for a wide range of skill levels. There are mountains to climb and valleys to wander. Rivers beckon for whitewater rafting. And everywhere, vast expanses of forest and farms are ripe for exploration, whether on foot, by bike or flying through the air on a zipline.

Left Zipline, Santa Elena (p133)
Right Mountain biking, Heredia (p63)
Below Whale shark (p219)

→ EXTREME BIKING

Mountains aren't just for hiking; bikers are welcome too. The Central Valley has numerous trails and adventure parks catering both to beginners and more experienced riders.

▶ Explore the many mountain bike trails (p63)

NATURE'S CHARM/SHUTTERSTOCK

WHITE-WATER SEASON

Generally speaking, heavy rain results in fast rivers. So the most challenging white-water rafting takes place toward the end of the rainy season.

▶ You can't beat riding the rapids on the Río Sarapiquí (p131)

RIGHT: WILDESTANIMAL/SHUTTERSTOCK
LEFT: JAN CSERNOCH/ALAMY

↑ SWIM WITH SHARKS

Snorkelers and divers come to Isla del Caño for the crystal-clear visibility and extreme biodiversity, including sharks, sea turtles and octopuses.

▶ Dive into the crystal waters of Isla del Caño (p219)

Best Extreme Experiences

▶ **Summit Cerro Chirripó, Costa Rica's highest peak.** (p214)

▶ **Soar through the cloud forest in Santa Elena on the longest zipline in Latin America.** (p133)

▶ **Ride the rapids and swim in the natural pools of Río Sarapiquí.** (p131)

Hike to La Leona Waterfall for cliff jumping and cavern crawling, in addition to waterfall swimming. (p143)

1,365,000 60kg bags of coffee are produced annually.

Costa Rica produces 1% of the world's coffee.

Cacao beans were used as currency as recently as the 1930s.

CAFFEINE **FIX**

Costa Rica's highlands provide ideal conditions for growing coffee beans – the country's most important agricultural commodity since the early 19th century. Meanwhile, the humid tropical climate is perfect for growing cacao fruit, cultivated for centuries by indigenous communities. Visit local *fincas* (farms) to learn about the enduring role of these products in the economy, culture and cuisine.

Best Coffee & Cacao Experiences

- **Discover how little red berries become coffee at Mi Cafecito coffee cooperative in San Miguel de Sarapiquí.** (p137)
- **Take a tour and sip coffee at Coopedota, a coffee cooperative based in Santa Maria.** (p213)
- **Learn about indigenous traditions and the cacao plant in Térraba.** (p216)

Participate in the chocolate-making process at Finca Köbö near Puerto Jiménez. (p229)

Volcán Rincón de la Vieja
Costa Rica's most recent major eruption (2022)

National geothermal capacity
13% to 15% of the power grid

Number of active volcanoes
Five

WOLLERTZ/SHUTTERSTOCK

VOLCANO **VACATION**

In Northern Costa Rica, the Cordillera de Guanacaste and the Cordillera Central are lined up in a row of hissing, sputtering, steaming volcanoes, bubbling with geothermic energy. Five of these mighty mountains are active volcanoes, but even the dormant ones show off their volcanic powers. Come to witness the tempestuous displays in the form of fumaroles, boiling mud pots and hot springs.

Best Volcano Experiences

- **Hike up hardened lava flow for epic views of Volcán Arenal.** (p118)
- **Visit Volcán Irazú, Costa Rica's highest volcano.** (p63)
- **Submerge your body in natural thermal pools and flowing turquoise rivers at Volcán Rincon de la Vieja.** (p140)
- **Witness a steaming volcanic lake at Volcán Poás.** (pictured above; p63)

San José rainfall
It rains 170 days of the year

Metro area population
1.8 million

La Sabana Park
Once was an international airport

HEMIS/ALAMY

CITY **SLICKERS**

San José is a densely packed city with traffic, markets, museums, live music, universities and more. It is a startling and intriguing interlude in this country so celebrated for its nature and tranquility. Spend a few days in the Costa Rican capital to sample its unexpected urban culture.

Best City Slickers Experiences

- **Eat your way around Barrio Escalante and Escazú to sample excellent international and creative Tico fare.** (p54)
- **Browse the historic Mercado Central for artisan crafts and souvenirs.** (p61)
- **Meander around local artists' exhibits and outdoor sculptures at Museo de Arte Costarricense.** (p50)

RURAL & RUSTIC

As many Tico farmers embrace organic agricultural practices, they are eager to show off how they work and what they have learned. All around the country, you are invited to tour family *fincas* to discover how small-time farmers are doing their part to save the planet (and how you can too).

LEFT: MASSIMILIANO FINZI/SHUTTERSTOCK; BOTTOM: JOHN COLETTI/GETTY IMAGES

WALK ACROSS THE COUNTRY!

The ultimate rural Costa Rica experience is hiking **El Camino de Costa Rica**, a two-week, 280km, coast-to-coast route that connects local villages.

▶ Immerse yourself in the ultimate Costa Rican hike (p93)

Best Rural & Rustic Experiences

▶ **Learn indigenous Bribrí farming techniques outside Cahuita.** (p96)

▶ **Be a cowboy for a day at Rancho La Merced, a working cattle ranch.** (p189)

Visit a working farm near Sarapiquí, meet the farmers and taste the fruits of their labor. (p136)

Tour the coffee plantation and meet the farm animals at Hacienda Orosí near Cartago. (p75)

↙ FARM FACTS

Costa Rica's most important agricultural product – in terms of land use and value of production – is coffee. Also important are bananas and pineapples, which are top exports.

▶ Go straight to the source (p136)

Opposite Mercado Central (p61), San José
Above Bribrí farmer (p96)
Left Pineapple farmer (p117)

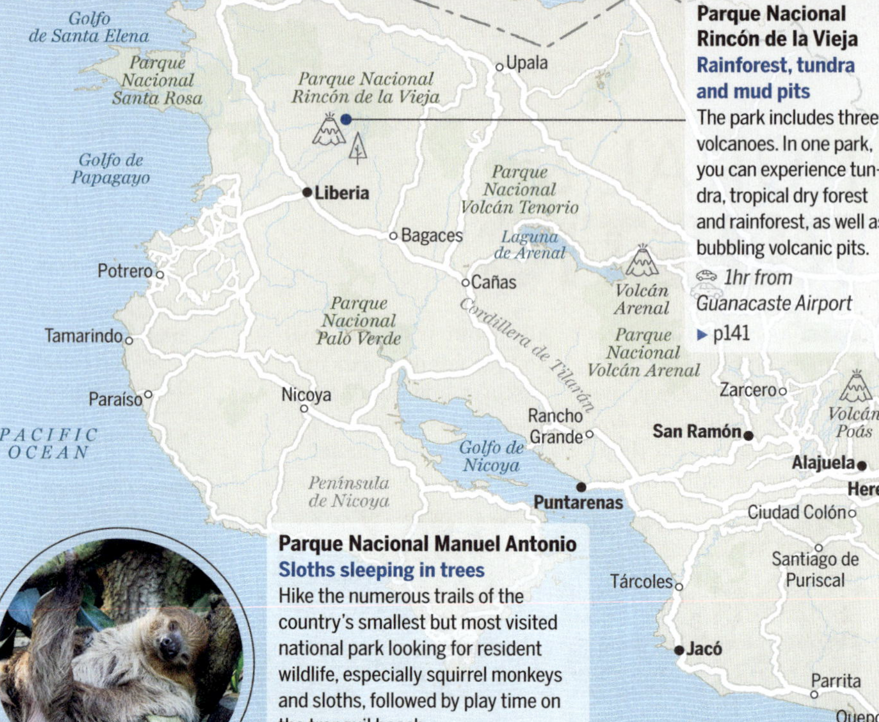

Parque Nacional Rincón de la Vieja

Rainforest, tundra and mud pits

The park includes three volcanoes. In one park, you can experience tundra, tropical dry forest and rainforest, as well as bubbling volcanic pits.

1hr from Guanacaste Airport

▶ p141

Parque Nacional Manuel Antonio

Sloths sleeping in trees

Hike the numerous trails of the country's smallest but most visited national park looking for resident wildlife, especially squirrel monkeys and sloths, followed by play time on the tranquil beach.

3hr drive from San José

▶ p191

GO WILD

From rainforest to cloud forest, from wetlands to dry tropical forest, Costa Rica harbors an incredible diversity of habitats – and a firm commitment to preserving them. As it turns out, preserving habitats goes a long way toward protecting the creatures that live there. Even if you don't take a dedicated wildlife tour, you'll encounter critters of all shapes and sizes.

Parque Nacional Marino Ballena

Whale-watching hub

On the Central Pacific Coast, Parque Nacional Marino Ballena is named for the humpback whales that migrate here to breed from July to November. Spot them from the beach or from the boat on a whale-watching tour.

20min from Dominical

▶ p191

PACIFIC OCEAN

0 100 km
0 50 miles

NICARAGUA

Refugio Nacional de Vida Silvestre Barra del Colorado

Caribbean Sea

Tortuguero

Puerto Viejo de Sarapiquí

Río Tortuguero

Parque Nacional Tortuguero

Parismina

Santa Clara

Guácimo

Parque Nacional Braulio Carrillo

Siquirres

Cordillera Central

Parque Nacional Barbilla

Limón City

SAN JOSÉ

Cartago

Cahuita

Puerto Viejo

Bribrí

Manzanillo

Parque Nacional Tapantí-Macizo Cerro la Muerte

Cordillera de Talamanca

Sixaola

Parque Nacional Chirripó

Parque Nacional Manuel Antonio

San Isidro de El General

Dominical

Río General

Uvita

Buenos Aires

Parque Nacional Marino Ballena

Bahía de Coronado

Guácimo

Sierpe

PANAMA

Bahía Drake

Rincón

Golfo Dulce

Parque Nacional Corcovado

Península de Osa

Puerto Jiménez

Parque Nacional Tortuguero

Crocodiles, turtles and manatees

The park consists of 172,000 hectares of protected land, canals and lagoons and is best explored by boat. Take an early morning tour to see leatherback turtles, herons, toucans, sloths, caimans and 'Jesus Christ' lizards who skip across the water.

30min from San José

▸ p92

Parque Nacional Corcovado

Monkeys and rare creatures

This sprawling park contains 2.5% of the world's biodiversity. Its expansive trails offer plentiful opportunities to scope out the rare Baird's tapir, watch scurrying coatis, observe monkeys swinging above your head and spy sleeping sloths.

1hr from Bahía Drake

▸ p224

CLOCKWISE FROM LEFT: MILAN NOGA/SHUTTERSTOCK, MARCO LISSONI/SHUTTERSTOCK, VACLAV SEBEK/SHUTTERSTOCK

Montezuma Waterfalls

Three cascading waterfalls

Three glorious waterfalls punctuate the Río Montezuma, creating a 40m drop in total. Visitors can swim under all three of these falls, which flow into each other and are connected by stairs.

40min from Montezuma

▶ p164

CHASING WATERFALLS

A sparkling cascade of water, cutting through the forest green and tumbling over the rocks, is always a sight to behold. In Costa Rica there are too many *cataratas* (waterfalls) to count, each with its own appeal, whether an adventurous hike, a soothing soak and dousing shower or just a spectacular scene.

FROM LEFT: JUHKU/SHUTTERSTOCK, DUARTE DELLAROLE/SHUTTERSTOCK

La Catarata Divina de Providencia

Waterfall swimming

The 3km hike to the falls through crisp cloud forest is enchanting with its changes in elevation and climate. Take a dip after the journey.

2hr drive from San José

▶ p213

Nauyaca Waterfalls

Refresh in canyon pools

The Río Barú creates two invigorating falls and multiple swimming holes for a family-friendly day excursion. You can access the falls by hiking, horseback riding or hitching a ride on a 4WD.

20min from Dominical

▶ p195

Naguala Falls

Serene rainforest waterfalls

Three separate stunning waterfalls are hidden within the rainforest on the grounds of Naguala Jungle Lodge, on the Península de Osa. Hike through creeks, streams and rivers to arrive at each of these unique, swimmable falls.

30min from Bahía Drake

▶ p221

Parque Nacional Tapantí-Macizo Cerro la Muerte

Quepos

Manuel Antonio

Parque Nacional Manuel Antonio

Río Savegre

Savegre

Río General

San Isidro de El General

Matapalo

Platanillo

Dominical

Uvita

Parque Nacional Marino Ballena

Peñuela

Tortuga Abajo

Bahía de Coronado

Palmar Norte

Sierpe

Río Sierpe

Chacarita

Río Chocuaco

Bahía Drake

Isla del Caño

Drake

Agujitas

Rincón

Rancho Quemado

La Palma

Parque Nacional Piedras Blancas

Golfo Dulce

Parque Nacional Corcovado

Laguna Corcovado

Península de Osa

Puerto Jiménez

0 50 km
0 25 miles

Noche Buena

Christmas Eve is when families gather, marking the main celebration of the Christmas holiday.

← Festival de los Diablitos

From December 30 to January 2, men in the Boruca community wear masks they made and play games commemorating indigenous resistance against colonization.

Boruca, p216

Festival de la Luz

On the second Saturday of December, Costa Rica's best bands join a massive parade of ornately lit floats followed by fireworks.

San José

← Tope Nacional

The Tope Nacional, National Horse Parade, occurs in San José on December 26, bringing expert riders and show horses from around the country.

San José

DECEMBER

Average daytime max: 27°C/82°F (Pacific coast)
Days of rainfall: 6

JANUARY

Costa Rica in SUMMER

FROM LEFT: LINDSAY FENDT/ALAMY, GILBERTO VELARDE/SHUTTERSTOCK, CFALVAREZ/SHUTTERSTOCK, LINDSAY FENDT/ALAMY
BOTTOM: MARGUS VILBAS/SHUTTERSTOCK

Carrera Chirripó

Held on the last Saturday of February, Carrera Chirripó is an annual 21km footrace running up and down Cerro Chirripó, Costa Rica's highest peak.

Cerro Chirripó, p214

▸ carrerachirripo.com

↙ El Rezo del Niño

January 6 marks the end of the Christmas season. Families take down their nativities over food and prayer.

↗ Envision Festival

A seven-day festival of yoga, meditation, beach dance parties and concerts in Uvita with a sustainability focus. Usually begins in late February and ends in early March.

Uvita

▸ envisionfestival.com

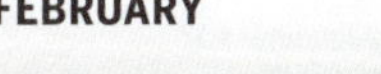

FEBRUARY

Average daytime max: 27°C/82°F (Pacific coast) Days of rainfall: 2

Average daytime max: 28°C/83°F (Pacific coast) Days of rainfall: 2

Packing Notes

Pack your rain jacket, rain boots and an umbrella to be prepared for spontaneous storms.

Semana Santa

Holy Week, the week between Palm Sunday and Easter Sunday, is the busiest for domestic tourism, so popular destinations, especially beaches, are packed.

← National Boyero Day

A joyous caravan of colorful carts pulled by oxen takes place in the last two weeks of March in downtown Escazú.

Escazú, San José

Feria del Agricultor de Orotina

The National Agricultural Festival in Orotina, an hour from San José, celebrates local agriculture with open-air produce markets, a beauty pageant and sustainable farming workshops. It takes place in mid-March.

Orotina

▸ facebook.com/p/Feria-del-Agricultor-de-Orotina

← Turtle Nesting

Peak nesting season for turtles in Parque Nacional Tortuguero begins, with leatherback turtles setting it off.

Parque Nacional Tortuguero, p92

MARCH

APRIL

Average daytime max: 28°C/83°F (Pacific coast)
Days of rainfall: 3

Costa Rica in

AUTUMN

FROM LEFT: KLAUS MOHR/SHUTTERSTOCK, ANDIPANTZ/GETTY IMAGES, XINHUA/ALAMY BOTTOM: SERGE GOUJON/SHUTTERSTOCK

→ Día del Trabajador y la Trabajadora

International Workers' Day, or Labor Day, is celebrated globally on May 1. In Costa Rica there are parades, marches and a 'State of the Union' address from the president in Limón City. It's also celebrated with cricket matches.

MAY

Average daytime max: 29°C/84°F (Pacific coast)
Days of rainfall: 8

Average daytime max: 28°C/83°F (Pacific coast)
Days of rainfall: 19

Packing Notes

Be prepared for a mix of sun and clouds – always bring a hat and sunscreen, even if it's overcast.

Rainy season begins for much of the country.

← LGBTIQ+ Pride

Thousands gather for Costa Rica's largest parade celebrating LGBTIQ+ Pride in San José, usually on the last Saturday of June. Manuel Antonio also hosts smaller Pride parties and events.

San José, p42
Manuel Antonio, p249

International Choral Festival for Peace

This festival features four days of singing by choirs from around the country and the world. Usually the last week of June.

Virgin of the Sea Day

Fishermen conduct a sea procession with decorated boats and pray for a fruitful year. On July 16 or the Saturday closest to that date.

Puntarenas

JUNE

Average daytime max: 27°C/82°F (Pacific coast)
Days of rainfall: 21

JULY

Costa Rica in WINTER

FROM LEFT: ADRIAN COTO RODRIGUEZ /SHUTTERSTOCK, MARCOS ANDRÉS COTO/ FLICKR/CC BY-NC-ND 2.0 ©, LBORGEPHOTO123/SHUTTERSTOCK BOTTOM: JAIME ESPINOSA/SHUTTERSTOCK

Whale-Watching

Peak humpback whale-watching season begins in July and lasts until November. Parque Nacional Marino Ballena and Bahía Drake are the best places to see them.

Bahía Drake, p220

Parque Nacional Marino Ballena, p200

↗ Annexation of Guanacaste

This historical event is celebrated in towns across Guanacaste on July 25 with marimba music concerts, dancing and carnival rides.

→ Recognizing Afro-Costa Rican Culture

August 31 is Día de la Persona Negra y la Cultura Afrocostarricense. There are vibrant parades with dancers, bands and food stalls, especially in Puerto Limón.

Puerto Limón, p106

Average daytime max: 27°C/82°F (Pacific coast)
Days of rainfall: 18

AUGUST

Average daytime max: 27°C/82°F (Pacific coast)
Days of rainfall: 22

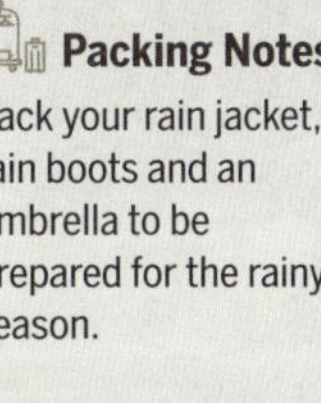

Packing Notes

Pack your rain jacket, rain boots and an umbrella to be prepared for the rainy season.

September is the rainiest month for most of the country.

Día de las Culturas

Held on October 12, this holiday coincides with Indigenous People's Day (Columbus Day) in the US. In Costa Rica, the holiday celebrates the mixing of immigrant and indigenous cultures.

Lantern Parade

On September 14, Ticos make homemade lanterns and parade with them around their neighborhoods to kick off Independence Day celebrations.

↑ Día de la Independencia

On September 15, Costa Rica celebrates its independence from Spain in 1821. Festivities include the running of the 'torch of Independence' and its arrival in Cartago.

Cartago, p71

SEPTEMBER

Average daytime max: 27°C/82°F (Pacific coast)
Days of rainfall: 24

OCTOBER

Costa Rica in SPRING

FROM LEFT: DRYADPHOTOS/SHUTTERSTOCK, CARA KOCH/SHUTTERSTOCK, MARCO DÍAZ/500PX
BOTTOM: DRYADPHOTOS/SHUTTERSTOCK

Limón Carnival

This 12-day celebration in Limón City vibrant celebration of Costa Rican Afro-Caribbean culture with parades, calypso and dancing in the streets, food festivals and fireworks. It typically begins on October 12.

Limón City, p88

Día de los Muertos

On November 1, families attend Catholic Mass and make pilgrimages to cemeteries to honor their ancestors and loved ones who have passed away.

↖ Día de la Mascarada

On Masquerade Day, October 31, locals make and wear elaborate papier-mâché masks depicting various characters, especially political and cultural figures or celebrities.

**Average daytime max:
27°C/82°F (Pacific coast)
Days of rainfall: 24**

NOVEMBER

**Average daytime max:
27°C/82°F (Pacific coast)
Days of rainfall: 15**

Packing Notes

Bring knee-high rain boots with solid traction to navigate muddy trails and deep puddles.

CENTRAL VALLEY HIGHLANDS & NORTHWESTERN COSTA RICA Trip Builder

TAKE YOUR PICK OF MUST-SEES AND HIDDEN GEMS

Sample Costa Rica's biodiversity in one road trip. This loop starts and ends in San José, but takes travelers on a journey to waterfalls, volcano hikes, cloud forest and beach.

Trip Notes

Hub towns San José, La Fortuna, Santa Elena, Jacó

How long Allow 10 days

Getting around Rent a car from Juan Santamaría Airport (SJO) in San José.

Tips Prepare for varying weather conditions and temperatures. Pack layers and a rain jacket, especially for Arenal evenings and cloud-forest excursions. Take hiking boots for navigating waterfalls, volcanoes and cloud forests. Bring a bathing suit and water shoes for hot springs in La Fortuna and the beach in Jacó.

Santa Elena Cloud Forest Reserve
Experience the ethereal cloud-forest ecosystem, meandering along misty trails or flying through the clouds.
20mins from Santa Elena

Monteverde
Feast on farm-to-table cuisine in unique settings, highlighting the unique flora and fauna of the surrounding cloud forest.
20mins from Santa Elena

CLOCKWISE FROM TOP: HENNER DAMKE/SHUTTERSTOCK, JORGE A. RUSSELL/ SHUTTERSTOCK, SAN LUCAS TREETOP DINING EXPERIENCE – WWW.SANLUCAS.CR

Río Arenal
El Tanque
La Fortuna
Parque Nacional Volcán Arenal
Roam through rugged trails that surround the park's namesake volcano and soothe your hiking muscles in natural hot springs.
30mins from La Fortuna
Parque Nacional Volcán Arenal
Ciudad Quesada
Volcán Platanar
Parque Nacional Juan Castro Blanco
Cordillera de Tilarán
Volcán Porvenir
Río Arunjue
Parque Nacional Volcán Poás
Cariblanco
Cordillera Central
Parque Nacional Braulio Carrillo
Zarcero
Volcán Poás
Vara Blanca
Volcán Barva
San Ramón
Río Barranca
La Paz Waterfall Gardens
Explore this wonderland of cascading falls and hiking trails, and visit the on-site wildlife park, the largest animal sanctuary in Costa Rica.
1hr from San José
Barva
Barranca
Esparza
SAN JOSÉ
San Pedro
San Mateo
Puerto Caldera
Orotina
Desamparados
Aserri
Santiago de Puriscal
Golfo de Nicoya
Parque Nacional Carara
Tárcoles
Playa Jacó
Swim, surf or sunbathe (or do all three) at Playa Jacó and nearby beaches.
5mins from downtown Jacó
Jacó
Playa Jacó
0
40 km
0
20 miles

CARIBBEAN COAST Trip Builder

TAKE YOUR PICK OF MUST-SEES AND HIDDEN GEMS

Home to Afro-Caribbean and Bribrí indigenous communities, this region has a distinct Caribbean Tico culture. The coast has its own cuisine, music and surf vibe, and ecotourism adventures are abundant.

Trip Notes

Hub towns Limón City, Puerto Viejo

How long Allow 1 week

Getting around Save time by flying into Limón from San José. Rent a car in Limón City to explore Cahuita, Puerto Viejo and neighboring beach towns along the southern Caribbean Coast.

Tips To visit Puerto Viejo by car, there's a two-lane coastal route and several one-lane bridges. Avoid 'rush hour' (mornings 8am to 9am, afternoons 4pm to 5pm) and factor traffic into travel time.

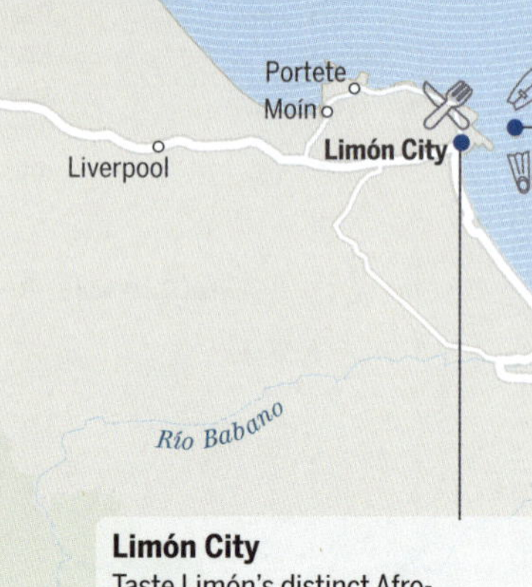

Limón City
Taste Limón's distinct Afro-Caribbean flavors at Jamaicatown's *sodas* (small local restaurants) and bakeries. Try the regional specialty, *rondón*, a delectable seafood soup with a coconut-milk base.
1hr flight from San José

Río Telira

Río Coen

Parque Internacional La Amistad

Isla Uvita

Sail out to Isla Uvita for surfing, scuba diving or just exploring this intriguing island. Experienced divers can explore an underwater shipwreck teeming with coral and marine life.

40mins Limón City

Cahuita

Drive down the coast to Cahuita to visit the eponymous national park. Hike the network of trails – crisscrossing coastal rainforest, beach and mangrove – to spot monkeys, sloths and more.

45mins from Limón City

Puerto Viejo & Playa Cocles

Surf bucket-list waves at these neighboring beaches. But beware – Salsa Brava, aka the 'Cheese Grater,' is for expert surfers only.

30mins from Cahuita

Manzanillo

Check out the southernmost town on Costa Rica's Caribbean Coast, with low-key beaches, reef snorkeling, inviting seafood restaurants and nesting sea turtles.

20mins from Puerto Viejo

Caribbean Sea
Pandora
Cahuita
Parque Nacional Cahuita
Puerto Viejo
Punta Uva
Manzanillo
Bribrí
Refugio de Vida Silvestre Gandoca-Manzanillo
Bratsi
PANAMA
0 20 km
0 10 miles

CENTRAL PACIFIC COAST Trip Builder

TAKE YOUR PICK OF MUST-SEES AND HIDDEN GEMS

A delightful mix of lazy beach lounging, national park hikes and waterfall swims, this route culminates with a mangrove tour into the Península de Osa, famously dubbed the most 'biologically intense place on the planet' by *National Geographic*.

Trip Notes

Hub towns Manuel Antonio, Dominical, Bahía Drake

How long Allow 2 weeks

Getting around As with many routes in Costa Rica, having a 4WD will be your best means of getting around, especially if you want to roam at your leisure. However, there are buses traveling between Dominical, Uvita and Sierpe, and from these towns you can book nature tours.

Tip Visiting Bahía Drake is easiest and most fun via motorboat ferry.

Parque Nacional Manuel Antonio
Hike through Costa Rica's most popular national park to spy sloths, toucans and monkeys in their natural habitat. Stop for a swim at the park's gorgeous beaches.
3hrs from San José

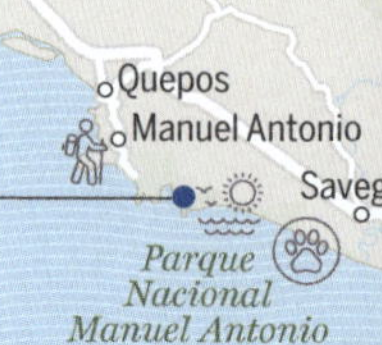

PACIFIC OCEAN

Bahía Drake
Hike through the coastal rainforest, lounge on deserted beaches, and take a trip to an offshore island, Isla del Caño, for snorkeling or scuba diving.
+ 2hrs from Palmar Norte

FROM LEFT: MATTHIEU GALLET/SHUTTERSTOCK, NATURE'S CHARM/SHUTTERSTOCK

Nauyaca Waterfalls
Take a detour from Dominical to visit these majestic mountain waterfalls on foot or via horseback. Spend a few hours swimming and enjoying the surrounding rainforest.
15mins from Dominical
Uvita
Stroll, snorkel and birdwatch along the tómbolo (aka the Whale's Tail) at the Parque Nacional Marino Ballena, where humpback whales come to breed and birth their young.
30mins from Dominical
Sierpe
Cruise through the mangroves of the Río Sierpe, rife with wildlife like monkeys, crocodiles, herons and iguanas. Mangroves protect the coastline and serve as a gateway to Bahía Drake and the Península de Osa.
90mins from Uvita
Rivas
San Isidro de El General
Parque Internacional La Amistad
Portalón
Matapalo
Platanillo
Dominical
Río General
Uvita
Parque Nacional Marino Ballena
Río Pejibayal
Isla Ballena
Peñuela
Tortuga Abajo
Paso Real
Rey Curré
Palmar Norte
Palmar Sur
Bahía de Coronado
Valle de Diquís
Sierpe
Río Sierpe
Río Chocuaco
Laguna Sierpe
Bahía Drake
Reserva Forestal Golfo Dulce
Isla del Caño
Drake
Agujitas
Rincón
Rancho Quemado
La Palma
Golfo Dulce
Golfito
Península de Osa
Laguna Corcovado
Parque Nacional Corcovado
Puerto Jiménez
Zancudo
Dos Brazos
Bahía de Pavon
Carate
Matapalo
Pavones
0
50 km
0
25 miles

PENÍNSULA DE NICOYA
Trip Builder

TAKE YOUR PICK OF MUST-SEES AND HIDDEN GEMS

Surfers and sun worshippers will have endless opportunities to ride the waves, lounge on the sand and marvel at the incredible Pacific sunsets on the Península de Nicoya.

Trip Notes

Hub towns Tamarindo, Nosara, Santa Teresa

How long Allow 2 weeks

Getting around A 4WD is necessary to navigate varying terrain, rough roads and river crossings.

Tips Fly directly into Guanacaste Airport (LIR) for easy access to Península de Nicoya destinations. From there, you can catch direct flights to Tamarindo or Tambor, near Santa Teresa.

Nosara
Witness thousands of olive ridley turtles build nests and lay their eggs on the deserted sands of the Refugio Nacional de Vida Silvestre Ostional.
2hrs from Tamarindo

Parque Nacional Palo Verde
0 40 km
0 20 miles
Reserva Forestal Taboga
Cordillera de Tilarán
Río Lagarto
Tamarindo
Get the party started in Tamarindo. Surf sweet swells all day and then dance under the stars all night.
2hrs from Guanacaste Airport
Guaitil
Parque Nacional Barra Honda
Nicoya
Mansión
Hojancha
Río Nosara
Península de Nicoya
Carmona
Isla Caballo
Puntarenas
Jicaral
Lepanto
Playa Naranjo
Isla San Lucas
Santa Marta
Sámara
The gentle waters at this family-friendly beach are perfect for swimming, beginner surfing and kayaking out to snorkel at Isla Chora.
1hr from Nosara
Golfo de Nicoya
Sámara
Carrillo
Islita
Bejuco
La Javilla
San Francisco de Coyote
Paquera
Pochote
Isla Alcatraz
PACIFIC OCEAN
Tambor
Cóbano
Santa Teresa
Salute the sun, ride the waves and feast on healthy food at this new-agey surf and yoga destination at the southern tip of the peninsula.
3hrs from Sámara
Santa Teresa
Montezuma
Mal País
Cabuya
Reserva Natural Cabo Blanco
Montezuma
Climb a rainforest river trail to the trio of cascades (with swimming pools) at Montezuma Waterfalls; or ride horseback to the singular El Chorro Waterfall, which tumbles directly onto the beach.
45mins from Santa Teresa

SOUTHERN COSTA RICA
Trip Builder

TAKE YOUR PICK OF MUST-SEES AND HIDDEN GEMS

Get to know Tico families and indigenous culture through homestays in remote and pristine landscapes. See rare quetzals, summit the country's highest peak and connect with its indigenous roots.

Trip Notes

Hub towns San José, San Isidro de El General, Buenos Aires, Palmar Norte

How long Allow 10 days

Getting around Rent a 4WD vehicle to access these outlying areas at your own pace.

Tips Download maps before leaving San José because cell service is spotty and wi-fi isn't readily available. This area has majestic mountain views but dangerous curvy roads, so drive cautiously. Fill up on gas and use ATMs in hub towns.

Santa María de Dota
Take a tour, sample the blends and buy some beans at Coopedota, a carbon-neutral coffee cooperative and plantation.
2hrs from San José

Santa María de Dota

Quepos

Manuel Antonio

Parque Nacional Manuel Antonio

Savegre

PACIFIC OCEAN

El Sitio Museo Finca 6
View the Diquís spheres and learn about the historical importance of these mysterious artifacts created by Costa Rica's indigenous people centuries ago.
30mins from Palmar Norte

CLOCKWISE FROM TOP LEFT: PIM PIC/SHUTTERSTOCK, YANNICK MARTINEZ/SHUTTERSTOCK, JAMES L. PEACOCK/ALAMY

Providencia de Dota

Spot the resplendent quetzal, hike to hidden waterfalls and drink the rich locally grown coffee in this misty highland region.

1hr from Santa María

San Gerardo de Rivas

Ascend Cerro Chirripó, Costa Rica's highest peak, and spend the night among the clouds. Less ambitious hikers can explore trails within the adjacent Cloudbridge Nature Reserve.

30mins from San Isidro de El General

Térraba

Learn about the past and present of the indigenous Brörán and Boruca tribes on their ancestral land. Take a cacao tour, do mask-making workshops and stop by the Boruca Museum.

2hrs from San Isidro de El General

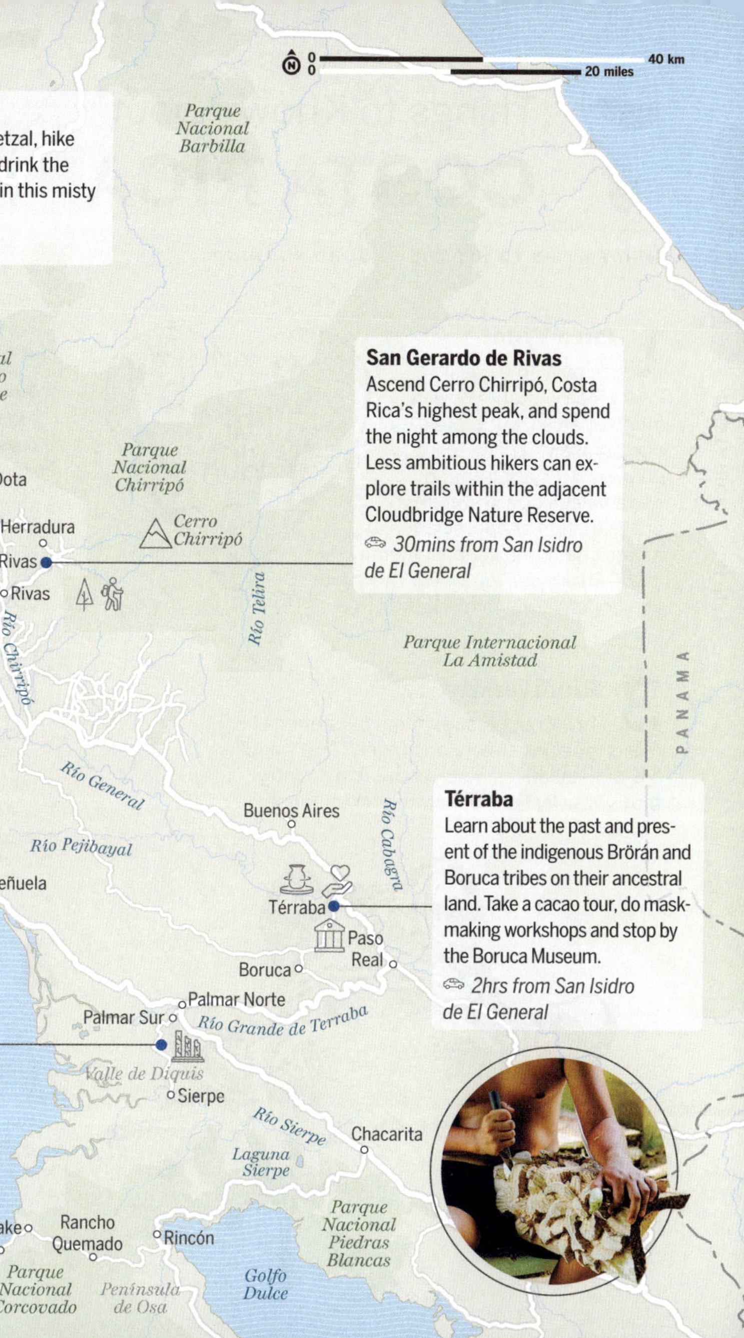

7 Things to Know About COSTA RICA

INSIDER TIPS TO HIT THE GROUND RUNNING

1 Pura Vida!

It's easy to travel in Costa Rica without knowing much Spanish, but there's one phrase you need to know: *pura vida!* It's a salutation and a valediction, a statement of affirmation or appreciation. It means that life is good, or literally, 'pure', *Pura vida!* You'll hear this a lot, and hopefully you'll feel it too.

2 Sodas

In Costa Rica, a *soda* isn't a carbonated beverage, but rather a small local restaurant. This is an ideal place to try a typical Costa Rican dish, known as a *casado.* This set meal includes a meat choice (chicken, beef or fish), *gallo pinto* (rice and black beans), a small salad and sweet plantains. Some *sodas* may offer a vegetarian *casado* on request. *Casados* have the dual advantage of being filling and relatively inexpensive.

3 Biodiversity

Tiny Costa Rica is home to about half a million species of flora and fauna. That's a full 5% of the planet's biodiversity, in a country that's smaller than the state of West Virginia.

4 It's Not Cheap

Costa Rica is the most expensive country in Central America. Travelers are often surprised at the cost of restaurants and hotels in particular. Budget accordingly.

CLOCKWISE FROM TOP LEFT: ANNE MATHIASZ/SHUTTERSTOCK, JSABIROVA/SHUTTERSTOCK, STACY DRAW/SHUTTERSTOCK, THE STUDIO/SHUTTERSTOCK, CHARLIE 91/SHUTTERSTOCK

5 Allow for Driving Time

Driving is one of the most stressful aspects of traveling in Costa Rica. Be prepared for heavy traffic in the cities and poor road conditions everywhere else. Recent years have seen many new roads and vast improvements to Hwy 1 (aka the Interamericana), which makes for safer, more pleasant driving. But you're likely to find yourself driving on some roads that are narrow, winding, unpaved and/or poorly maintained. Here's how to stay safe:

- Take your time! Don't be in a rush to reach your destination.
- Travel during daylight hours (that is, before 6pm), as it gets very dark very quickly after the sun goes down.
- Rent a 4WD for ease of travel over unpaved roads and for the occasional river crossing.
- Fill up on gas when passing through towns.
- Download maps and routes before you set out, as you're likely to lose your connection en route.

6 Microclimates Aplenty

The weather can change drastically as you travel around the country. While much of the country has a tropical, humid and warm climate, the mountains and cloud forests can have chilly temperatures around 10°C. Areas like San Gerardo de Rivas, Providencia and Monteverde require a jacket and even hats or scarves depending on the time of year.

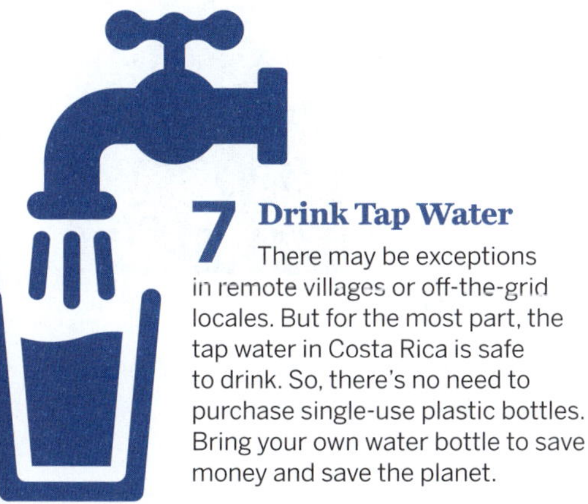

7 Drink Tap Water

There may be exceptions in remote villages or off-the-grid locales. But for the most part, the tap water in Costa Rica is safe to drink. So, there's no need to purchase single-use plastic bottles. Bring your own water bottle to save money and save the planet.

Read, Listen, Watch & Follow

READ

Finding La Negrita (Natasha Gordon-Cipembere; 2022) A rich reinterpretation of the Black Madonna story, set in an Afro community.

The Adventurer's Son (Roman Dial; 2020) A father's memoir about searching for his son in the wilds of Corcovado.

The Island of the Lonely Men (José León Sánchez; 1973) Fictionalized account of Sanchez' time imprisoned as an innocent man.

Única Looking at the Sea (Fernando Contreras Castro; 1993) Moving novel about a family of 'dump divers' who have been abandoned by society.

LISTEN

Manuel Obregón Musician, composer and former Minister of Culture who integrates nature and culture into his music.

Cocofunka A wildly popular funk-blues-reggae-Latin rock group from San José.

Walter 'Gavitt' Ferguson A Costa Rican calypso legend from the Caribbean coastal town of Cahuita.

Toledo One of the country's biggest reggae artists. Some of his music has a political slant, such as calling out police corruption.

CHRISTOPHER POLK/BILLBOARD VIA GETTY IMAGES

Debi Nova
A Grammy-nominated pop singer who has collaborated with Sergio Mendes, Q-Tip, Ricky Martin and more.

WATCH

Maikol Yordan Traveling Lost (Miguel Alejandro Gomez, 2014) Comedy about a farmer on a mission to save his land.

Caribe (Esteban Ramírez, 2004) Drama about Caribbean banana farmers fighting land-grabbing oil corporations.

Endless Summer II (Bruce Brown, 1994; pictured right) Documentary about local surf culture, particularly in Tamarindo.

Clara Sola (Nathalie Álvarez Mesén, 2021) A woman goes on a mystical journey to escape her repressive religious upbringing.

2.5% – The Osa Peninsula (Marco Bollinger and Eytan Elterman, 2017) Documentary by Lokal Travel highlights Península de Osa and tourism's impact on its biodiversity.

NEW LINE CINEMA/CINEMATIC COLLECTION/ALAMY

FOLLOW

Two Weeks in Costa Rica (*twoweeksincostarica.com*) Excursions resource, especially for families.

Descubre Costa Rica (*@descubrecostarica*) Costa Rica bucket-list inspiration.

MyTanFeet (*mytanfeet.com*) Travel tips and stories.

Caribeando (*@caribeandocr*) Caribbean landscape and culture.

Tico Times (*ticotimes.net*) *English-language daily digital news.*

Sate your Costa Rica dreaming with a virtual vacation

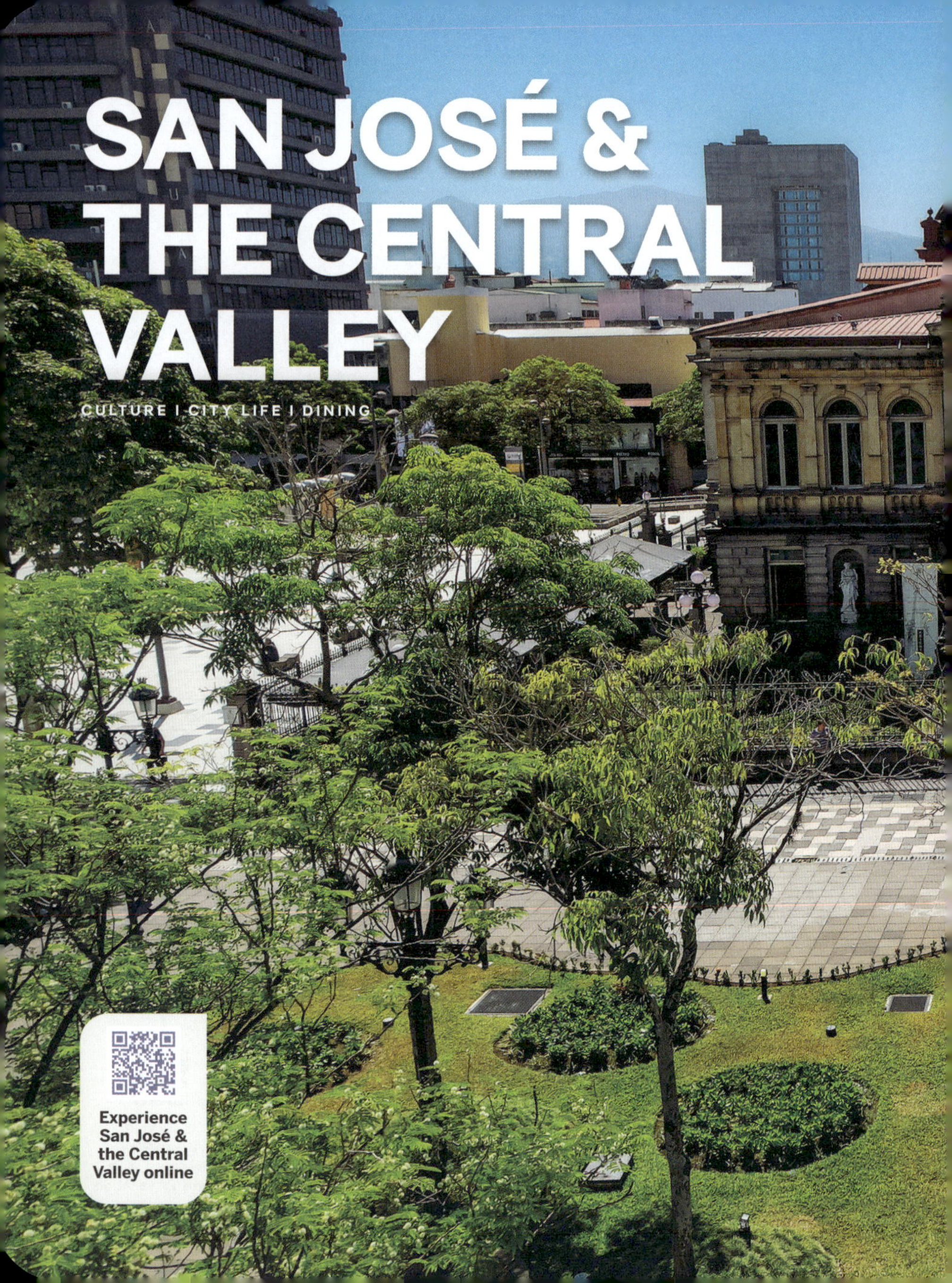
SAN JOSÉ &
THE CENTRAL
VALLEY
CULTURE | CITY LIFE | DINING
Experience
San José &
the Central
Valley online

TEATRO NACIONAL

Stroll among the enchanting hedge sculptures of **Parque Francisco Alvarado** (p68)
1½hrs from San José

Concepción

San Ramón

Palmares

San Pedro de Poás

Santa Bárbara

Alajuela

San Joaquín de Flores

Learn about Costa Rica's singular war hero at the **Museo Histórico Cultural de Juan Santamaría** (p59)
30mins from San José

San Antonio

La Guácima

Santa Ana

Escazú

Zona Protectora Cerro de Escazú

SAN JOSÉ & THE CENTRAL VALLEY

Trip Builder

Hike through mountainous coffee groves at **Hacienda La Chimba** (p63)
20mins from San José

The Central Valley is the fertile crescent of Costa Rica. Enjoy spring-like weather, charming *pueblos* (small towns) and mountain ranges punctuated with volcanoes. In the middle lies San José, a diverse capital city jammed with museums and dining options.

Zona Protectora Caraigres

PREVIOUS SPREAD: GIANFRANCO VIVI/SHUTTERSTOCK
FROM LEFT: ROBERT ISENBERG/LONELY PLANET, MIX TAPE/SHUTTERSTOCK, MICHAL SARAUER/SHUTTERSTOCK

Practicalities

MARCO LISSONI/SHUTTERSTOCK

ARRIVING

Juan Santamaría Airport The busiest airport in Costa Rica, and the most direct route to the Central Valley. The airport is technically in Alajuela, a 25-minute drive from downtown San José. A crowd of *taxistas* (taxi drivers) will accost you at the terminal exit, and US$30 is a reasonable price for a metered ride into town. Walk a little further to the main road, and you can catch an express bus for US$1.50 or less.

HOW MUCH FOR A

Breakfast with *gallo pinto* US$8

Gourmet coffee US$2

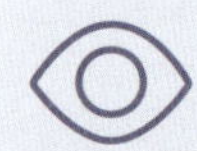

Authentic Boruca mask US$100

GETTING AROUND

Bus The Central Valley has a comprehensive bus system (p72), which is cheap (US$1 to US$1.50) and safe to ride. Routes can be confusing, but nearly all buses circle back to San José depots.

Taxi The default cab in San José is the *taxi rojo* (red taxi), which you can find almost anywhere. Make sure the *taxista* has a visible *maría* (meter). Rides around the inner city should cost between US$10 and US$30, depending on traffic.

Car Driving in the Central Valley can be a jaw-clenching thrill, and rental cars are affordable by US standards.

WHEN TO GO

NOV–JAN
Breezy, perfectly temperate, with possible showers.

FEB–APR
Dry and hot, with clear skies and lots of crowds.

MAY–JUL
Pleasant temperatures and afternoon rain.

AUG–OCT
Humid but agreeable mornings followed by frequent thunderstorms.

TOP: WOLFGANG KAEHLER/ALAMY
BOTTOM: MABELIN SANTOS/SHUTTERSTOCK

EATING & DRINKING

San José has the most dynamic dining scene in the country. True, you'll find a lot of familiar fast-food chains, plus windows selling cheap *empanadas* (turnovers stuffed with meat and cheese; pictured top right) and *arroz con pollo* (chicken rice). But the city is the best place to find Indian, Pan-Asian and South American cuisines, plus a range of chic gastropubs. You could spend days noshing your way through Barrio Escalante or Escazú. The options become more traditional in the smaller towns, but there's everything to love about a good *casado* (set meal; pictured bottom right).

Best craft-beer pub
Wilkcr (p66)

Must-try traditional meal
Nuestra Tierra (p74)

WHERE TO STAY

The city is packed with hotels of every budget and style. Small towns offer more boutique experiences. As a rule, prices are highest in the dry season.

Neighborhood	Pros/Cons
Downtown San José	Museums and dining. Mixed quality. Withering crowds.
Barrio Escalante	Superlative accommodations and nightlife. Often sold out.
Escazú/ Santa Ana	Top-notch hotels. Family-friendly resorts. Often expensive and generic.
Alajuela	Near airport. Economical. Isolated and varying quality.
Heredia	Authentic town. Easy drive to sights and good access to Caribbean. Fewer options.
Orosí Valley	Beautiful landscape. Tourist-friendly. Very quiet.

CONNECT & FIND YOUR WAY

Wi-fi SIM cards are widely available in the airport and city, and the biggest carriers are Claro and Kölbi. Free wi-fi (pronounced 'wee-fee') is standard in hotels and guesthouses. Take the usual precautions installing cards and logging onto networks. You'll find less access in the mountains.

Navigation Ticos rely on the Waze app, preferring crowdsourced landmarks to street addresses.

MONEY

Cards are widely accepted, but it's wise to keep a small bundle of cash. Bus drivers carry boxes of exact change, so riding somewhere is a great way to break medium-value bills.

SAFETY

San José can be rough around the edges, but the most common concerns are pickpockets and scammers. Men often try to catch women's attention with an annoying 'ts-ts-ts' sound, which is best ignored.

01 Capital CULTURE

CITY I MUSEUMS I PERFORMING ARTS

San José is the cultural heart of Costa Rica, where world-class museums and cultural institutions await the curious traveler. This capital isn't known for beaches and biodiversity, but is a hotbed of artists, academics and entrepreneurs.

MABELIN SANTOS/ALAMY

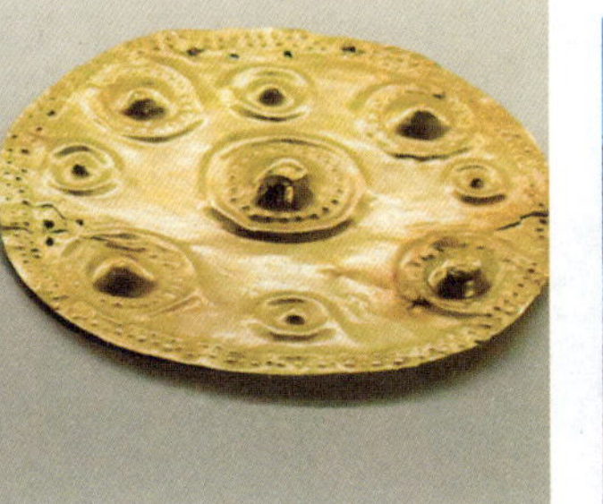

How To

Getting around Downtown San José has a ton of attractions located within a small area: walking is the best way to get around. For outlying neighborhoods, a *taxi rojo* (red taxi) is easy to spot.

When to go San José is ready for you anytime.

Dress the part Most *josefinos* wear trousers or dresses in this pleasant climate, and we advise sturdy shoes for weather-beaten sidewalks. Nothing says 'tourist' like shorts and sandals.

MIHAI-BOGDAN LAZAR/SHUTTERSTOCK

Pre-Columbian Museums

Two of Costa Rica's most impressive museums explore the culture of indigenous people before the arrival of Europeans. The **Museo del Jade** displays stone carvings, ancient artifacts and elaborate dioramas of everyday tribal life. The enormous modern building is packed with sophisticated multimedia exhibits. The **Museo del Oro Precolombino** is an underground museum dedicated to the importance of gold to the early *caciques* (chiefs). See the many ways gold was used for dress, decoration and spiritual rites.

STEFANO PATERNA/ALAMY

Live Music

Superstar vocalists from around the world make regular stops in San José. Better yet, the city has garnered a well-earned reputation for indie bands, which you can see at these

The Teatro Nacional

First opened in 1897, the Teatro Nacional is the historic flagship of San José's performing arts scene. Visitors can explore a small museum and grand auditorium, then order a beverage at the elegant **Alma de Café**. The theater remains as active as ever, holding performances year-round.

Top left Museo de Oro Precolombino
Top right Teatro Nacional
Bottom left Museo del Jade

smaller venues. **Amón Solar** is a converted house in the bohemian neighborhood of Barrio Amón, and you'll find everything from Latin to blues bands on its stage. **El Observatorio** is a brick-walled showroom in the party district of Barrio California. **StarView CR**, near Barrio Amón, has the feel of an underground bar from the 1990s, with music to match.

Arts Galore

San José has a good number of art galleries, which display experimental and avant-garde works you won't find anywhere else in Costa Rica. **TEOR/éTica**, in Barrio Amón, is an old corner building painted with a new mural every few months. In each room artists build installations that address social concerns. In Santa Ana, **Casa Negra** is an art gallery that showcases local crafts; you can also join a workshop in the studio, where a creative professional will guide you through the basics of ceramic sculpting or experimental photography. The **Museo de Arte Costarricense** stands on the eastern entrance of Parque La Sabana. This elegant building is constructed in a traditional Spanish style,

Fiestas de Zapote

Around the New Year, the **Fiestas de Zapote** commandeer this sleepy San José neighborhood, attracting thousands of families from across the valley. The streets are cordoned off to traffic, and you'll find the gamut of roller coasters, sugary snacks and well-stocked beer stalls. One of the draws is the **Toros a la Tica**, Costa Rica's traditional rodeo, which takes place in the **Redondel de Zapote** (Zapote Arena). Nightfall brings festive lights and fireworks displays over the town. Travelers have about two weeks after Christmas to enjoy the ranching atmosphere. Cowboy hats are encouraged.

with bleached white walls and tile roofs, making it hard to believe that the museum once served as an airport terminal.

Specialty Museums

The **Museo de los Niños** was once a prison, but today this jaunty yellow children's museum has castle-like towers and stands proudly on a hill. Inside you'll find dinosaur skeletons, science activities, an auditorium and even the **Galería Nacional**. In a similar vein, the **Museo Nacional de Costa Rica** was once a military barracks, but today it looks like a fairy-tale castle, with its yellow walls and medieval turrets. Themed exhibits circulate through the museum on a regular basis, and the indoor butterfly garden is open year-round. Once a distillery, the **Centro Nacional de la Cultura** (CENAC) is a cluster of different buildings, including the **Museo de Arte y Diseño Contemporáneo** (Museum of Contemporary Art and Design) and **Teatro 1887**, which hosts a range of Spanish-language performing arts.

Left Redondel de Zapote
Below Museo de los Niños

02 Park Yourself HERE

OUTDOORS | SPORTS | ARTS

San José has lots of urban parks, but none of them compare to **La Sabana**. This sprawling green space is famous for its open fields and shady trees, and Ticos come from all over the city to jog or play ball. La Sabana served for 44 years as an international airport; today, the park helps urbanites escape San José's crowds and din.

JOSHUA TEN BRINK/SHUTTERSTOCK

How To

Getting here La Sabana is centrally located in San José and easy to reach by bus, taxi or foot.

When to go La Sabana is open all day, every day. The outdoor facilities are best enjoyed when it's not raining, but there's always somebody on the turf.

Bring water There aren't a lot of water fountains or corner stores near La Sabana, so bring your own hydration.

SALVADOR AZNAR/SHUTTERSTOCK

Top left Estadio Nacional and La Sabana
Bottom left Museo de Arte Costarricense

Go solo **La Sabana** is covered in paths and walkways, so you can take a refreshing promenade through the trees or even run laps along the perimeter. The small 'lake' is surrounded by foliage and grass, making it the perfect spot for a picnic. There's also a public racetrack and a rink for inline skating.

Join a team The park has several soccer fields, attracting players of all skill levels, and it's perfectly normal for random travelers to join a friendly game. The same goes for the baseball fields and volleyball court. There's even a small playground on the north side for the kiddos.

Browse the art One of the most beautiful buildings in San José is the **Museo de Arte Costarricense**, a former airport terminal built in traditional Spanish architectural style. Today, the structure serves as a museum with rotating art exhibits and historical retrospectives. The sculpture garden outside is a peaceful place to rest and regroup. The best part: admission is free.

Replenish calories La Sabana is lined with diverse restaurants, especially on the western side of the park. Pick from Asian, Mexican and South American menus. Two favorites are **Soda Tapia**, a popular diner with great breakfasts located near Paseo Colón, and **El Social Sabana**, a modern *cantina* (canteen) serving traditional dishes alongside a party atmosphere.

Sports Capital

The **Estadio Nacional** (National Stadium) is considered the most modern in Central America, and the 35,000-seat venue is used for all kinds of major events. The stadium is best known as the home base of La Selección, Costa Rica's national soccer team, and international matches often take place here during the season. The field has also hosted regional matches and the Women's World Cup. Sports aside, the stadium serves as a main stage for some of the most famous musicians in the world; Shakira herself performed the first concert here in 2011, and big names perform here every month of the year.

03 Eat & Drink in SAN JOSÉ

FOOD I BEVERAGE I NIGHTLIFE

San José is the epicenter of Costa Rican nightlife, where the dining options are most diverse and the bars stay open longest. Each neighborhood overflows with epicurean options, and places like Barrio Escalante and Escazú have garnered global attention for their dynamic nightlife.

ROBERT ISENBERG/LONELY PLANET

How To

Getting around San José is walkable and well connected by buses, but if you're staying out late, taxis are a smart option.

When to go San José is always a happening city. Prices are best in the rainy season, but the city is most active in the drier months.

Plastic is golden In the wake of COVID-19, credit and debit cards are welcomed in most San José businesses.

VDB PHOTOS/SHUTTERSTOCK

Barrio Escalante

You could eat every meal in Barrio Escalante for weeks and still find something new and delicious to try. The center of the action is **Calle 33**, a walkable street of cafes, restaurants and entertainment. The **Calle 33 Mercadito** food hall boasts numerous different kitchens under one roof. You can order anything from ramen and burgers to soups and tacos, then sit down anywhere in the funky cafeteria. True fine dining comes in the form of **Isolina**, an elegant eatery known as much for its wine as for its international cuisine, and **Sikwa**, which elevates pre-Columbian and indigenous culture and cuisine.

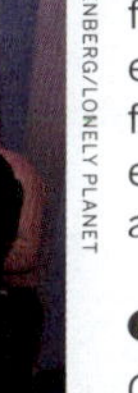

ROBERT ISENBERG/LONELY PLANET

Cerveza Artesanal

Costa Rica has fallen fully in love with *cerveza artesanal* (craft beer), giving Ticos far more

Classic Cinema

Movie buffs will get a kick out of **Cine Magaly**, a one-screen movie house in Barrio California. It is a true cinema, in the tradition of old-school art houses. The marquee shines like a beacon in the night for culture seekers, and its single screen is busy with classic, indie and international films.

Top left Calle 33
Top right Beer tasting
Bottom left Cine Magaly

options than the bottles of Imperial and Bavaria stocked in every refrigerator. Gastropubs are everywhere in San José, inviting you to sample the many local beers and high-quality imports. The **Beer Factory** is an enormous Tyrollean *Biergarten* located smack-dab in the middle of Barrio Escalante. A couple of blocks down Calle 33 is **Wilk**, a bar with a slacker vibe, diverse brews and an entire wall covered floor-to-ceiling with beer bottles. The ever-popular Stiefel Pub now has two locations – one **downtown** and one in **Escazú** – both with a dozen craft beers on tap and good vibes.

Escazú

Swank Escazú is great for shopping and high-end service, but it positively excels at dining. The suburb is drenched in upscale restaurants, and you could spend weeks sampling them all. The real pride of Escazú is its global

San Pedro's College Scene

If you want to connect with a younger crowd, consider a night in **San Pedro**, home to the **Universidad de Costa Rica**. More than 40,000 students attend UCR, and most of them study, shop and party in San Pedro. The campus is upbeat, welcoming and open to the public. Visitors can stroll past academic buildings or grab a snack at a local cafe, but the real attraction here is the resident sloth that lazes around the campus greenery. The biology department has its own butterfly garden, and the **Planetario** is a few blocks away.

Left Blue morpho butterflies
Below Indian food

flavor: **Taj Mahal** is the best place in Costa Rica to find Indian cuisine, with Mogul-inspired decor. **Kololo Ramen** serves excellent Japanese and Korean noodles and soups in a trendy restaurant in Plaza Tempo. **El Mestizo Mercado Gastronómico** food court in Plaza Tempo is a wallet-friendly destination that is also downright delicious. Choose between Caribbean, Peruvian, Argentine, Spanish, Mexican and more, then grab a seat at a private or communal table.

FAR LEFT: MARGUS VILBAS PHOTOGRAPHY/SHUTTERSTOCK
LEFT: FINN STOCK/SHUTTERSTOCK

Food Halls

An exciting trend in local dining can be translated roughly as 'food hall.' In these communal settings, tiny restaurants are packed together and seating is shared. Patrons can order from one or several different windows and sit wherever they want. In Barrio Escalante, **Jardín de Lolita** describes itself as a 'gastronomic community,' and that feel-good vibe pervades the industrial space and verdant decor. You can pick from nine different eateries with fare from Mexican to Japanese. Over in Santa Ana, **Container Platz** is a colorful construct made of repurposed shipping containers. Patrons can pick and choose from 17 different eateries, and specialties include burgers, poké bowls and fine Italian. Container Platz has become one of the best spots in Santa Ana for DJs and karaoke nights.

04 War STORIES

HISTORY I MONUMENTS I MUSEUMS

Costa Rica abolished its military on December 1, 1948, making it one of a few countries in the world without a standing army. Ticos were never warmongers, but traces of their martial past remain. Scattered monuments in Alajuela and Heredia are some of the most iconic of the Central Valley, both for their distinctive architecture and their significance to Costa Rica's formative years.

OLAF SPEIER/ALAMY

How To

Getting here Alajuela and Heredia are located near the airport. Scores of buses ferry passengers from San José to these cities and back, as do commuter trains.

When to go These landmarks are open most days, and they're worth visiting in any season.

Stay central All of the best sights in Alajuela and Heredia are within a couple of blocks of these central landmarks.

ROBERT ISENBERG/LONELY PLANET

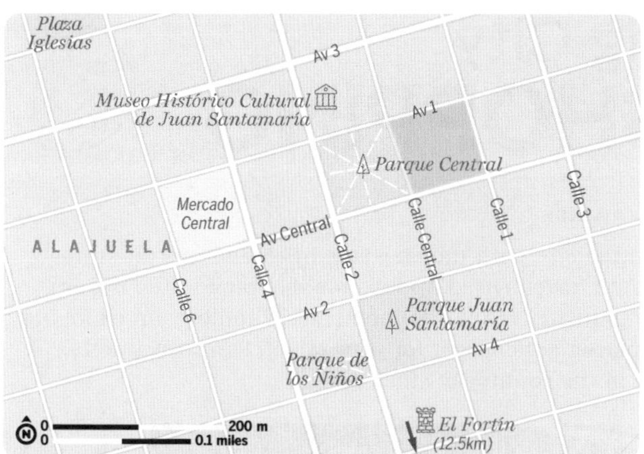

Hero's legacy Drummer boy Juan Santamaría was killed during a daring one-man assault on enemy lines in 1856. The **Museo Histórico Cultural Juan Santamaría** in Alajuela transports visitors back to the Filibuster War, a bitter face-off between US mercenaries and Central American militias. Using dioramas and period artifacts, these exhibits explain the importance of Costa Rica's most celebrated war hero. The fortified structure has dominated Alajuela's downtown since 1895, adding to the museum's historical ambience.

Military monuments There aren't a lot of sword-waving statues in Costa Rica, thanks to its many years of peace, but you can find a significant few. **Parque Juan Santamaría** is just a couple of blocks from the museum, where the young soldier's likeness is sculpted in bronze. **Parque Central** in Alajuela is a busy plaza with a gazebo, fountain and statue of the bearded General Tomás Guardia, who twice served as president of 19th-century Costa Rica.

Towering achievement One of the most peculiar structures in Costa Rica is a former watchtower in the middle of Heredia called **El Fortín**. The stout brick cylinder and oval windows are unlike any other fortification from the 1870s, and the remaining three towers of the original plan were never completed. Today, El Fortín is the official symbol of Heredia, and visitors can enter the structure and view the town from its battlements.

Top left Parque Juan Santamaría
Bottom left El Fortín

Milestone Holidays

Costa Rica has several patriotic holidays, which recall major moments in the nation's history. Celebrations are biggest in the cities of the Central Valley, where thousands turn out to wave Costa Rican flags. The **Día de la Independencia** (September 15) commemorates Central America's hard-won secession from Spain in 1821 with parades across the country. During the **Día de Juan Santamaría** (April 1), the streets of Alajuela fill with marching bands in honor of their native son. In 2020, the government declared December 1 to be **Día de la Abolición de Ejército** (Abolition of the Army Day) to observe the many years of peace.

05 Big City SHOPPING

SHOPPING I WALKING I URBAN LIFE

San José is a mercantile city, with thousands of brick-and-mortar stores competing for customers. You have myriad options for shopping in the big city, from a century-old bazaar to luxury retail developments. Whether you're looking for gifts for family or a replacement charger for your tablet, San José and its suburbs are the best place in the country to stock up.

ANNE RICHARD/SHUTTERSTOCK

How To

Getting around San José and Escazú are well connected by bus routes, and taxis are a great option for shorter distances.

When to go You may want to avoid the outdoor malls on rainy afternoons. Lots of merchants tend to close their shops on Sundays as well.

Cards are good Credit cards are widely accepted across San José, especially since COVID-19.

LUIS ALVARADO ALVARADO/SHUTTERSTOCK

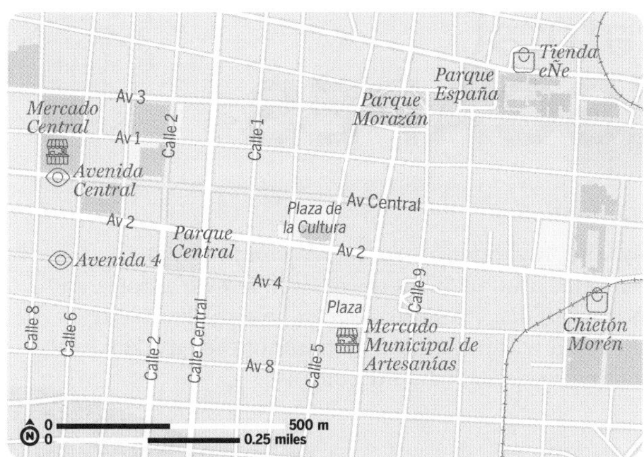

Top left Mercado Central
Bottom left Avenida Central

Browse historic markets Vendors have sold their wares in the **Mercado Central** since 1880. This indoor complex has narrow walkways and a mishmash of shops and restaurants. You can find a lot of stock souvenirs here and easily score a cheap plate of *gallo pinto* (a rice and beans medley). A similar marketplace is the **Mercado Municipal de Artesanías**, where artists hustle to sell their crafts among densely packed stalls.

Hit the avenue The suburb of **Escazú** is a chic shopper's paradise, where plazas overflow with upmarket stores. The crème-de-la-crème is **Avenida Escazú**, a mixed-use development with high-rise condos, luxury chains and top-notch restaurants. The outdoor walkways are a spotless concourse along which you can while away an afternoon. For a more traditional experience, head down the road to **Multiplaza**, a massive indoor shopping mall.

Stroll pedestrian malls San José is a fairly walkable city, largely thanks to **Avenida Central** and **Avenida 4**. These two downtown avenues run parallel to each other for almost a kilometer, and both are almost entirely blocked off to motor traffic. The brick walkways are lined on either side with clothiers, department stores and electronics depots. Shopping here can be a hit-or-miss experience, but the *avenidas* are a common place to start exploring San José, and the people-watching alone is worth a visit.

Costa Rican Creations

There are a few standalone stores in San José that are worth a special trip, if you are in the market for some truly representative Costa Rican craft. **Tienda eÑe** is a stylish boutique specializing in Costa Rican–made designs. These are not traditional handicrafts, but rather modern but creative clothing, bags, jewelry and more. By contrast, **Chietón Morén** sources traditional handicraft items from Indigenous communities, such as Boruca masks and bags, Chorotega ceramics, Huétar baskets and Ngöbe clothing and textiles. This operation is staffed completely by volunteers and all profits go to the artisans.

06 Natural ESCAPES

HIKES I WATERFALLS I VOLCANOES

When you put 'valley' and 'highlands' together, you end up with spectacular views. The mountains around San José are webbed with trails, and studded with volcanoes and waterfalls. These routes can be a workout, but they're also safe, well marked and within striking distance of the city. You can expect at least one breathtaking *mirador* (lookout point).

JURATEBUIVIENE/SHUTTERSTOCK

How To

Getting here While it is possible to reach some of these trailheads by bus or taxi, a car is easiest.

When to go The dry season is best for all routes. Hit the trails early in the day, especially at the volcanos, where the entrance closes at 2pm.

Altitude sickness At 3432m, Irazú is high enough to induce symptoms of altitude sickness. Stay hydrated and bring along painkillers for sudden headaches.

REBECA BOLANOS/SHUTTERSTOCK

Top left Volcán Poás
Bottom left Hacienda La Chimba

Volcán Poás The 2697m **Volcán Poás** is an active volcano, covered with cloud forest, about one hour northwest of Alajuela. At the summit, you can gaze into the turquoise-colored Laguna Caliente. It's a 10-minute hike from the parking lot to the crater. Helmets are required and available on-site.

Mantra Trail In the hills above Santa Ana, **Hacienda La Chimba** is a sprawling coffee farm with ecotourism staples like ziplining and canopy tours. You can also hike the Mantra Trail, which takes you through the groves and past a succession of sculptures. The trail concludes with La Mano, a massive wicker hand that extends over the ridge.

La Paz Waterfall Gardens Thanks to five epic waterfalls, **La Paz Waterfall Gardens** has become the most-visited private preserve in Costa Rica. The twin delights of five fantastic cascades and a massive animal sanctuary certainly contribute to its acclaim. Don't miss the waterfall garden, a whimsical joining of nature and architecture, where you can weave in and out of the thundering cascades on perfectly designed paths.

Volcán Irazú The country's highest volcano rewards travelers with rocky craters, emerald-colored lakes and, on a clear day, views of both the Caribbean and Pacific. The 2km Craters Sector Loop yields views of the five craters, while the more rugged Micaela Trail shows off the region's flora and fauna over the course of a 1.6km loop.

Biker's Paradise

Mountain biking is all the rage in Costa Rica, and certain regions are crisscrossed with single-track trails. For a more curated experience, the Central Valley has several mountain-bike parks, where rated routes and constructed jumps cater to all skill levels. **Valle Escondido** is a playground for new and casual riders in suburban Santa Ana. In Heredia, **Adventure Park** provides epic alpine routes along with ziplining and canopy tours. **La Angelina** is a 40-hectare MTB park located between San José and Cartago, with 19km of trails and platforms. Note that none of these parks rent bikes, so make sure to bring one.

To Bus or Not to Bus?

YOU CAN GET THERE FROM HERE

How you get around Costa Rica will determine how you interact with it. A cross-country bus can be sublime and economical – the ideal choice for first-time visitors. But there are benefits to driving, despite the many roadblocks you may encounter along the way. The best option may be a mix of both.

Top left La Suiza
Top center Cariari bus station
Top right River crossing

BOB POOL/SHUTTERSTOCK

The Beauty of Buses

The seats are soft, the riders are quiet and cool air eases through open windows. All around, the tropical countryside reveals itself, the forests and farms, the mountains and rivers. You have nothing to do for the next couple of hours but watch the scrolling scenery and maybe take a siesta. If you don't mind mass transit, the Costa Rican bus is about as good as it gets. And it's cheap.

For years, backpackers have zigzagged across the landscape by bus, rarely paying as much as US$20 to cross entire provinces. These roads can be rough and full of switchbacks, even in the city; swallow a little Dramamine and let a professional driver take the wheel. This is the way most Ticos travel, and riders tend to be courteous and keep to themselves.

The vast majority of these buses end up in San José, the nation's transportation super-hub. City buses travel to every barrio and suburb, usually costing a dollar or less. Long-distance buses can take you to the Caribbean, the Pacific, volcanoes, national parks and almost any major town. The bus is a great option for travelers on a budget, and you can usually stow extra luggage in a handy undercarriage compartment. It's romantic and carefree, and you'll meet a lot more locals this way.

The 4WD Advantage

The Costa Rican bus system has its flaws, of course. For starters, there is no central terminal in San José, but rather several different stations and services, which are

MATYAS REHAK/SHUTTERSTOCK

RAINER LESNIEWSKI/SHUTTERSTOCK

generally located in dodgy neighborhoods. Depots can be grimy and full of characters, especially in the darker hours.

The main drawback is the limited movement. Costa Rica is full of secret nooks, which are often impossible to reach without four-wheel-drive. Renting a car is vastly more expensive than the bus, and you do risk fender benders and mud traps. But you can also take control of your route, grinding over rocky roads to a little-known beach or waterfall. Such nooks can be just too far to trudge on foot, and you may find yourself rolling the dice on a taxi.

For years, backpackers have zigzagged across the landscape by bus, rarely paying as much as US$20 to cross entire provinces.

The Best of Both Worlds

If you're wrestling with your budget, the most rewarding option is to bus for a while, get a sense of what you'd like to see, and then rent a car for a couple of days and double-back to all the spots you've missed. Costa Rica is geographically complex, and it's often hard to gauge travel time before you arrive. The bus will help you understand what you're dealing with, from road conditions to micro-climates. You'll figure out which neighborhoods in San José are worth fighting all that traffic. If all goes well, you'll put your time, and mileage, to good use – and probably hear about a dozen more sights for your next trip.

Hit the Rails

The most overlooked transport in the Central Valley is the commuter train, which can carry you to several major towns for a pittance. Its central hub is the humble **Estación Atlántico** in downtown San José, where passengers gather on the platform each morning and afternoon. The train is a little rickety, but it can take you all the way from Alajuela or Heredia to San José, and then beyond to Cartago. The 32-station system is the last remnant of a defunct national railroad network, and its wide windows offer unique vistas of the urban landscape.

07 Animals up CLOSE

WILDLIFE I ENVIRONMENT I ECOTOURISM

In a nation that boasts 5% of the world's biodiversity, *refugios* serve a double purpose: to help injured and abandoned animals, and to offer visitors an intimate encounter with native species. The Central Valley is hardly Costa Rica's wildest province, but a refuge is a safe place to see critters up close before you seek them in their natural habitats.

TADAS_JUCYS/SHUTTERSTOCK

How To

Getting here *Refugios* in Escazú and Santa Ana are on established bus lines from San José. Locations in Alajuela and Heredia are easiest to reach by taxi or rental car.

When to go Each *refugio* has its own hours of operation. All have outdoor exhibits, so rain can be a factor.

Donations welcome If you're looking to support a good cause, note that most *refugios* work on a shoestring budget.

ONDREJ PROSICKY/SHUTTERSTOCK

Top left Keel-billed toucan
Bottom left Zebra longwing butterfly

Rescate Wildlife Center On the outskirts of downtown Alajuela, Rescate receives more than 2700 at-risk animals per year. A further 800 animals are on permanent exhibit, representing 125 species. Guests can walk the paved paths and see the gamut of wild cats, tapirs, monkeys and birds in a leafy setting. Covering 34 acres, the Wildlife Center is the largest sanctuary in the area.

Refugio Animal de Costa Rica This *refugio* is located on a twisty road between Escazú and Santa Ana, and more than 1500 individual creatures find their way to the facility each year. Visitors are required to take the 90-minute tour, which is led by a trained naturalist. After meeting crocs and white-faced capuchins, order some lunch at in-house **Kivu Restaurant**.

Butterfly Kingdom Mariposario The organized tours at this butterfly preserve in Escazú are mostly designed for children and families, but honestly, who doesn't love butterflies? Learn about metamorphosis, migration patterns and the many butterfly species of Costa Rica while watching them flit around the small garden.

Toucan Rescue Ranch You'll find toucans, of course, but also sloths and barn owls. This ranch is headquartered in the hills of Heredia, where animals are rehabilitated and bred. If you can't find time to get here, the Rescue Ranch also hosts virtual tours.

Hope for Endangered Macaws

Scarlet macaws have long been a darling of illegal pet traffickers, so these vivid-plumaged creatures are now endangered in their natural habitats. At Rescate Wildlife Center, a breeding programs focuses on restoring the scarlet macaw population. Volunteers ensure that macaws have a safe place to build private nests, and they regularly check for new eggs. Once the eggs hatch, the veterinary staff monitors the health of each chick. The goal is to release strong, healthy birds back to their natural home in the Península de Nicoya, so they can continue to reproduce in the wild.

08 Alajuela Rural ROAD TRIP

DRIVE | GARDENS | SMALL-TOWN CHARM

In rural Alajuela, you'll find storybook towns full of fabulous topiaries, tiny cloud forests populated with life-size dinosaurs, and glorious gardens with neon-colored blooms. Leave early, and you can hit up every spot on this road trip and return to Alajuela in time for dinner.

GIANFRANCO VIVI/ SHUTTERSTOCK

Trip Notes

Getting around These towns are accessible by public transportation but you'll need your own car to complete this itinerary in one day.

When to go These destinations are delightful at any time of year.

Stop and smell the hedges Break up your trip from Alajuela (or San José) to La Fortuna with this detour through rural Alajuela.

Crisp Air, Fresh Coffee

My favorite spots in the Central Valley are Heredia and Poás. You can visit the great coffee plantations and the air is crisp and fresh. You can experience local life, taste the food and learn about the culture here. The people are good, friendly and open.

Insight by **Alejandro Aleman**, Alejandro Trips and Tips *(alejandrotripsandtips.com)*

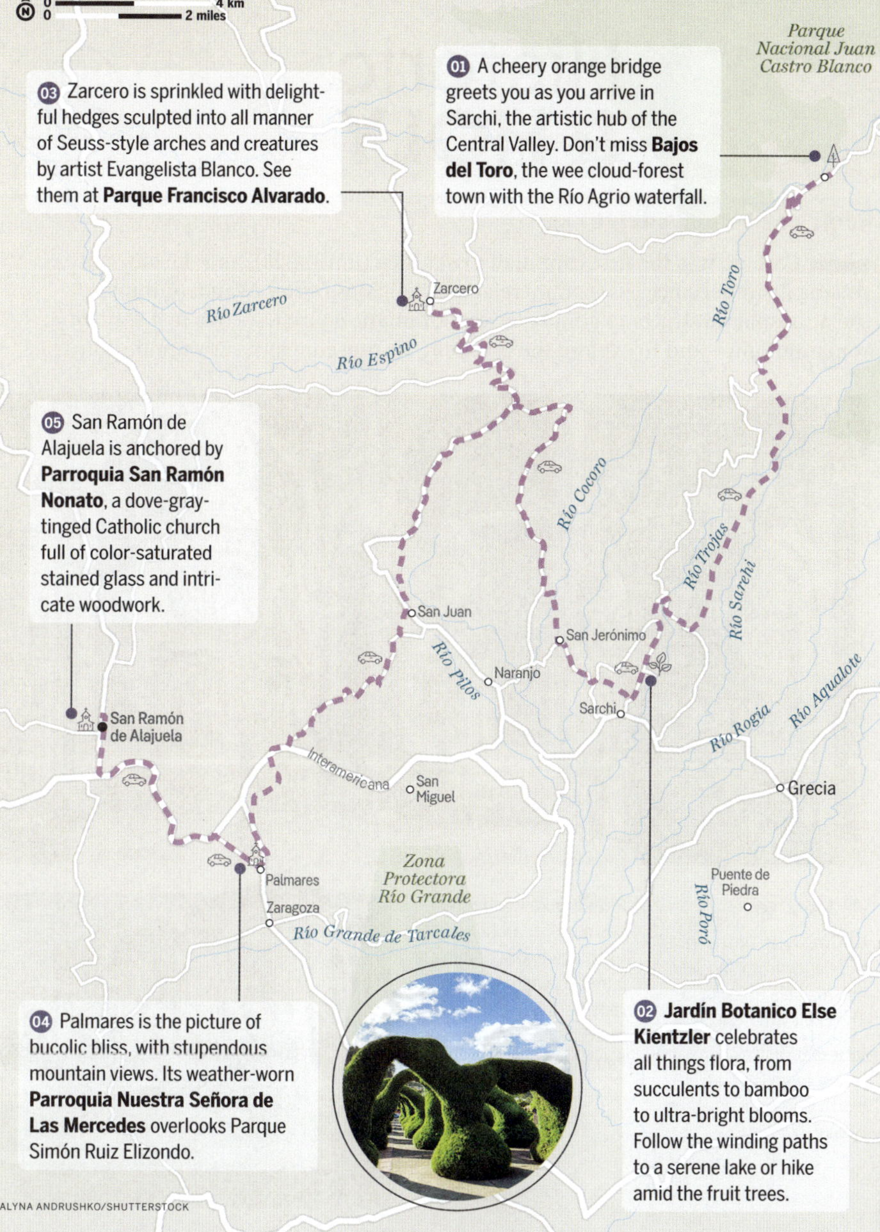

GALYNA ANDRUSHKO/SHUTTERSTOCK

09 Historic & HOLY

RUINS I RELIGIOUS SHRINE I ART

Cartago was the first capital of Costa Rica (until 1823), and the city still retains its importance as a commercial and religious center. Wander around the atmospheric streets to admire several dramatic churches – one in a state of romantic ruin – and to explore the excellent art museum and surrounding gardens.

MILOSK50/SHUTTERSTOCK

How to

Getting here Buses travel frequently from San José and Alajuela to Cartago. The city center is easy to navigate on foot.

When to go Cartago is worth visiting at any time of year.

Ride a bike Cartago has a well-maintained, usable network of bicycle lanes, as well as many rental shops, making it a great place to explore on two wheels.

SVETLANA BYKOVA/SHUTTERSTOCK

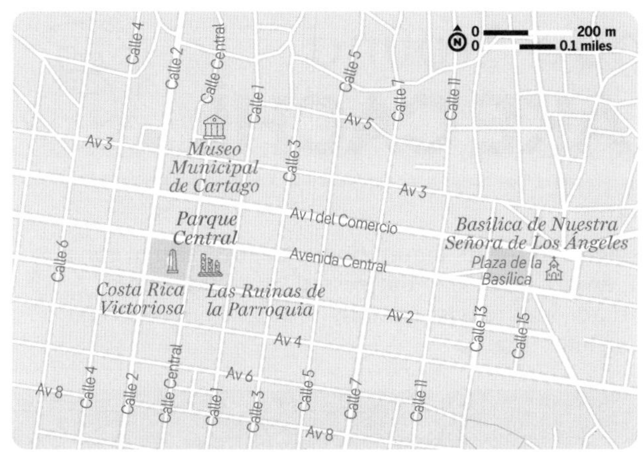

Left Basílica de Nuestra Señora de Los Ángeles
Below Las Ruinas de la Parroquia

Plaza Mayor has been the hub of Cartago life since the city was founded in 1563. The centerpiece of the plaza, **Costa Rica Victoriosa** celebrates 200 years of national independence. On its eastern flank, **Las Ruinas de la Parroquia** are the remains of the multiple churches that have been built and destroyed on this site since the 16th century. While the lore is rife with restless ghosts and natural disasters, the ruins now occupy a tranquil and beautiful park, mixing old masonry and inspired landscaping.

Museo Municipal de Cartago Two blocks north, the Museo Municipal de Cartago is one of the best places to see well-preserved regional art and relics. Multiple rooms feature the art of luminaries like Rafa Fernández, and a big mural depicts the triumphant struggle for Costa Rican independence. The museum is surrounded by lovely manicured gardens, dotted with statuary.

Beautiful Basilica Five blocks east of Plaza Mayor, the iconic **Basílica de Nuestra Señora de Los Ángeles** is a visually epic cathedral – the crown jewel of the city – with ornate pillars reaching up to a golden-arched ceiling. This is the home of La Negrita, a revered black stone icon of the Virgin Mary. Every year, a million devotees participate in the **Romería**, a pilgrimage from San José to Cartago to bring her their prayers.

The Torch of Independence

Every year on September 15, a rare patriotic celebration takes place in Plaza Mayor: the arrival of the torch of independence. The torch is carried from Nicaragua and through the Central Valley, before arriving in the former capital of Cartago. It symbolizes the news of Costa Rican independence, which traveled the same route, after the Central American countries shook off their colonial yoke. Along with the arrival of the torch, the celebration includes parades, festivals, national dances, music and fireworks. Simultaneous celebrations also take place in nearby cities and towns, including Alajuela and San José.

10 Loop Around LAKE CACHÍ

LAKE I NATURE I ECOTOURISM

The Orosí Valley is beloved for its mountainous beauty, and at its center lies Lago de Cachí, an artificial lake buttressed by a major dam (pictured below). Gentle roads and tourist-friendly towns around the lake make for a blissful drive or bike ride.

KRYSSIA CAMPOS/GETTY IMAGES

Lake Cachí

Lake Cachí marks the intersection between the **Río Orosí** and **Río Reventazón**. The lake itself is a little swampy and hard to access, but the dam provides clean electricity to the valley, and the rivers are popular for fishing and white-water rafting. Several tour companies in the town of Orosí can arrange river trips.

Trip Notes

Getting here Buses pass daily between Cartago and local towns, but these gently curving roads are a pleasure to drive or cycle.

When to go The rivers are strongest in the rainy season, but landslides are also possible.

Early to bed Most businesses in the Orosí Valley are closed by 9pm, so make sure to buy everything you need before then.

FROM TOP: CARMELA SOTO/SHUTTERSTOCK, ROBERT ISENBERG/LONELY PLANET

JOSHUA TEN BRINK/SHUTTERSTOCK

The City & the Country

A JET-SETTING NATION, A HUMBLE PAST

Five-star restaurants. Luxury condos. Billboards advertising jewelry and electronics. San José is a 21st-century boomtown, and signs of its success are everywhere. But this image contrasts sharply with Costa Rica's agrarian roots. As Central Valley development amps up, we must remember what makes Ticos special: their connection to the land.

Top left Estadio Nacional
Top center *Casado*
Top right Catedral Metropolitana

In the middle of San José, you'll see the colorful facade of **Restaurante Nuestra Tierra**. Sculptures of a woman and man, dressed in traditional costume, stand next to the entryway. The tables are designed to look like rustic wood. Eating a meal here is like a tutorial on Costa Rican cuisine, from brothy *olla de carne* (pot roast) to *gallo pinto* (blended rice and beans) served on banana leaves. Even coffee is steeped in the canvas sock of an old-fashioned *chorreador*. Nuestra Tierra means Our Land, and the restaurant doubles as a monument to Costa Rican pride. Across from the Plaza de la Democracia, on one of downtown's busiest roads, Nuestra Tierra is an idyllic getaway of wagon wheels and woven baskets. The easygoing dining room contrasts sharply with the diesel fumes and panhandlers just outside.

Costa Rica has changed rapidly in the past few decades. As recently as the 1980s, outsiders perceived this country as a sleepy Central American backwater, known mostly to intrepid backpackers with a high tolerance for rutted jungle roads. Since then, ecotourism has exploded and San José has rapidly modernized. Suburbs have sprung up between disparate towns, and sprawl extends for miles in every direction. The capital is full of cultural institutions, from the historic **Catedral Metropolitana** to the state-of-the-art **Estadio Nacional**. San José has become a city of entrepreneurs, restaurateurs, hoteliers and nonprofit founders. Three-quarters of Costa Rica's population now live in the Central Valley, among them thousands of expats.

Still, the soul of Costa Rica is in its *campo* (countryside). The nation's economy first prospered because of its fertile

SALVADOR AZNAR/SHUTTERSTOCK

MIROSLAV DENES/SHUTTERSTOCK

volcanic soil. Today, urbanites flee to the beaches and mountains every weekend. Family remains the strongest bond, and even the hippest city slickers make time to gather with their kin for dinner. The preferred meal is still some variation of rice and beans, the same staples eaten by farmers for generations. Tico humor has always been bawdy and down-to-earth. These are folks who love simplicity, who don't like to rush things. You won't find a lot of hoarders here; most people only have enough possessions to furnish their homes.

> The soul of Costa Rica is in its *campo* (countryside). The nation's economy first prospered because of its fertile volcanic soil.

The further you venture from the city, the more relaxed the people seem. In the small *pueblos* of the Central Valley, locals wave to strangers and help with directions. *'Pura vida'* isn't just a phrase, but a way of life. The government may have disbanded the army in San José, but the passion for living in peace is the hallmark of the *campesino*. The same goes for environmental stewardship; farmers carefully tended the fields long before the first carbon-neutral resort.

Nuestra Tierra is a sentimental restaurant, but it also reminds visitors of those agrarian roots. Costa Rica had embraced its new roles as global playground and environmental champion, and Ticos should be proud of all they have accomplished. But, as many Ticos have observed, *'Costa Rica es un pueblo.'* You could translate this two ways: 'Costa Rica is a small town,' or 'Costa Rica is one people.'

La Vida Rural

The Tico connection to the land is not only about rainforests and wildlife. Agriculture still plays a significant role in the culture and economy, especially in the Central Valley, where sugarcane and coffee farms blanket the undulating hills. Touring a local farm (or better yet, spending a few days) is a wonderful way to get a more complete understanding of this connection to the land. **Hacienda Orosí** allows visitors to experience the processes of growing and harvesting coffee beans, while the on-site farm, aka La Granja, shows off the farm animals. It's an idealized version of farm life, for sure, but still an insightful one.

THE VALLEY
at a Glance

01

02

03

04

01 Chifrijo
No San José pub crawl is complete without this hearty stew of *frijoles* (beans) and *chicharrones* (pork rinds).

02 Museo Nacional
This castle-like facade (p51) is easy to spot in downtown San José, and exhibits include art galleries and a butterfly garden.

03 Juan Santamaría
This bronze statue (p59) in Alajuela honors Costa Rica's only major war hero, who died on a daring one-man raid.

04 Las Esféras
These mysterious stone orbs are attributed to pre-Columbian peoples. Original spheres and facsimiles decorate major buildings, including the Estadio Nacional.

05 Estadio Nacional
This 35,000-seat sports complex (p53) is the envy of Central America and home to La Selección, Costa Rica's soccer team.

06 Guaro
This clear liquor is made from sugarcane. Cacique Guaro distills the national spirit, which mixes well with anything.

07 Central Clock
An ornate clock and fountain stand on the edge of the Plaza de la Cultura, marking a common rendezvous point.

08 Taxi Rojo
Hail a *taxi rojo* (red taxi) just about anywhere in the Central Valley to quickly zip to your destination.

09 El Fortín
This distinctive lookout tower (p59) was once part of a colonial fort. and is now the proud symbol of Heredia.

Listings

BEST OF THE REST

Food Halls

Por Media Calle Mercado Gastronómico $$

This is an eclectic food hall in Heredia, with regular live music between 7pm and 9pm nightly.

Calle 33 Mercadito $$

This Escazú spot takes its name from the neighborhood's busiest corridor. Browse 10 windows for tacos, ramen or ceviche, then settle on a pet-friendly patio.

Jardín de Lolita $$

Polished picnic tables, strung-up lights and more styles of cuisine than you could try in a single night. This edenic food hall in Barrio Escalante serves everything from sushi to burgers.

Container Platz $$

Shipping containers make for cool architecture, especially when each contains a different mini-restaurant. Mosey over to Santa Ana for wraps, ice cream or poké bowls.

El Mestizo Mercado Gastronómico $$$

In the commercial sprawl of Escazú, El Mestizo Mercado Gastronómico is a flavor oasis. Morning waffles, noontime tapas and a full night at the *Biergarten*.

Unique Stays

Gran Hotel Costa Rica

This handsome hotel from the 1930s stands next to San José's Plaza de la Cultura. The hotel was recently renovated but retains its vintage ambience. Notable guests include John F Kennedy.

URBN Escalante

This 29-story apartment complex towers over Barrio Escalante in San José. Many tenants rent their apartments to guests, who enjoy a rooftop pool and one of the best views in the city.

Peace Lodge

The La Paz estate in Alajuela is best known for its waterfall gardens, but you can also stay the night, giving you time to savor the on-site restaurants and animal sanctuaries.

Xandari Resort & Spa

Drive 15 minutes north of Alajuela and find lush countryside, expansive verandas and all the wellness treatments you could hope for. Easy access to the airport makes this a pampering vacation-ender.

IMAGESYNC LTD/ALAMY

Peace Lodge, La Paz Waterfall Gardens

Finca 360

It doesn't look like a farm, but the 360-degree views are soul-stirring. With only five rooms, this mountainside lodging in rural Alajuela offers a spa, a kitchen and yoga sessions.

 Cultural Encounters

Mercado Central

Browse among the same stalls where Ticos have done their shopping for generations. Hundreds of vendors sell everything from spinach to handbags in this feisty indoor environment.

Teatro Melico Salazar

You might walk right by this hallowed auditorium in downtown San José, but don't let it's bland facade deceive you: professional concerts, theater and dance all take place on its stage.

Antigua Aduana

Once a customs house, this voluminous brick building on the edge of Barrio Escalante holds large-scale cultural events. Expect to walk into a concert or craft market on any given day.

Teatro el Triciclo

'Tricycle Theater' in San José specializes in comedies and farces. Triciclo is one of many black-box theaters designed for crowd-pleasing, Spanish-language entertainment.

ChepeCletas Tours

Walking and cycling tours around San José, focusing on themes such as coffee, *cantinas* (canteens), food markets and history, guided by locals who love Chepe.

Parque Diversiones

For old-school roller coasters, you can't do better than Parque Diversiones on the outskirts of San José. Founded to fund the Hospital de los Niños, this amusement park is entertaining for all ages.

ROAMING PANDA PHOTOS/SHUTTERSTOCK

Mercado Central

Sibö Chocolate

This little chocolate company in Heredia celebrates Costa Rica's underrated cacao industry. Learn about the history of chocolate in its hilltop location, or visit the second shop and cafe in Escazú.

Museo Histórico Cultural Juan Santamaría

This museum in downtown Alajuela celebrates Costa Rica's role in the Filibuster War of the early 19th century. It's also close to the Mercado Municipal, a historic indoor bazaar.

Casa de la Cultura Alfredo Gonzáles Flores

This vintage house in downtown Heredia is located right next to El Fortín and curates both gallery shows and lecture series. A permanent exhibit honors historic Costa Rican president 'Don Alfredo.'

Monumento Nacional Guayabo

This pre-Columbian town mysteriously thrived several hundred years ago, but no one knows who built it or why its society disbanded. Hike around this well-excavated archaeological site.

Hacienda Orosí

Come for the hot springs, stay for the crash course in agriculture. Laze in Hacienda Orosí's five thermal pools, dine in its upscale restaurant and take a farm tour.

Sacred Sites

Catedral Metropolitana

The cathedral is a colossal church in San José, standing on one end of the Parque Central. This is also the site for a recreated crucifixion scene during Holy Week.

Tres Cruces Trail

This rigorous hike in the mountains above Escazú is no task for beginners, but climbers will be rewarded with divine views – plus three crucifixes scattered across the peaks.

Parroquia San Antonio de Padua

This red-roofed church in Escazú yields a divine view of the Central Valley. It's also nestled in the middle of town, next to an attractive flower garden.

Iglesia de Santa Ana

This historic church is an anchorpoint in the middle of Santa Ana. Admire its simple stone architecture, then come back on Sunday for the weekly farmers market just outside.

Parroquia Vázquez de Coronado

No church in Costa Rica looks more like it was transported directly from the French countryside. This church in Coronado is a gothic masterpiece, although it was notably finished in 1930.

Basílica de Nuestra Señora de los Ángeles

The magnificent basilica in the middle of Cartago is an active church, but it's also a destination for pilgrimage. See 'La Negrita,' a carved stone with a miraculous 17th-century past.

Iglesia Colonial de Orosí

This simple church across from Orosí soccer field is considered the oldest Costa Rican church to hold continuous services, having survived earthquakes and social tumult. Visit the adjacent museum to learn more.

Coffee Experiences

Cafeoteca

This bright former ranch house has a spacious atrium and sophisticated local coffees. Cafeoteca was a pioneer in Barrio Escalante, where many similar high-end cafes have sprung up.

Britt Coffee Tour

Local coffee giant Britt has its headquarters in Heredia, where visitors can join a multimedia plantation tour, savor a cappuccino in the open-air cafe and browse the coffee-scented gift shop.

Hacienda La Chimba

In the hills above Santa Ana, Hacienda La Chimba hosts coffee tours plus dinners in its restaurant. Make a day of it with ziplining, ropes courses and independent hiking.

Hacienda Alsacia

Best known as a Starbucks supplier, Hacienda Alsacia in rural Heredia offers a compelling tour for a well-known product. Stop here on the way to or from Volcán Poás.

Finca Rosa Blanca

You may love visiting the Finca Rose Blanca farm so much, you'll want to stay over. Luckily, the *finca* doubles as a boutique hotel, with jaw-droppingly beautiful accommodations and surroundings.

SALVADOR AZNAR/SHUTTERSTOCK

Basílica de Nuestra Señora de los Ángeles

Grab a Drink

El Cuartel $$

In the throbbing Barrio California party district of San José, El Cuartel is a cozy, old-school tavern. Order from a classic bar menu, swig an Imperial and catch a match.

Mandrágora $$

This Barrio Escalante gastropub is modeled on the Harry Potter franchise, complete with robed servers, entrees named after characters, and 'broomstick parking' outside. The cocktails work magic.

LA Buenos Aires $$

This is your classic San José pub with a long, L-shaped bar. Located next to Santa Taresita Church, LA Buenos Aires has a long history of wedding after-parties.

Café Los Deseos $$

Romantic lighting and superlative pub food make this place a must-visit in Barrio Carmen. Come for the artful decor, stay for the margaritas thick with chopped fruit.

Club Alemán $$

The German Club is popular among Central European travelers, but all are welcome. The food is meaty and well prepared, and there's no better place to celebrate Oktoberfest.

Soberanos $$

The first thing you'll see is a big porch and cartoon cats painted on the facade. Step inside this Escalante pub for burgers, noodle bowls and a discriminating beer selection.

La Criollita $$

The classic San José restaurant has white tablecloths, framed paintings and a lively little bar. Professionals often come here after work, and the menu lives up to its 'Creole' namesake.

ROBERT ISENBERG/LONELY PLANET

Hacienda La Chimba

Central Pub $$

Just a stone's throw from La Sabana Park, step into the English-style pub for inventive cocktails and live music in the adjacent London Room.

Jazz Café $$

Tucked into an Escazú frontage road, Jazz Café is a state-of-the-art performance venue drawing some of the best musicians in Costa Rica. Expect energetic concerts and expert cocktails.

Bar Chubbs $$

Chubbs is an archetypal American sports bar, with Buffalo wings, buckets of beer and global sports on TV. When you're in Escazú and need the 'Cheers' experience, hit up Chubbs.

República Casa Cervecera $$

A voluminous brewpub next to La Sabana Park, Republica Casa showcases brightly colored taps and crispy fish and chips. The beer and festive atmosphere make this a major hot spot.

Scan to find more things to do in San José & the Central Valley online

CARIBBEAN COAST

NATURE | HISTORY | ADVENTURE

Experience the Caribbean Coast online

CARIBBEAN COAST
Trip Builder

El Caribe's vibe is like nothing else in Costa Rica: part Tico, part Rastafarian, part Jamaican, with fusion spins on classic dishes, stunning beaches and jungle, and lively, historically relevant big cities that reveal fantastic art and culinary scenes if you peek below the surface.

Eat your way around **Jamaica Town**, sampling Costa Rican and Caribbean flavors (p89)
20min from central Limón City

Marvel at the traditional water-enveloped village of **Parismina** (p92)
+ 90min from Siquirres

Snorkel **Isla Uvita**, Limón's uninhabited island paradise (p87)
40min from Limón City

Explore hidden waterfalls and jungle trails at **Cahuita** (p94)
10min from Cahuita

Observe the leatherback nesting ground at **Manzanillo** (p104)
20min guided walk from Manzanillo

Tackle apex-level surfing at **Salsa Brava** in Puerto Viejo (p98)
3min from central Puerto Viejo

PREVIOUS SPREAD: STUART PEARCE/ALAMY
ABOVE: DAMSEA/SHUTTERSTOCK

Practicalities

ARRIVING

Fly into San José's **Juan Santamaría International Airport** and take the direct bus to Limón, or fly to **Limón International Airport** and take a six-minute taxi ride into the city.

MONEY

Eat at local *sodas* (small local restaurants) and stay at homestays to save cash. Don't expect good wi-fi at budget options.

CONNECT

Wi-fi tends to be spotty in remote places in El Caribe, so it's a smart idea to have an international plan or get a local SIM card.

WHERE TO STAY

City/Town	Pros/Cons
Puerto Viejo	Excellent nightlife, accommodations for every budget. Better nature elsewhere.
Limón City	Great food, amazing history. Difficult to navigate.
Cahuita	Amazing music scene. Fewer amenities.
Manzanillo	Tons of nature and animals. Little nightlife.

GETTING AROUND

Car Renting a car is the easiest way to travel El Caribe.

Public transportation Ample public transportation in Limón City, including taxis, and buses arriving from Terminal de Autobuses, and Terminal MEPE.

Taxi, shuttle and public bus Services run between Limón City, Cahuita and Puerto Viejo.

TOP: PAUL_BRIGHTON/SHUTTERSTOCK
BOTTOM: CLARA MURCIA/SHUTTERSTOCK

EATING & DRINKING

El Caribe's cuisine is Jamaican influenced. As such, you'll find traditional rice and beans served with coconut milk, jerk-style dishes (pictured top left), garlic potatoes, *patis* (small savory pastries), and Caribbean-influenced sweets like yucca rolls (pictured bottom left) and ginger biscuits. People on the Caribbean coast don't just eat *gallo pinto* (rice and beans) for breakfast, and their *casados* (set meals) have rice and beans mixed together.

Best *patis*
Taylor's (p89)

Must-try *casados*
Restaurante Kalisi (p110)

SEP–OCT
Dry weather means exceptional snorkeling and diving

DEC–FEB
Find epic waves in Puerto Viejo during these months

FEB–APR
Usually rainier, cheaper accommodations, fewer crowds

AUG–SEP
Best time to spot turtles

11 Uninhabited ISLAND

DIVING | SURFING | EXPLORATION

Whether it's called Quiribri, Little Grape Island or Isla Uvita, Limón City's long and lush offshore isle was Christopher Columbus' primary landing spot on his final trip to El Caribe. It's adorned with *alemandra* (almond), tobacco, Spanish cedar, and Peruvian Poro trees and plants. Snorkel, paddleboard or dive to the hidden shipwreck on this uninhabited stretch, a quick 30-minute sail from Limón's port.

How To

Getting here A public boat from **Transporte Acuático Island Uvita Eco Tour** on Río Cieneguita *(US$20)* runs to the island several times daily, depending on demand.

When to go Go during El Caribe's dry season (September to October) for the best visibility.

Lighthouse When not diving or exploring Isla Uvita's rugged landscape, pay homage to the lighthouse and its cultural significance.

SEAPHOTOART/ALAMY

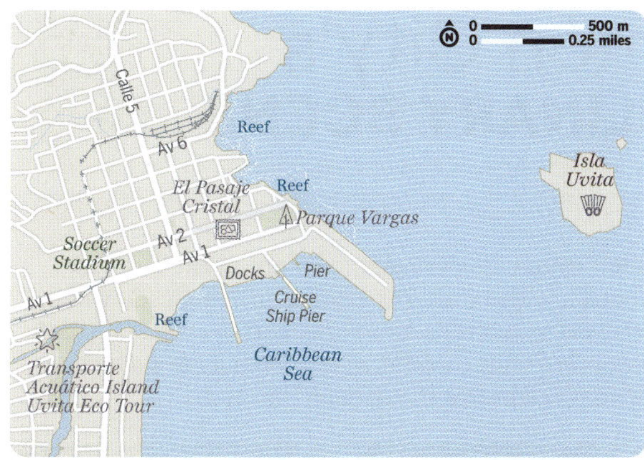

Island Life Disembark at the south end of **Isla Uvita** and hike through thick tropical vegetation to the remains of an 1886 hospital. Here, nuns cared for people with incurable illnesses (leprosy, smallpox, tuberculosis etc). Continuing around the island, you'll scale hills for views of coral colonies and tide pools below; look out for brown boobies (large seabirds related to gannets) nesting on a neighboring islet.

Surfing The reefs create gnarly, unpredictable but undeniably fun surf with barrel-heavy waves and sharp breaks. Bring your shortboard if you want a challenge, but be prepared for unforgiving waves and a super-sharp coral bottom if you get stuck in the washing machine. Jellyfish are also common near Isla Uvita.

Diving Massive coral reefs surround Isla Uvita, perfect for experienced divers who don't mind navigating nooks and crannies and discovering at least one shipwreck tangled below. Marine life and coral have reclaimed Isla Uvita's shipwreck, the *Phoenix*, and exploring the wreck is one of the most popular and rewarding things to do there. Full of twisty nooks and glorious bright coral and sea life, the *Phoenix* is a cool interplay of sunken maritime technology and marine life habitat.

Bring your own gear Isla Uvita is also good for paddleboarding and snorkeling. In all cases, you need your own gear, as there are no facilities on the island.

Far left Snorkeling

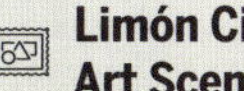

Limón City's Art Scene

Sharp-eyed visitors will spot street art near Parque Vargas on Limón City's dock, right across from Isla Uvita, where Christopher Columbus famously made his fourth and final voyage to Costa Rica. There are also many smaller museums near Parque Vargas, directly across from where the cruise ships dock, showcasing historical oil paintings. If you're looking for super local, new art, visit **El Pasaje Cristal**, reasonably close to Parque Vargas, where local artists set up shop.

Insight by
Sadie Jordan, *Soul Life Travel*
@Soullifetravel

12 Limón City's CULINARY SCENE

SEAFOOD | PASTRIES | SWEETS

Firmly but politely hidden from outsiders and folks not in the know, Limón City's culinary scene spans a wide berth. It's evident in Jamaica Town, in Caribbean bakeries that serve sweet yucca rolls and *patis*, and in *sodas* (small local restaurants) offering *gallo pinto* with coconut rice, as well as *rondón*, a traditional Jamaican fish stew that celebrates the African diaspora.

CENTRAL AMERICA/ALAMY

How To

Getting around Public buses are the easiest and cheapest way to get around, but taxis are available too. Always use the meter.

When to go Lunchtime

Try It In Limón, your *casado* (set meal) is likely to come with coconut-milk-flavored rice and beans instead of the more standard *gallo pinto*.

HOPE PHILLIPS/SHUTTERSTOCK

Culinary heritage Part of Limón City's charm is tied to its culinary heritage. Food is intrinsically linked to the culture here, and it has deep roots dating back to when seeds were taken from Jamaica to grow in El Caribe. The fusion of traditional Costa Rican foods with Caribbean-inspired ingredients is one of Limón City's critical contributions to the foodie world.

Where to try it Visit the **Mercado Municipal**, an open-air market near Parque Vargas for fresh, organic fruits and vegetables. **Jamaica Town** is famous for fried chicken. Hit up the local bakeries for sharp ginger biscuits or yucca rolls.

Eateries Follow your nose to **Soda El Patty**, a beloved, long-standing restaurant, for savory or sweet *patí* (essentially a Caribbean *empanada*). If the line's too long, locals recommend **Taylor's** a few blocks east. Sidle up to the counter at **Restaurante Kalisi** and request a plate of coconut rice, red beans, meat and veggies, with a glass of *sorrel* (a Jamaican hibiscus-ginger drink); save room for a slab of chewy cassava pudding. True to its name, **Red Snapper** restaurant serves delicious whole fried snapper and fried plantains from its mountainside perch just west of Jamaica Town; the views are as good as the food. Out on Playa Piuta, **Lizzie 1879** is a favorite with a staunch local following. The name is a nod to the first ship to bring Jamaicans to Costa Rica.

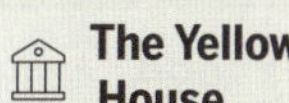

Top left Open-air market, Limón City
Bottom left Red snapper and fried plantains

The Yellow House

The **Casa de la Cultura Marcus Garvey**, also known as Liberty Hall or the 'Yellow House,' is an essential piece of Puerto Viejo's history. Created by activist Marcus Garvey, the humble yellow house was a place for migrant workers who didn't have a place to live. It was and continues to be a community hub and marketplace. Today it hosts farmers markets, health fairs, English classes and dance and documentary screenings. It also offers an on-site library, regular art exhibitions and children's entertainment and education. Murals inside and out depict its history, and a banner honors the first families of Puerto Viejo.

Unpacking Limón City

FABULOUS FOOD, ESSENTIAL HISTORY AND WELCOMING VIBES

Limón City is among the most important historic areas in Costa Rica, thanks to Marcus Garvey's Black Star Line and his UNIA organization. From its tantalizing Caribbean takes on traditional Costa Rican foods to its essential history, Limón City beckons you toward a whole new appreciation of this complex country.

Top left Marcus Garvey
Top center United Fruit Company workers
Top right Stock certificate, Black Star Line

SCIENCE HISTORY IMAGES/ALAMY

Undeserved Reputation

Despite its incredible historical relevance and food scene, many visitors to Costa Rica give Limón City a miss, as the town has been unfairly maligned as a risky no-go zone. That's a shame because, while parts of the city are best avoided, and you should always exercise caution with your valuables, it's no worse or better than other major tourist cities in Costa Rica.

Jamaican Immigration

Limón City, and El Caribe in general, have a predominately Black population due to the influx of Jamaican migrants and the United Fruit Company's history in Limón City. Jamaican people emigrated to Costa Rica during the mid-1800s to work on the new railroad and for the United Fruit Company. They brought their cuisine with them, and the merging of Jamaican staples like jerk spices with Costa Rican dishes created the amazing food culture El Caribe enjoys today.

Marcus Garvey

Jamaica native and (short-term) Costa Rica resident, Marcus Garvey was a Black activist who sought ways to unite Africans and African-descended peoples and fought for their rights around the world.

Like many Jamaican-born people, Garvey emigrated to Costa Rica for job prospects and worked at the United Fruit Company. There, Garvey witnessed exploitation and terrible working conditions, prompting him to launch *The*

PHOTO-FOX/ALAMY

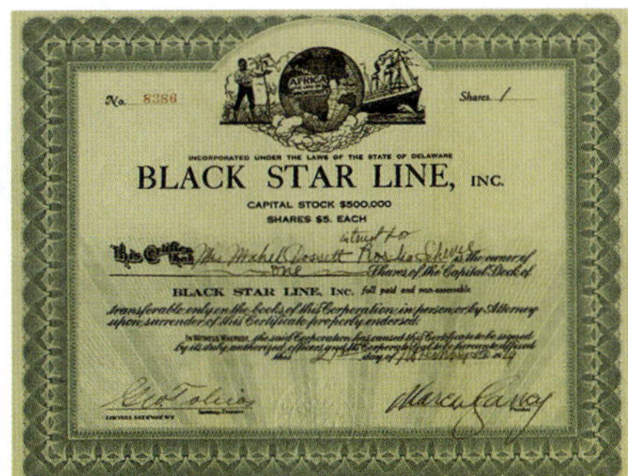

EVERETT COLLECTION HISTORICAL/ALAMY

Nation, a publication aimed at supporting workers. He also founded the Black Star Line with the objective of facilitating trade with Africa, and giving Black people the agency to return to Africa if they wished. Garvey went on to found the Universal Negro Improvement Association (UNIA), a Black rights organization with members worldwide.

Garvey's legacy is evident all over Limón City. The fruits of his labor continue in places like Puerto Viejo, where Garvey set up a haven house for migrant workers who didn't have anywhere else to go. Today, it's a thriving community center.

> Limón City's charm comes from its historic significance, a legacy of overcoming the odds, friendly, proud people, and remarkable food and arts scenes.

Limón City Today

Despite being long overlooked in favor of the Pacific coast, weathering decades of economic recession, and taking a huge hit from the cruise-ship industry, Limón City retains its dignity and culture. The city's charm comes from its historic significance; a legacy of overcoming the odds; friendly, proud people; and remarkable food and arts scenes.

So, don't believe the hype about Limón City. Instead have a *pati*, a yucca roll, or a steaming bowl of *rondón,* visit the old site of the Black Star Line, learn about Garvey's profound legacy, and walk away with an appreciation for the grit and dignity of El Caribe's people.

United Fruit Company

While the American-owned United Fruit Company, known as Chiquita today, promised jobs and mobility to Limón City's residents, the reality was sadly much different. Workers were paid abysmal wages, sometimes in company coupons rather than actual cash, and expected to work long hours with no time off. Additionally, vast banana plantations destabilized the natural environment and negatively affected the soil, impacting future generations. Workers often suffered through bouts of tropical diseases, like yellow fever or even malaria, and sanitary conditions were poor at best. At its peak, the United Fruit Company owned as much as 9% of Costa Rica's land.

13 Sea Turtles & SECLUSION

SEA TURTLES | SPORTFISHING | BIRDWATCHING

Parismina sits at the mouth of Parque Nacional Tortuguero and is known for its leatherback sea turtles, laid-back village life, and phenomenal sportfishing and birdwatching. Visit on your way to the park, or spend a few days soaking in the local vibe, horseback riding, or fishing for bonito, snook or tarpon in the local canals or beachside.

How To

Getting here Take the Caño Blanco water taxi from Siquirres to Parismina. Or, take a tour or private boat from Moín and ask to be dropped in Parismina.

When to go Visit between February and July for leatherbacks, and July and October for green turtles.

Money and language There are no reliable ATMs in Parismina and credit cards are not widely accepted; bring cash. You'll also need functional Spanish to communicate.

A different vibe Parismina's vibe is light years away from anything you'll find in Puerto Viejo or Limón City. It's a laid-back, eco-centric atmosphere, where local homestays are the lodging of choice, village culture is traditional, and there are leatherback and green turtles aplenty. You won't find a party scene here. Parismina is for those who don't mind working for an exceptional experience, including taking public transportation and water taxis to land on something wholly unique.

Sea turtles **Asociación Salvemos Las Tortugas de Parismina** (ASTOP) is a local association dedicated to protecting the sea turtle population. The group maintains a turtle hatchery on a section of 6km beach. Travelers can volunteer to help guard the hatchery and patrol the shoreline alongside professional turtle guides (most of whom are former poachers). Depending on the time of year, volunteers also help with nest

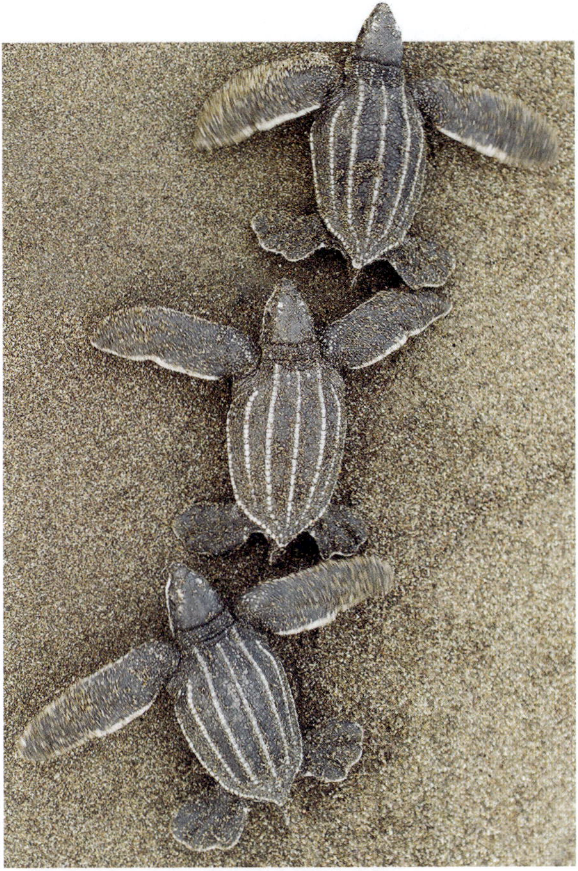

CAVAN IMAGES/GETTY IMAGES

JORY F/SHUTTERSTOCK

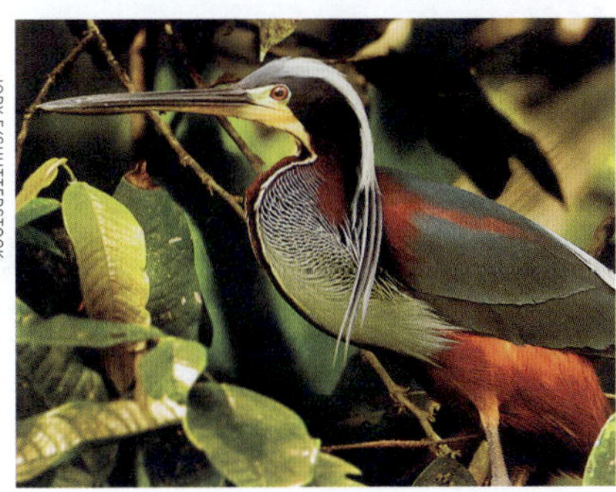

Above Leatherback sea turtles
Left Agami heron

Walk Across Costa Rica

Pick up **El Camino de Costa Rica** – a walk that traverses Costa Rica from El Caribe to the Pacific Coast – outside Parismina at Pier Goshen. Your 280km walk takes about two weeks and connects Costa Rica's internal rural villages. You'll trek through different ecosystems, stay at local houses, enjoy curated experiences and support the local economy.

Certain parts of the trail are strenuous, so you'll need a relatively high endurance and physical aptitude, and a desire to experience authentic Tico culture. Recommended tour companies include **UrriTrek** *(urritrekcostarica.com)*, **Walk CR** *(walkcr.com)* and **Ticos A Pata** *(ticosapata.com)*.

excavation, collecting data and hatchery building, or other community projects.

Wildlife Situated right near Parque Nacional Tortuguero, **Parismina** is a veritable haven for local fish and birds, such as Agami herons and toucans, which, in addition to its famed turtles, flock to the beaches between February and October. For the whole experience, stay with a local family, and try your luck at sportfishing right from the beach. Rudimentary Spanish and a willingness to go with the flow are musts here.

14 Caribbean Jungle VIBES

WATERFALLS | WILDLIFE | CALYPSO

Cahuita has a unique vibe, played to the tune of Calypso music from local legend Walter 'Gavitt' Ferguson. Explore coastal rainforest and clandestine waterfalls, meet the Bribrí indigenous people, and experience an authentic, unforgettable slice of Afro-Caribbean paradise.

F.J. JIMENEZ/GETTY IMAGES

How To

Getting here Cahuita is a 50-minute bus ride from Limón, or 30 minutes from Puerto Viejo. The town is small enough to explore on foot or by bike.

When to go Visit between June and September to glimpse leatherback turtles nesting on Cahuita's *playas*.

Caution The hiking trail requires a river crossing. Respect the red flag: it means that crossing is unsafe.

PATDU PHOTOGRAPHY/SHUTTERSTOCK

Walter 'Gavitt' Ferguson

Also known as 'Segundo,' Ferguson is Cahuita's most famous resident and the king of Calypso in this chilled-out Caribbean town. Mr Gavitt died in 2023, at the age of 103, but his legacy endures in Cahuita's refreshing music scene. Check it out on Friday nights at **Reggae Bar** or Saturday nights at **Coco's Bar**. Better yet, come for the annual weekend-long **International Calypso Festival** in July.

SIMON DANNHAUER/SHUTTERSTOCK

Beachy Fun

Cahuita is bookended by two beaches: Playa Negra and Playa Blanca. At the northwestern end of Cahuita, **Playa Negra** – a long, black-sand beach – flies the *bandera azul ecológica*, meaning that it meets the highest ecological standard. Most parts of the beach are good for swimming. When the swells are big, there's also

Yellow Eyelash Vipers

Yellow eyelash vipers wink at their prey before they strike, landing a heavy dose of neurotoxic and hemotoxic venom that immediately attacks the nervous system. Death is quick but terrifying, making these brightly hued snakes one of the most fearsome creatures in Central America. Fortunately, if you give them a wide berth, you'll avoid their wrath.

Top left : Playa Blanca
Top right Natural pool, Cahuita
Bottom left Playa Negra

a good beach break for beginner surfers. Just south of Cahuita, the undeveloped white-sand **Playa Blanca** is beautiful but perilous for swimmers due to rip tides.

Leatherback Turtles

Turtle Rescue Cahuita nurtures and protects resident leatherback turtles that nest on the beach between June and September. During these months, travelers can volunteer to assist with nest monitoring, beach cleanup and turtle releases. If you're lucky, you might see these beautiful behemoths emerge from the sea and lay their eggs.

Parque Nacional Cahuita

One of the country's most popular national parks, **Parque Nacional Cahuita** comprises diverse habitats, including white-sand beach, coral reefs, coastal rainforest and mangrove swamp. The park is bisected by a hiking trail connecting its two entrances, Playa Blanca and Puerto Vargas, off Hwy 36. It's about 11km end to end; along the way you have a good chance of spotting sloths, monkeys, coatis and raccoons – maybe even a venomous eyelash pit viper. Bring plenty of water and don't miss a delicious dip at Punta Cahuita.

Visiting the Bribrí People

The indigenous Bribrí people live 20 minutes outside Cahuita. Although it's not advisable or respectful to go alone, local guides from Cahuita can take you to the village, where you'll learn how to make chocolate, fashion a rope of local leaves and learn about Bribrí farming techniques. There are also three incredible waterfalls near the Bribrí village and a lookout point from which you can spot the Cordillera de Talamanca mountains, Panama and Puerto Viejo. Visiting the Bribrí people is an honor and a privilege. If you go, refrain from photographing them or their homes without permission.

Insight by **Alexander Mullins Aymerich (Tito Cahuita)**, owner of Cahuita Green Tours, Cahuita *@tito_cahuita*

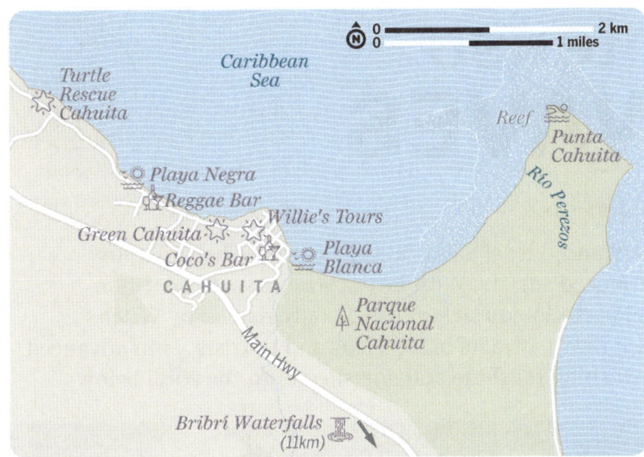

Left Sloth, Parque Nacional Cahuita
Below Yellow eyelash viper, Parque Nacional Cahuita

Punta Cahuita is surrounded with white-sand beaches and full of tropical fish like loro (parrotfish), angelfish, red snapper, kingfish and friendly nurse sharks – making it an excellent snorkel spot. Snorkeling is best during the dry season, as Costa Rica's green season can stir up sediment from the bottom and disturb the fish. You must be accompanied by a guide to snorkel in the park; hire one through **Willie's Tours** or **Green Cahuita**.

Waterfall Magic

Between Cahuita and Puerto Viejo, several impressive waterfalls offer an enticing cooldown on a sweltering day. On the grounds of the private farm Finca Las Brisas, the smallish **Catarata Dos Aguas** has a refreshing dipping pool for a small parking fee.

A little further west, another signposted road leads to **Catarata Ma-Cu**, aka Bribrí Sparkling Waterfalls. The falls are a steep 10-minute walk down, so you'll want water shoes with good grip.

In the rainforest on the Bribrí reservation, the gorgeous 15m **Catarata Volio** has a deep natural swimming pool. Getting there requires two shallow river crossings and a short jungle walk. A guide is recommended; try **Green Cahuita**.

15 Intense WAVES

SURFING | ADRENALINE | ADVENTURE

Consistently gnarly, advanced level Salsa Brava, aka 'The Cheese Grater', is a wild ride, even for experienced surfers. With heavy, sizable surf and a skin-shredding coral bottom, it's Puerto Viejo's sickest break, only rivaled by Witch's Rock in intensity. While Salsa Brava attracts brave Ticos and tourists, even advanced surfers are sucked into the washing machine and smashed onto the coral below.

ADRIAN HEPWORTH/ALAMY

How To

Getting here Access Salsa Brava from the very south end of Puerto Viejo on the way to Playa Cocles. Look for the small park with beach access and plenty of seasoned surfers with shortboards.

When to go You'll get awesome waves year round, but if you're really seeking a divine surf experience, visit during April or November when the swells are the biggest.

Beware! Watch out for super-sharp coral and big egos on the breaks.

LMSPENCER/SHUTTERSTOCK

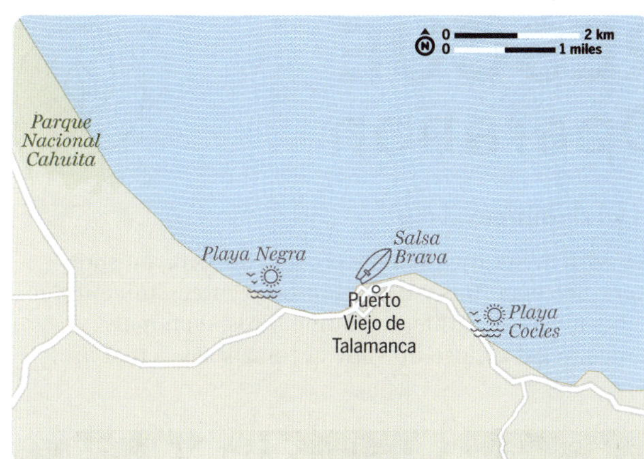

Breaking the Pacific monopoly Puerto Viejo's Cheese Grater proves once and for all that the Península de Nicoya and the Pacific coast don't have a lockdown on fab surfing in Costa Rica. **Salsa Brava** not only rivals anything you'll find in Tamarindo, Jacó, or even intermediate-level Dominical, it blows it out of the water. Massive swells coupled with lacerating coral make this break a fun but ferocious ride that can give you bragging rights forever or land you in the nearest ER; no in-betweens.

Local territory Shortboards are the best way to navigate the perils and barrels of the Cheese Grater, although they won't protect you against the break's other menace: territorial surfers who stake claim to the juiciest and heaviest waves. Don't expect any courtesies or favors from salty surfers whose turf you're paddling on. If you drop in on the line, you'll get slammed with worse than Salsa Brava's notorious coral.

Takeoff zones Salsa Brava has two takeoff zones: First and Second Peak. Top surfers and locals usually flock to First Peak, and the lineup can get jammed. Second Peak tends to be less congested, and it's just a little northwest of First Peak. You can catch barrels from either takeoff point, but the Second Peak is slightly better for shoulder surfing.

Playa Negra If the Cheese Grater is too intense for your tastes, nearby **Playa Negra** has chiller surf and a calmer vibe.

Top left Playa Cocles
Bottom left Playa Negra

Surfing Playa Cocles

A 10-minute walk or two-minute bike ride from Salsa Brava, **Playa Cocles** is a sweet alternative to the Cheese Grater, with intermediate to advanced waves and a less-aggressive lineup than the infamous surfer skinner.

Bring your shortboard and head to Cocles during high tide, when you'll find magnificent, hearty waves and a lengthy run. There are left and right breaks near the shore and ample room for everyone.

If your surfing skills are a little rusty and you want to warm up properly before heading to Salsa Brava, Playa Cocles is a smart play, and since it's so close, you can easily kick off both places in a day.

■ Insight by **Alexander Tapia**, of Alexander Tourist Driver Costa Rica, Puerto Viejo

16 RESCUE Operation

WILDLIFE | BIRDWATCHING | ENVIRONMENTALISM

It's easy to fall in love with Costa Rica's many creatures when you spot them in their natural habitats. See what folks at local rescue centers are doing to protect and rehabilitate this diverse wildlife, including birds, mammals and more. This is also a chance to get a close-up view of some species that are otherwise elusive.

LEAENA/SHUTTERSTOCK

How to

Getting here Located 5km to 10km east of Puerto Viejo, Jaguar Centro de Rescate and Ara Manzanillo are accessible by bicycle, car or taxi.

When to go Both facilities receive visitors at very specific times. Double-check the schedule (and reserve, if necessary) before showing up.

Volunteer **Jaguar Centro de Rescate** hosts volunteers who are able to commit to at least four weeks working with the animals.

EXPATPOSTCARDS/SHUTTERSTOCK

Left Great green macaw, Ara Manzanillo
Below Sloths, Jaguar Centro de Rescate

Great green macaws Located between Punta Uva and Manzanillo, **Ara Manzanillo** is devoted to saving the endangered *lapa verde* (great green macaw.) This NGO has successfully reintroduced dozens of endangered birds to the lowland tropical forests of the southern Caribbean. Learn about their efforts and watch the macaws fly and feed in the forest every afternoon at 3pm. This is the best chance you'll get to behold these wondrous creatures in their natural habitat. Reserve in advance on the website.

Creatures great and small At the east end of Playa Cocles, the well-run **Jaguar Centro de Rescate** takes care of ill, injured and orphaned wildlife. (Sadly, their numbers are rising in step with development in the region.) The furry friends that are unfit to be released back into the wild are the animal ambassadors you can meet on a tour of the facility. These might include Bobo the booby bird, who lost his fear of humans; Kivu, an ocelot with feline leukemia; and Sansa, an abandoned spider monkey who needed eye surgery. Tours take place twice a day in the morning.

Birdwatching Spots

I have lived on the southern Caribbean coast all my life. These are my favorite spots in the Caribbean to birdwatch:

Tucán Rd
On this one road just behind Playa Cocles, I can regularly spot anywhere between 40 and 60 species of birds.

Gandoca
There are around 40 to 50 species in Gandoca, and right outside my door I can usually find hawks, toucans, tanagers, woodpeckers and hummingbirds.

Moín
The canals in Moín are a great place to see and photograph wading birds like herons and kingfishers. There are just so many.

Insight by **Haniel Rodriguez Rojas**, tour guide specializing in wildlife and bird photography *@haniel_tourguiderodriguez*

17

Rainforest RELAXATION

REEFS | RAINFOREST | REFUGE

Manzanillo is an oft-overlooked fishing village in the Gandoca–Manzanillo Wildlife Refuge near the Panama border, with scores of protected reefs, white-sand beaches and gentle leatherback turtles. Shrouded in rainforest and low-key, Manzanillo is a bright-and-early alternative to Puerto Viejo's raucous nighttime party scene.

AMANTE DE LUZ/SHUTTERSTOCK

How To

Getting here/around Manzanillo is 14km south of Puerto Viejo. Arrive by bus from San José or Puerto Viejo. Once here, you'll only need your feet to get around.

When to go September to October for snorkeling, July to September for turtle-watching.

Practicalities You'll need some Spanish, as many locals aren't bilingual. There aren't reliable ATMs, so stock up on colones in Puerto Viejo.

DAMSEA/SHUTTERSTOCK

Village Life

A quarter of a century old, and full of quaint curving streets and brightly colored stilted buildings, **Manzanillo** is a charming coastal village. If you're looking for a break from Puerto Viejo's party scene and want some peak *pura vida*, this place is the place for it.

Manzanillo isn't the southernmost stop on the way out of Costa Rica (that honor belongs to Sixaola), but it's only a few miles shy of the border. So if you want to tick off Panama's Caribbean coast and El Caribe in one go, it's a smart, time-sensitive choice because you can be in Panama's Bocas del Toro in a matter of hours.

PESEK PHOTO/SHUTTERSTOCK

Sea Creatures Galore

Narrow walking paths, bright azure waters and stretches of white sand protected as part of the **Gandoca–Manzanillo Wildlife**

Dark Nights

Bright lights spook turtles, sending them plodding back into the sea. During nesting season, guides use ruby-colored flashlights to gently illuminate the creatures, allowing the turtles to do their business undisturbed. Before your turtle tour, it's essential to make sure your flash is off.

Top left Manzanillo Beach
Top right Comet sea star, sea sponge and anemone
Bottom left Capuchin monkey

Refuge are the prime draws here. Plus, you can stay in humble accommodations and homestays, wake up to sea birds and chattering monkeys every morning, and see leatherback turtles nesting between February and September.

Manzanillo's reefs provide plenty of snorkeling opportunities. You may spot tropical *loros*, angelfish and nurse sharks in these waters. If you're extra-fortunate, you might even come across a manatee. Sea kayaking and swimming are also popular activities. Manzanillo's calm waters are good for swimming year-round, but dry-season snorkeling when there's less loose sediment and better visibility tends to be better. Bring your own gear, as the snorkel shop in town is open sporadically.

Hiking Trails

Gandoca-Manzanillo Wildlife Refuge features several hiking trails. A **coastal trail** extends

Reefs Under Threat

There are two snorkeling reefs along the Caribbean coast of Costa Rica – the larger **Cahuita reef** (6 sq km), which receives more visitors, and the **Gandoca-Manzanillo reef** (5 sq km). They are home to over 120 species of fish, plus spiny lobster, turtles and other denizens of the sea. Coral species include brain coral, grey deer-horn coral, reddish moose-horn coral, plus purple fan coral in deeper waters. Unfortunately, dead coral is also not uncommon. Both reefs are facing significant challenges from upriver industries. Mainly, silt (from logging) and agricultural runoff (from banana plantations) pollute the rivers, which feed into the sea and destroy the coral.

DAMSEA/SHUTTERSTOCK

Far Left Green sea turtle
Left Gandoca-Manzanillo Wildlife Refuge
Below Green iguana

5.5km east from Manzanillo. The first part of this path from Manzanillo to Tom Bay (about a 90-minute walk) is clearly marked, with excellent snorkeling at the end (bring your own mask). Once you pass Tom Bay, however, the trail is not well maintained.

The 4km-long **La Trocha** trail takes visitors through thick forest along a mix of dirt track and boardwalk. In both cases, hiring a guide maximizes your chances of spotting and identifying plants, birds and animals.

Humans & Animals Side-by-Side

Firmly rooted in traditional Costa Rican life, Manzanillo is rustic and unapologetically itself. The town goes to bed and wakes up early. Manzanillo's human residents live side-by-side with giant iguanas, sloths and howler monkeys. Capuchins, tapirs and *pacas* (small rodents) also reside nearby. The rainforest climate and underdeveloped beauty of Manzanillo make it an apex place for jungle bugs, scorpions and sometimes snakes.

These rugged brushes with the animal kingdom are all part of Manzanillo's charm. It's the textbook definition of the overused and often poorly applied term 'off the beaten path' and an unconventional place to lay your head in El Caribe.

FROM LEFT: CHRISONTOUR84/SHUTTERSTOCK, JPCOLLINSPHOTOGRAPHYUK/SHUTTERSTOCK

18 CRUISING THE Caribbean Beaches

BEACH | WILDLIFE | MARINE ACTIVITIES

To really soak up the Caribbean vibe, rent a beach cruiser in Puerto Viejo and head east along the coast with vague plans, stopping at unique beaches, swimming at will and lounging even longer.

IAN BOTTLE/ALAMY

Trip Notes

Getting here/around Start in Puerto Viejo (pictured above) and cycle east along the coast for a total of 14km.

When to go Go early in the day before the heat and rains hit their peak. Be sure to leave yourself time (and energy) to get back.

Bike rental Rent a beach cruiser in Puerto Viejo from **Manú Bikes** or **Puerto Viejo Bike Rentals**.

Accessible Beach

In 2024, **Playa Manzanillo** became Costa Rica's third accessible beach. Nine tons of plastic bottle tops were recycled into plastic lumber and used to build a retractable walkway to the beach. The 33m-long boardwalk allows visitors with mobility issues to reach the beach using an amphibious wheelchair.

01 Leave the buzz of Puerto Viejo behind and pedal out of town along the coastal road to **Playa Cocles**. Here you can rent a surfboard, play beach volleyball or indulge in a beach massage.

04 About 2km further, there are several entrances to **Punta Uva**, and all of them lead to a blissful beach, with opportunities for kayaking, snorkeling or surfing.

0 5 km
0 2.5 miles

Salsa Brava

Puerto Viejo de Talamanca

Casa de la Cultural

Punta Uva

Manzanillo

Refugio de Vida Silvestre Gandoca-Manzanillo

02 Cruise south along the coast for 3km, and consider popping into one of several chic beach clubs, such as **Da Lime**, for a coconut water or cocktail.

03 It's another 4km to **Playa Chiquita**, a coco-palm-lined stretch of sand where you can escape the crowds in an isolated cove and take a dip in the Caribbean waters.

05 Another 4km of cycling along jungle roads brings you to Manzanillo, a quiet outpost of Afro-Caribbean culture. Treat yourself to a fine meal at **Cool & Calm Cafe**.

Río Saxaola

PANAMA

ICONIC IMAGES
of El Caribe

01 Pati
This tasty specialty in Limón City is a El Caribe spin on *empanadas* containing savory, traditional Costa Rican fillings.

02 Nurse Shark
Snorkel Parque Nacional Cahuita, and you could have a chance encounter with these majestic ancient and completely non-aggressive creatures.

03 Fusion Cuisine
Coconut-scented rice and hearty meats offer a spin on *gallo pinto,* a terrific nod to the Jamaican influence in El Caribe.

04 Howler Monkey
Some of Manzanillo's loudest but most lovable residents, these small black monkeys make a racket disproportionate to their diminutive size.

05 Yellow Eyelash Viper
One of the most venomous snakes in Cahuita, eyelash vipers are shy, vibrant, and amazing creatures indigenous to El Caribe.

06 Shortboard
Ideal for making sharp turns on Salsa Brava's 'Cheese Grater', shortboards allow you to slice through tough waves with ease.

07 Playa Negra
Cahuita's Playa Negra (p95), a black-sand beach, is an otherworldly place to spend your day and is symbolic of the town's natural beauty.

08 Black Star Line Logo
Marcus Garvey's famous transportation line designed to connect to the African diaspora and transport goods and people around the world.

09 Red Hummingbird
Costa Rica's Camino de Costa Rica, which starts in Parismina and continues to the Pacific, is marked with red hummingbirds.

10 Marcus Garvey
Limón City's influential activist, orator, and Black Star Line and UNIA founder (p90) who advocated tirelessly to unite the African diaspora.

01 BONCHAN/SHUTTERSTOCK, **02** AVETPHOTOS/SHUTTERSTOCK, **03** ERICKBOLANOS506/SHUTTERSTOCK, **04** ANTON_IVANOV/SHUTTERSTOCK, **05** ERIC ISSELEE/SHUTTERSTOCK, **06** SANIT FUANGNAKHON/SHUTTERSTOCK, **07** SIMON DANNHAUER/SHUTTERSTOCK, **08** EVERETT COLLECTION HISTORICAL/ALAMY, **09** CHASE D'ANIMULLS/SHUTTERSTOCK, **10** EVERETT COLLECTION/SHUTTERSTOCK, RANGIZZZ/SHUTTERSTOCK, JOINTSTAR/SHUTTERSTOCK

Listings

BEST OF THE REST

Best Eats in El Caribe

Taylor's $$

A great spot for authentic *patis* and coconut rice and beans, situated across the street from the former location of Marcus Garvey's Black Star Line.

Mercado Municipal $

Visit this large market right near Limón City's port for authentic souvenirs and great local food at a fraction of the price you would pay elsewhere.

Soda El Patty $

Enjoy *patis* and live music at this affordable Limón City *soda*. It's got a welcoming vibe and fun atmosphere that will make you feel right at home.

Tsunami Sushi $$

Nice spot for fresh sushi rolls and a party vibe in Limón. Prices are higher than local *sodas*, but are still reasonable enough for budget travelers.

Restaurante Kalisi $$

An ideal brunch spot in Jamaica Town in Limón. Visit for some of the best and strongest coffee in El Caribe and generously portioned plates of traditional Caribbean Costa Rican fare.

Shugga Place $$

Slightly more expensive than your typical local *soda*, but has great ambience and really good artisanal coffees. It's a nice place to chill and get your bearings while in Limón City.

Café Rico $

Puerto Viejo's top spot for fast, delicious breakfasts and traditional *soda* fare.

Staying in Puerto Viejo

Pagalù Hostel

Welcoming hostel in Puerto Viejo with airy doubles and dorms (with lockers and bunkside lamps), open-air kitchen and quiet lounge with hammocks.

Villas Piña

Adults-only resort close to Puerto Viejo and Playa Negra, with a sizable pool, plenty of hammocks, amenities, and a relaxed and secluded location.

Rocking J's Hostel

In the middle of Puerto Viejo, this hostel has a party vibe, huge grounds and strong wi-fi. There are only private rooms, so if you need a dorm, go elsewhere.

Jaguar Inn Bungalows

Set back slightly into the jungle near the Jaguar Centro de Rescate, this secluded natural hotel has plenty of gardens and decent wi-fi. It's a good respite from the beach parties of Puerto Viejo.

PHORTUN/SHUTTERSTOCK

Traditional *soda*, Puerto Viejo

 Best El Caribe Nightlife

Coco's Bar $$

Cahuita rasta bar with Calypso and reggae music, a great menu and plenty of regular drink specials.

Reggae Bar $

Decent Cahuita spot for food. Great place for drinks and socializing very close to Playa Negra.

Ricky's Place $

Solid spot for big portions of fresh seafood and a wide selection of different drinks and beers. In Cahuita.

Maestros Wine & Grill $$$

Limón City's premier wine and craft-beer bar, with tasty tapas and a nice vibe.

Reina's $$

On the beach at Playa Bonita, 5km west of Limón City. Loud reggaetón and salsa, good vibes, *mariscos* (seafood) and fruity cocktails.

Tasty Waves Cantina $$

Chilled-out Playa Cocles haunt with excellent food, occasional live music and a friendly atmosphere.

The Kat House $$

This breezy, elegant spot pairs natural wines and cocktails with tuna *tiradito* (Peruvian raw fish), shrimp tacos and sushi.

 Top Tour Companies in El Caribe

Soul Life Travel

Located in Puerto Viejo but running tours in Limón City and Puerto Viejo, Soul Life Travel works with the community providing local experiences that put money in local people's pockets.

Caribe Fun Tours

Offering a variety of cultural and adventure-oriented experiences, Caribe Fun Tours will help you understand and appreciate El

IAN BOTTLE/ALAMY

Salsa Brava

Caribe on a whole new level. It's based in Puerto Viejo, but serves all of El Caribe.

Green Cahuita

Locally owned and operated, in El Caribe's town of Cahuita, Green Cahuita specializes in taking tourists to hidden waterfalls and beaches, and meeting the Bribrí people in a respectful and educational fashion.

 El Caribe Bars with a View

Salsa Brava $$

Named for the famous surf spot, Salsa Brava offers incredible views of the break and drink specials to go along with it.

Sol Mar Cocktails $$

Skip the food and go straight for the strong cocktails, paired with sea views, in Puerto Limón.

Johnny's Place $

Whether you're watching the surf or checking out the game on the bar's large TV, Johnny's Place is a humble spot at which to soak up the sun with a cold one.

Scan to find more things to do in the Caribbean Coast online

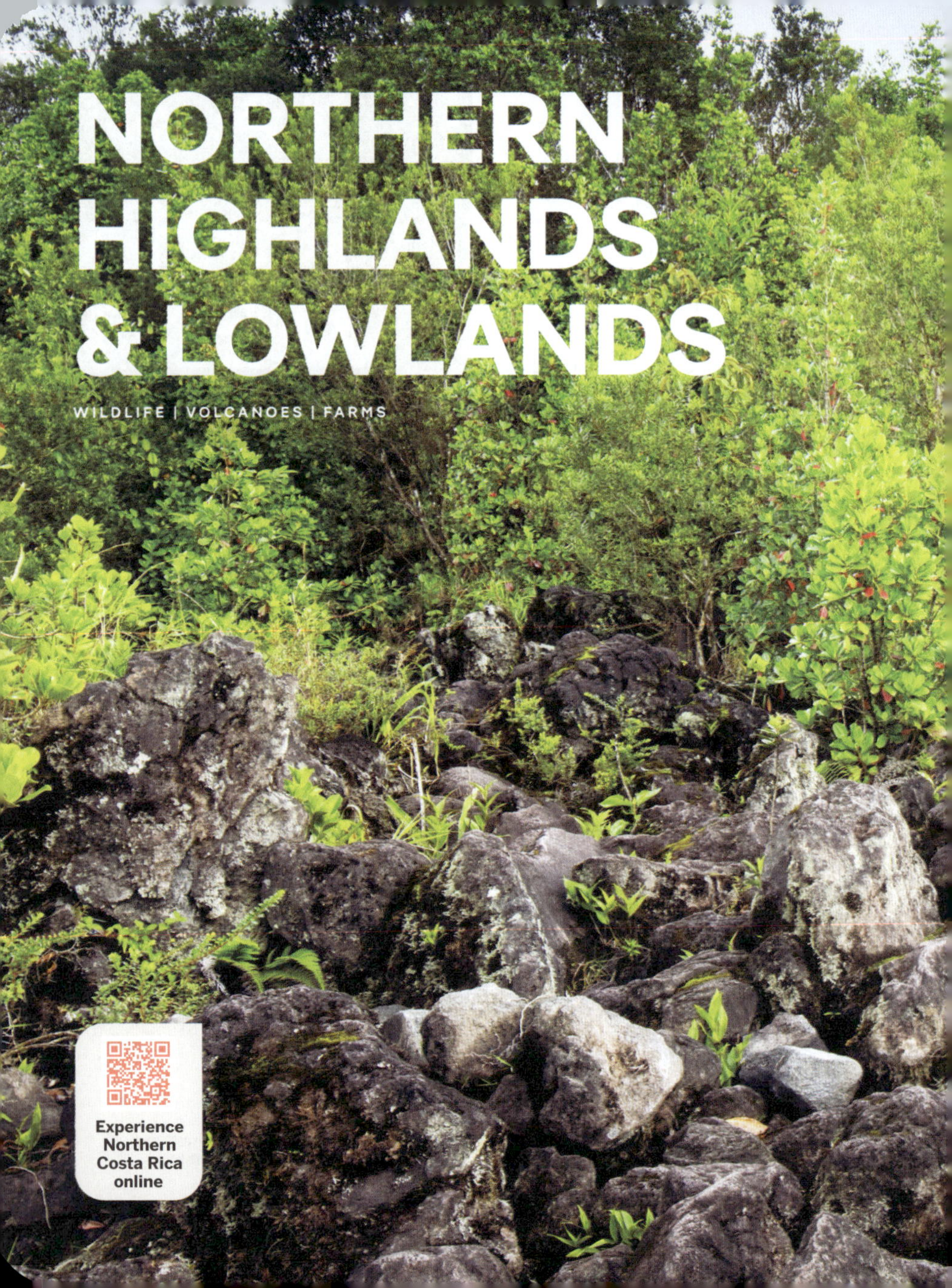
NORTHERN HIGHLANDS & LOWLANDS
WILDLIFE | VOLCANOES | FARMS
Experience Northern Costa Rica online

NORTHERN HIGHLANDS & LOWLANDS

Trip Builder

A microcosm of Costa Rica itself, this diverse region shows off the country's highlights, from the steaming volcanoes and misty cloud forests of the Cordillera de Guanacaste, to the inky lagoons and dense rainforest of the Northern Lowlands.

PREVIOUS SPREAD: JOHN COLETTI/GETTY IMAGES
FROM LEFT: REBECA BOLANOS/SHUTTERSTOCK, GAIBRU PHOTO/SHUTTERSTOCK, NICK FOX/SHUTTERSTOCK, EL JARDÍN IN MONTEVERDE LODGE & GARDENS

0 50 km
0 25 miles
Lago de Nicaragua
NICARAGUA
Río Indio
Hike (or fly) through the clouds at **Santa Elena Cloud Forest Reserve** (p133)
20mins from Santa Elena
Ride the rapids or float through the forests of the **Río Sarapiquí** (p130)
10mins from Puerto Viejo de Sarapiquí
Río San Juan
Spot wildlife at **Sloth's Territory** and other rainforest nature preserves (p125)
30mins from La Fortuna
Río San Carlos
Refugio de Vida Silvestre Mixto Maquenque
Río Sarapiquí
San Rafael
Venado
Unión
Río Arenal
Boca Arenal
La Fortuna
El Tanque
Laguna de Arenal
Volcán Arenal
Follow the lava flows from the biggest eruptions of **Volcán Arenal** (p118)
20mins from La Fortuna
Chachagua
Platanar
Parque Nacional Volcán Arenal
Florencia
Santa Elena
Ciudad Quesada
Monteverde
Volcán Platanar
Cordillera de Tilarán
Parque Nacional Juan Castro Blanco
Parque Nacional Volcán Poás
Cordillera Central
Parque Nacional Braulio Carrillo
Guacimal
Río Arunjuez
Volcán Barva
Rancho Grande
Visit **Monteverde restaurants** to feast on tantalizing food in surprising settings (p134)
30mins from Santa Elena
SAN JOSÉ

Practicalities

EQROY/SHUTTERSTOCK

ARRIVING

Daniel Oduber Quirós International Airport, Liberia This smal airport provides easy access to destinations in the northern parts of Costa Rica. Private shuttles run from the airport to various destinations, and public buses run from the terminal in Liberia.

Juan Santamaría International Airport, San José The main international airport is closer to destinations in the northeast, including the Sarapiquí region. Private shuttles run from airport, and public buses from the terminals in San José.

HOW MUCH FOR A

***Casado* (set meal) US$5–8**

250g bag of coffee beans US$5–8

Birding tour US$60

WHEN TO GO

JAN–APR
Peak tourist season sees the driest weather and highest prices.

MAY–AUG
'Green' season brings more rain and slightly lower prices.

SEP–OCT
Low season, with the most rain and lowest prices.

NOV–DEC
Rain eases and the tourists return in droves during holiday season.

GETTING AROUND

Car Renting a car gives the greatest access to destinations and activities all around the northern region. It's worth upgrading to a 4WD vehicle, especially during the rainy season.

Shuttle service A few different private shuttle services provide transportation to the main tourist destinations, including both airports, Monteverde (Santa Elena), La Fortuna and Puerto Viejo de Sarapiquí. These vans are significantly faster and more comfortable (though more expensive) than public buses.

Public bus Liberia is a major transportation center for buses traveling the Interamericana, from Santa Cruz to San José. Ciudad Quesada (San Carlos) is a transportation hub for the region further east.

EATING & DRINKING

In Guanacaste, the staple ingredient is corn, featured in corn tortillas, corn rice and especially *chorreadas* (corn pancakes; pictured top right). This is also cattle country, so this is the place to feast on grilled steaks (pictured bottom right) and burgers. Further east, the landscape is dominated by agriculture, especially plantations growing banana, pineapple and palmitos. This region is big on farm-to-table cooking, so you'll see all of these items on menus.

Best coffee
Café Monteverde (p155)

Must-try *chorreadas*
La Choza del Maíz (p154)

TOP: WELANIE PANSA/SHUTTERSTOCK
BOTTOM: IGNACIO GUEVARA/SHUTTERSTOCK

CONNECT & FIND YOUR WAY

Wi-fi Wi-fi is available at most lodges, hotels and restaurants, though the speed varies. Some places to stay may offer wi-fi only in common areas, not in the rooms.

Navigation Car-rental companies no longer offer GPS units, but navigation apps like Google Drive and Waze are reliably accurate.

WHERE TO STAY

Depending on the length of your trip, you may want to stay in a few different towns or villages to sample this diverse region.

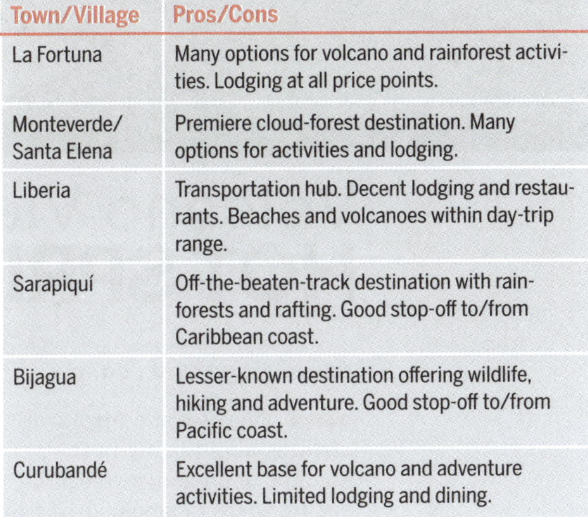

Town/Village	Pros/Cons
La Fortuna	Many options for volcano and rainforest activities. Lodging at all price points.
Monteverde/ Santa Elena	Premiere cloud-forest destination. Many options for activities and lodging.
Liberia	Transportation hub. Decent lodging and restaurants. Beaches and volcanoes within day-trip range.
Sarapiquí	Off-the-beaten-track destination with rainforests and rafting. Good stop-off to/from Caribbean coast.
Bijagua	Lesser-known destination offering wildlife, hiking and adventure. Good stop-off to/from Pacific coast.
Curubandé	Excellent base for volcano and adventure activities. Limited lodging and dining.

STAY IN THE LOOP

La Voz de Guanacaste *(vozdeguanacaste.com)* A great source for news and articles about current events, culture, the environment and human-rights issues

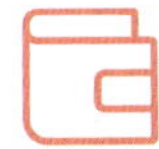

MONEY

Credit cards are widely accepted, but some lodgings and tour companies accept cash payment only (Costa Rican colones or US dollars). ATMs – accessible in most towns – may dispense dollars and/or colones.

19 Volcano Views & HOT SPRINGS

GEOLOGY | HIKING | SOAKING

There's something awe-striking about being in the shadow of an active volcano – seeing wisps of smoke drift from its conical top, following trails of volcanic rock and soaking in waters heated by volcanic thermal energy. Volcán Arenal may no longer be spitting fire, but its power is still on full display.

MARA VORHEES/LONELY PLANET

How To

Getting here/around This trip requires a vehicle, although any tour agency in La Fortuna can arrange transportation to the volcano parks or to the hot springs.

When to go It's best to hike in the morning to avoid the afternoon heat. (Volcano hikes are not as shady as forest hikes.) Thermal springs are open for daytime admission (9am to 4pm) or evening admission (4pm to 9pm).

How much Admission to the national park is US$17. Eco Termales is US$44.

JOHN KEATES/ALAMY

Hike the Lava Flows

The mighty **Volcán Arenal** is surrounded by protected land in the form of the eponymous national park, as well as private reserves, which offer chances to explore the volcano and witness its effects. The **Parque Nacional Volcán Arenal** (Sector Volcán) is the natural starting point.

There are basically two interconnected circular trails. The **Sendero Las Coladas** (Lava Flow Traill) branches around the volcano for 2km, passing the lava field that remains from an eruption in 1992. You can actually hike up the old lava flow – now hardened into volcanic rocks – which culminates with a vista of Arenal in all its glory. A challenging but rewarding detour! The 3km **Sendero El Ceibo** is a semicircular loop that branches off from Las Coladas and heads deeper into the

Arenal 1968

Note that Arenal 1968 is a private reserve right next to the national park that offers a very similar hiking experience on and around the lava flows from the 1968 eruption. The entrance fee is slightly higher, but it's a solid alternative to the national park.

MATYAS REHAK/SHUTTERSTOCK

Top left Volcán Arenal
Top right Arenal 1968 trail (p120)
Bottom left Warning signs, Parque Nacional Volcán Arenal

rainforest. Circle back to the parking lot and end your hike at the **Mirador Principal**, or main lookout point, which is the closest you can get to the volcano.

Get a Ride

If hiking doesn't get your heart pumping, there are other ways to explore the unique, post-eruption environment around Volcán Arenal.

- Go mountain biking with **Bike Arenal** at **Arenal 1968**, where the 16km of single- and double-track trails are separate from the lava hiking trails.
- Take a wild ride with **Original Arenal ATV** on a private farm near the national park, with volcano views all around. Along the way, you can cool off (and clean off) with a dip in the river.
- Ride a horse from **Arenal Wilberth Stables** through forest and farmland, near the base of the volcano. Enjoy lake and volcano views from the saddle.

Local Soak

Tourists flock to the hot-springs facilities around town, but locals know where to soak for free. Opposite the entrance to Tabacón Hot Springs (7km east of the national park), a gravel path leads down to **Río Chollin**, a bubbling, volcano-heated, thermal river, carefully crafted by Mother Nature. It is less luxurious and less safe than the private hot springs around town, but it's also less expensive (aka free). Be careful of strong currents and slippery rocks: water shoes are recommended. But if you're up for a mini-adventure, this is a fun, low-investment and decidedly authentic experience for travelers in the know. Enjoy!

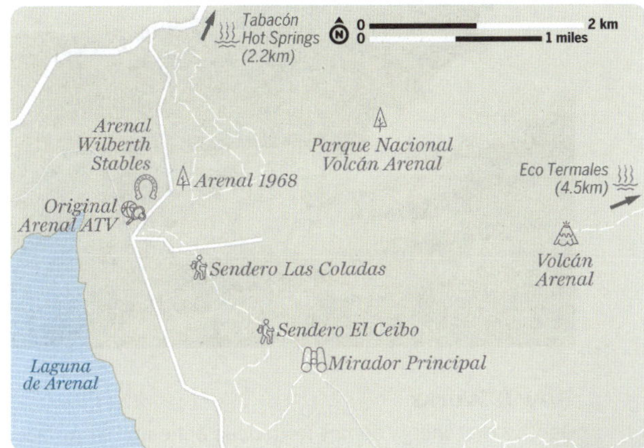

Left Thermal springs, Parque Nacional Volcán Arenal
Below Eco Termales Fortuna

Hot Stuff

After a day of hiking (or biking or riding), it's time to soothe your aching bones. Drive 7km back toward town to **Tabacón Hot Springs** to soak in volcano-heated waters amid gorgeous greenery and cascading waterfalls. Tabacón is unique in that it's the only facility built around a nature-made, free-flowing hot river (as opposed to pumping the heated water in from below). A more affordable option is **Eco Termales Fortuna**, which is set amid a verdant secondary forest. Although Eco Termales is not the fanciest 'hot springs' experience in La Fortuna, it does benefit from a gorgeous natural setting, with lush greenery all around.

In either place, you can soak in the mineral-rich pools, stand under waterfalls for a hydro massage, and cool off in plunge pools. This is nature at its most luxurious. Order a cocktail from the bar and sink into the warm healing waters.

FAR LEFT: RYAN HENKE/500PX
LEFT: ECOTERMALES

Volcano Power

HARNESSING GEOTHERMAL ENERGY TO SAVE THE PLANET

Since 2015, Costa Rica has generated more than 98% of its electric energy from renewable resources – one of only four countries in the world to do so. While most of this energy comes from hydropower, some 15% is geothermal power – that is, the power of the earth itself.

JOSHUA TEN BRINK/SHUTTERSTOCK

How It Works

Geothermal energy comes from deep beneath the surface of the earth, where a continual process of radioactive decay generates intense heat. These extreme temperatures create the semi-molten material at the earth's core known as magma. This energy is visible to us at the surface in places where cracks or fissures allow the heat to escape, such as geysers, fumaroles and hot springs. Sometimes the magma itself bubbles to the surface and flows out as lava, in a volcanic eruption.

To generate electricity, geothermal plants tap into reservoirs of hot water several kilometers beneath the surface. The hot liquid is pumped up to the surface and into a depressurizing system. The resulting steam powers a turbine, which connects to a generator to produce electricity. This 'flash-steam' system is the most common type of geothermal power plant.

Geothermal energy is a renewable resource. It is relatively clean, producing little waste or byproduct. It is also not dependent on the weather, unlike solar, wind and hydro power. It is – arguably – the ultimate 'green' energy.

Where It Works

Costa Rica is perfectly placed to tap into this practically unlimited source of energy (as evidenced by its many volcanoes). The country's first facility was the Miravalles geothermal power plant, constructed in 1994 in Bagaces. Volcán Miravalles is officially dormant, but it still generates an abundance of geothermal energy. There are now five geothermal power plants operating at Miravalles.

Top left Las Pailas geothermal power plant
Top center Fumarole, Volcán Poás
Top right Volcán Turrialba

MABELIN SANTOS/SHUTTERSTOCK

PACO GUTI/SHUTTERSTOCK

In 2011, Costa Rica tapped into an additional energy source in Curubandé de Liberia, near Volcán Rincón de la Vieja, with the addition of a second plant in 2019.

The Challenge

Considering all the benefits, it seems like a no-brainer for the country to expand its capacity for geothermal power. However, there is a significant obstacle: geothermal energy is location specific, which means the plants must be built in areas where the energy is accessible. In Costa Rica's case, most of these areas are contained within national parks. As such, they are designated for recreation, education and conservation. And they are legally protected from commercial use.

> Geothermal energy is a renewable resource. It is relatively clean, producing little waste or byproduct. It is – arguably – the ultimate 'green' energy.

The Costa Rican power company ICE and other geothermal advocates are trying to find compromises (or to change the legislation). But the Ministry of Environment and Energy is dead against it, arguing that it sets a dangerous precedent for commercial exploitation of a public natural resource. It's a legitimate point, which highlights the fact that no resource is unlimited and no activity is inconsequential. Saving the planet is never simple, but every small step helps.

Five Active Volcanoes

- **Volcán Arenal** (p119) It's not safe to go to the crater, but you can hike along the lava flows of past eruptions.
- **Volcán Irazú** (p63) At 3400m, this is Costa Rica's highest volcano, topped with green crater lakes.
- **Volcán Poás** (p63) Has one of the largest active volcano craters in the world. Since 2017 it has been active, so strict safety measures are in place.
- **Volcán Rincón de la Vieja** (p140) It's not safe to go to the crater, but there is plenty of geothermal power on display in Las Pailas sector.
- **Volcán Turrialba** Intense activity means that the surrounding park and trails have closed frequently since 2016.

20 Where the WILD THINGS ARE

WILDLIFE | PHOTO OPS | VOLUNTEERING

Want to watch howler monkeys swing through the trees or glimpse the smile of a sloth? On the outskirts of La Fortuna, private nature reserves are allowing wildlife to reclaim the territory and inviting visitors to take a peek. Here are some opportunities to see wild animals in their natural habitat and to learn about keeping wildlife wild.

JUAN CARLOS VINDAS/GETTY IMAGES

How To

Getting here You'll need a car to get to most of these wildlife destinations, which are all located on the outskirts of La Fortuna.

When to go All of these tours and experiences require advance reservations, with the exception of the 'iguana bridge,' which is an easy stop at any time of day.

Protect yourself Always wear close-toed shoes to protect from snakes and insects. Don't forget a rain jacket and insect repellent!

TYLER WENZEL/SHUTTERSTOCK

Top left Three-toed sloth
Bottom left Red-eyed tree frog

Spot a sloth Support a reforestation effort and see the national symbol at **Sloth's Territory**, a private reserve 5km east of La Fortuna. Expert guides have an amazing ability to locate these charismatic creatures, even when they are camouflaged amid the leaves high above. Their scopes ensure that you will get a good look too.

Iguana bridge Drive 20km east to Muelle, where Rte 35 takes a sharp turn to cross a narrow bridge. Here, a mess of green iguanas hangs out in the trees above the river. Some of them are massive. You can walk across the bridge or get a good look from the **Centro Turístico Las Iguanas**. This is also a good place to grab lunch or ice cream before your next stop.

Rescue operation About 24km south of La Fortuna in San Carlos, **Proyecto Asis** is a rescue center that rehabilitates animals for release back into the wild. The goal here is to educate visitors about the importance of keeping wildlife wild. While the animals are endearing and the tour is mildly interesting, the highlight is the 'volunteer' part of the experience, when guests help to prepare the food and make animal enrichment toys for the animals.

Creatures of the night Almost every nature preserve offers a night tour to show off the frogs and spiders and insects – and even some mammals – that only come out at night. **Ecocentro Danaus** seems to specialize in frogs, including that other much sought after national symbol, the red-eyed tree frog.

Sloth Hangout

For the untrained eye, it is not easy to spot a sloth: one trick is knowing where to look. In Costa Rica, most animal lovers can tell you that the best place to look for a sloth is a cecropia tree, known locally as *guarumo*. Sloths like to suck on the spongey interior of the cecropia stalks (which happen to have hallucinogenic properties). And wouldn't you know it? They often fall asleep there too. Fortunately for us, the leaves are not as dense as some other trees, which gives us a chance to get a peek.

Insight by **Alex Araya Carvajal**, sloth guide at Bogarin Trail *@bogarintrail*

21 Check Off Your BIRD LIST

BIRDS | RAINFOREST | WETLANDS

Does your heart flutter at the sight of a new feathered friend? Follow this multiday itinerary – traversing rainforest, cloud forest, dry forest and wetlands – to see how many of the country's 900 species you can check off your bird list.

MALLARDG500/ GETTY IMAGES

Trip Notes

Getting here/around If only we could be like the birds and fly into these avian habitats. Instead, you'll need your own wheels (preferably 4WD).

When to go While birding in Costa Rica is fabulous any time of year, the bird life is more concentrated during the dry season (December to April).

Guide the way Hire a guide and see more species. Most guides travel with a scope, and they can talk to the birds.

Birdwatching Tips

- We're in a rainy area, so don't go birding without a rain jacket or poncho. You'll also want waterproof hiking shoes or rubber boots.
- You'll need binoculars to see the details of each bird up close.
- Bring a guide from the area with you. They're an unending source of knowledge about each of the species.

Insight by **Adolfo González**, Manager of Laguna del Lagarto Lodge *@lagartoecolodge*

FROM LEFT: RICHARD CONSTANTINOFF/SHUTTERSTOCK, KAREL CERNY/SHUTTERSTOCK

BIRD BRIGADE

01 Scarlet Macaw
This big beauty has made an amazing comeback since the 1980s, and is now easy to spot along the southern Pacific coast.

02 Blue-Crowned Motmot
Commonly sighted, but uncommonly gorgeous. One of six species of motmot found in Costa Rica – all of them pretty spectacular.

03 Montezuma Oropendola
You'll hear the distinctive gurgling call before you see this handsome blackbird, named for the Aztec Emperor.

04 Great Green Macaw
Critically endangered and stridently protected, but sometimes possible to spot in all its spectacular plumage in Sarapiquí and Boca Tapada.

05 Clay-Colored Thrush
Not much to look at, but it sings a lovely, melodic song. And it is the national bird of Costa Rica.

06 Coppery-Headed Emerald Hummingbird
Of the country's 50 species of hummingbird, this is one of two that are endemic to Costa Rica.

07 Resplendent Quetzal
Resplendent, indeed. Depending on the season, look for them in the cloud forests around Monteverde or Providencia de Dota.

08 Three-Wattled Bellbird
Another cloud-forest favorite, this elusive and odd-looking cotinga gives itself away with its metallic call.

09 Ornate Hawk Eagle
The most distinctive of the country's three hawk eagles, due to its spiky crest and bold, barred plumage.

10 Keel-Billed Toucan
Toucan Sam – with the rainbow beak – is the most colorful of the six species of toucans that live in Costa Rica.

01 PASSAKORN UMPORNMAHA/SHUTTERSTOCK, **02** JO CREBBIN/SHUTTERSTOCK, **03** DAVID HAVEL/SHUTTERSTOCK, **04** SUPER PRIN/SHUTTERSTOCK, **05** WILLIAM BERRY/SHUTTERSTOCK, **06** ROSALIE KREULEN/SHUTTERSTOCK, **07** ONDREJ PROSICKY/SHUTTERSTOCK, **08** AGAMI PHOTO AGENCY/SHUTTERSTOCK, **09** ZEN WILD EXPEDITIONS/SHUTTERSTOCK, **10** BUTEO/SHUTTERSTOCK

22 Run the RIVERS

RAPIDS | NATURE | ADVENTURE

The rivers are the lifeline of the Northern Lowlands, watering the fertile farmlands, transporting the produce and providing endless entertainment for adventure seekers and wildlife-watchers. Whether you float among the flora and fauna on the Río Puerto Viejo, ride the rapids on the Sarapiquí or just go for a dip, a day on the river is a day to relish and remember.

GABBRO/ALAMY

How To

Getting here/around The tour companies offer transportation from hotels and lodges in the area.

When to go The rapids run fastest at the end of the rainy season (say, November or December) or anytime that it's been raining.

Lunch break Stop for lunch at **Rancho Magallanes** for succulent chicken, roasted in a brick oven and served with tortillas and banana salsa.

MARCO LISSONI/SHUTTERSTOCK

Top left White-water rafting, Río Sarapiquí
Bottom left Iguana

White-water rafting For a fantastic day out on the water, you can't beat riding the rapids on the **Río Sarapiquí**, guaranteed to get your body moving and your heart racing. Most rafting trips take place on 14km of 'extreme' white water near the town of San Miguel. Here you'll find Class II and III rapids, giving novice and experienced wave runners a thrill ride. The rapids are broken by natural pools where you can jump from cliffs, cool off with a swim and gear up for the next run. Trips on Class IV rapids are also available for more experienced wave riders.

Wildlife-watching For a more serene adventure, the same rafts (or canoes or inner tubes) go floating down the **Río Puerto Viejo**, with passengers on the lookout for birds and animals that inhabit the lush surrounding forest. The variety of water birds is incredible, not to mention stoic caimans, playful otters, sleepy sloths, two kinds of monkeys, and countless iguanas sunning themselves on the muddy riverbanks.

Excellent companies offering both kinds of trips include **Green Rivers** in Puerto Viejo de Sarapiquí, **Aventuras de Sarapiquí** in Chilamate and **Sarapiquí Outdoor Center** in La Virgen.

Take a Dip

The Northern Lowlands are steaming hot, and there's no better way to beat the heat than to take a dip in the glorious cooling waters of the **Río Sarapiquí**. Access the river from the road to Linda Vista (which is also the road to Chilamate Rainforest Retreat). After crossing the bridge, look on the left side of the road for the path down to the river. A small sandy beach and a rope swing make for a perfect picnic and swimming spot.

Insight by **Lluvia**, **Aeden** and **Kiara Azofeifa**, resident kids at Chilamate Rainforest Retreat *@chilamaterainforestretreat*

23 Head in the CLOUDS

HIKING | ECOLOGY | ADVENTURE

Swirling with mist, echoing with birdsong and literally dripping with life, the tropical cloud forest is an environment unlike any other. If you have ever wondered what it's like to walk (or fly) through the clouds, Santa Elena is your chance to find out. Slow your steps for a sensory overload, or pick up the pace for an adrenaline rush. Or do both.

JORDI CAMI/ALAMY

How To

Getting here/around Both Santa Elena Cloud Forest Reserve and Selvatura Park offer transportation to/from area hotels.

When to go Nonstop precipitation during the rainy season makes for muddy trails. Hiking is easier from January to April.

Top tip If you can't see much from the observation tower, wait around. Clouds come and go, as do the views.

MILAN ZYGMUNT/SHUTTERSTOCK

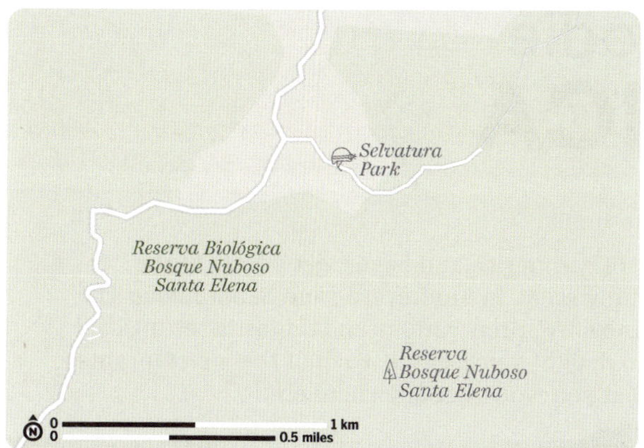

Feast for the senses All your senses are in for a treat at the **Santa Elena Cloud Forest Reserve** (Reserva Bosque Nuboso Santa Elena), from the lush greenery and ethereal bird calls to the ever-encroaching humidity. The place is dense with life, and the slower you go, the more you notice. Keep your eye out for high-profile highland bird species, including the resplendent quetzal, the three-wattled bellbird, the long-tailed mannakin and the emerald toucanet. A guide also helps, but there is plenty to see and hear if you prefer to go it alone. Just take your time. There are 12km of well-marked trails of varying difficulty and length. Finish up with a stop at the observation tower, which on a clear day yields a view of four volcanoes.

Boost for the heart rate For a different perspective on the cloud forest, pick up the speed and go soaring through the canopy at **Selvatura Park**. This high-speed canopy tour is a favorite among kids (age four and up) and anyone who appreciates a good adrenaline rush. One of the larger zipline courses in town, Selvaura has 13 cables (plus a Tarzan swing for extra fun) strung out over an incredible stretch of primary cloud forest. Because Selvatura is right next door to the Santa Elena reserve, it has magnificent, unbroken cloud-forest views – not to mention the highest altitude for a zipline course. So if you want to fly through the clouds, this is the place to do it.

Top left Santa Elena Cloud Forest Reserve
Bottom left Emerald toucanet

What Is a Cloud Forest?

Cloud forests are tropical, evergreen forests, found at high altitudes (between 1000m and 2500m). Moist air flows inland from the sea, cooling and collecting into clouds when it hits the mountains. This gives the forest its misty, otherworldly appearance. Moisture from the clouds collects on vegetation, and the constant humidity allows flora to flourish, including large numbers of epiphytes (plants that grow on other plants), such as lichens, mosses, ferns, bromeliads and orchids. Trees are often short, gnarly and dense, lending a unique primordial feel. Globally, cloud forests are at risk due to deforestation and climate change, which makes protected areas like Santa Elena and Monteverde all the more important.

24 Foodie RICA

DRINK | FOOD | VIEWS

When you grow weary of eating rice and beans, get a taste of the surprisingly sophisticated dining scene in Monteverde and Santa Elena. The focus on local ingredients, innovative preparations and fantastic settings are sure to sate your appetite and delight your senses. Each of these restaurants offers an eating experience that you won't get anywhere else.

ROLANDO MENDOZA FERNÁNDEZ

How To

Getting here/around These restaurants are within walking distance of downtown Santa Elena or Monteverde.

When to go For dinner, book a table for 5pm or 5.30pm to enjoy the scenery in the late afternoon glow. Reservations are recommended for El Jardín and San Lucas Dining Experience.

Get your drink on From home-brewed beverages to specialty cocktails, each of these venues will also serve you something special to drink. Cheers!

Garden party You'll dine on fantastic gourmet fare, surrounded by hanging greenery and blooming fleurs at **El Jardín**, the acclaimed restaurant at Monteverde Lodge and Gardens. The greenhouse setting is a delight – especially when the orchids are in bloom (January to April). And there are plenty of options for vegetarians and vegans.

Locavore's delight You can't get more local than **Farm to Table Escondida** at Valle Escondido Nature Reserve Hotel and Farm, which grows most of its ingredients on-site. The result is irresistible fresh salads and brick-oven pizzas. While you're here, you can explore the lovely grounds and gardens to see where your meal came from. Bonus: stunning views over the 'hidden valley,' especially wonderful at sunset.

Tico time At venerable Hotel Belmar, **Restaurante Celajes** epitomizes farm-to-table cuisine, using ingredients that are cultivated in the hotel's organic garden or nearby family farm. From the balcony, you'll enjoy sweeping views of the cloud forest all the way to the Golfo de Nicoya. Even the lounge serves beers that are brewed on-site and craft cocktails made from fresh seasonal ingredients (also from the farm). Come for 'Tico time' (aka happy hour), from 4:30pm to 5:30pm, to take in the sunset vistas and drink a toast to *pura vida*.

Top left Farm to Table Escondida
Bottom left Restaurante Celajes

Dining in the Sky

High up on a hillside overlooking Santa Elena, eight glass pods are suspended in the sky, looking down through the clouds to the world below. Here, **San Lucas Treetop Dining Experience** promises (and delivers) a 'gastronomic adventure.' The menu is a secret – a multicourse extravaganza that celebrates the region and the country. Every course tells a story, through which diners learn about the geography and cuisine and culture of Costa Rica. The food and the setting are truly unique. There are two seatings per night: go for the early one.

25 Play with Your FOOD

FOOD | FARMS | SUSTAINABILITY

Tantalize your tastebuds with some Tico specialties and find out where they come from. Go straight to the source at local organic farms and hone your skills with some hands-on harvesting.

MARA VORHEES/LONELY PLANET

Trip Notes

Getting here/around Most *fincas* (farms) and facilities are in rural locations, so a car is essential.

How much Most tours cost between US$25 and US$35, including a generous degustation.

Reservations Book tours in advance, especially during the high season.

Souvenirs Consumables make excellent souvenirs (and gifts!). Load up on chocolate, coffee and other goodies at the on-site shops.

Choco-History

Cacao has been a critical product in Costa Rica since pre-Columbian times. Cacao beans were used as currency (as recently as the 1930s) and *la hora de chocolate* (chocolate hour) was an evening ritual. In the 1980s, a blight devastated the country's cacao production. Today, production is on the rise again, as scientists work to develop disease-resistant varieties.

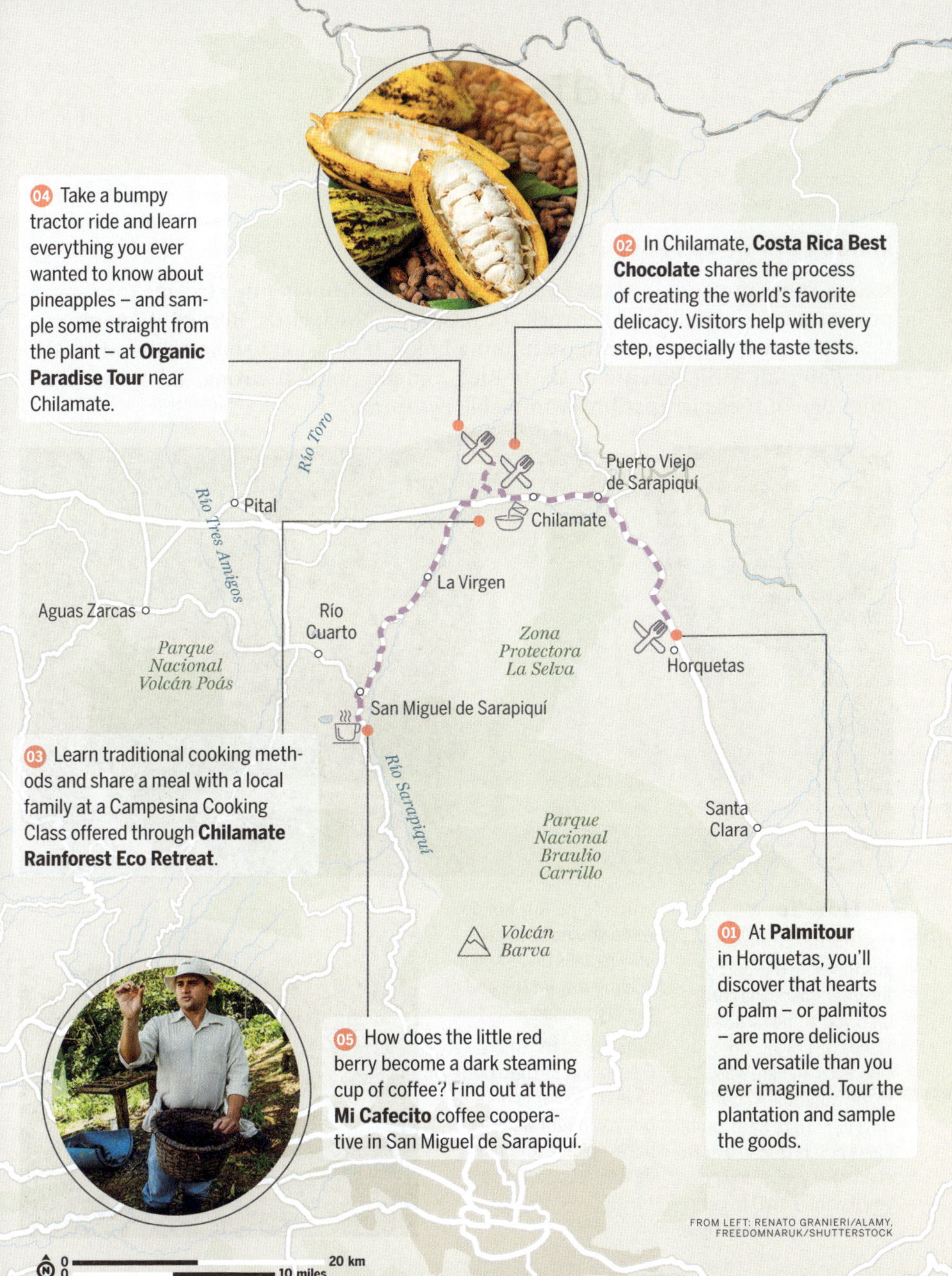

FROM LEFT: RENATO GRANIERI/ALAMY, FREEDOMNARUK/SHUTTERSTOCK

26 Waterfall MAGIC

HIKING | SWIMMING | ADVENTURE

There are a *lot* of waterfalls in Costa Rica – from gentle streams to powerful ragers, rushing over rocks or dropping down cliffs. Best of all, many of these beauties end in enticing swimming holes. If you don't swim under at least one waterfall while you are in Costa Rica, you are doing it wrong. Take your pick from one of these irresistibly swimmable *cataratas*.

KRYSSIA CAMPOS/GETTY IMAGES

How To

Getting here/around Any bus traveling this part of the Interamericana can drop you at the turnoff to Llanos de Cortés, from where it's a 1.5km walk to the waterfall. A shuttle runs to El Tigre from Santa Elena hotels (for an extra charge). If you're driving, you'll want a 4WD to get to Viento Fresco or El Tigre.

When to go Any hot day when you need to cool off. The falls do lessen in volume toward the end of the dry season.

What to eat Viento Fresco and El Tigre both have restaurants on-site, but you might want to pack a picnic for Llanos de Cortés.

KIM HAMMAR/ALAMY

Llanos de Cortés Just north of Bagaces, this is one of the widest, most welcoming waterfalls you will find. A short but steep trail leads from the parking lot down to a cascade of loveliness, 28m high and 12m wide, dropping into a tranquil pond. It's a picture-perfect swimming hole with a sandy beach for your picnicking pleasure. (Bring your lunch, as there is no food for sale here.)

Viento Fresco A perfect place to break up the drive between La Fortuna and Monteverde. The hiking trail is steep and sometimes precarious. But it leads past three picturesque waterfalls of varying sizes, with one more within view in the distance. The highlight is the 75m **Arco Iris**, which casts a rainbow in the lower right corner of the pool. You can climb up behind the cascade and jump off the rocks on the right side. Scary, but not as scary as it looks!

El Tigre An adventurous and sometimes challenging 8km hike that includes four gushing falls, 10 hanging bridges and countless swimming holes along the way. The trail is well marked but often muddy, so wear your boots. If you want to avoid the uphill slog on the way back, spring for the 'full package' admission price, which includes a ride back on horseback or by 4WD. This is an all-day outing from Santa Elena.

Top left Catarata Llanos de Cortés, Guanacaste
Bottom left Catarata El Tobogan, Viento Fresco

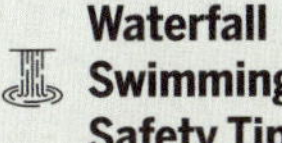

Waterfall Swimming Safety Tips

Waterfalls and plunge pools are fluid (obviously). That means that the conditions may change dramatically, especially depending on recent rainfall. It's important to assess the risk each time you swim at any given location:

- Always comply with posted warnings and restrictions.
- If your guide says it's safe, it's probably safe.
- Check for underwater hazards and adequate depth before jumping into plunge pools.
- Be careful of currents that can force swimmers into rocks or boulders.
- Be cautious about swimming directly under the waterfall, as the weight of the water can be bone crushing, depending on the level of water flow.

27 La Vida VOLCANO

GEOLOGY | ADVENTURE | HIKING

Volcán Rincón de la Vieja is one of Costa Rica's most active volcanoes, with sizeable eruptions as recently as 2023. While it's too dangerous to hike to the crater, you can still witness the volcanic activity – gurgling mud pots, steaming fumaroles and boiling hot springs – in the surrounding national park.

BRIAN LASENBY/SHUTTERSTOCK

How To

Getting here/around It helps to have your own wheels. Otherwise, tours run from Liberia and from beach towns on the Península de Nicoya.

When to go Las Pailas sector is closed Monday; Santa María sector closesTuesday and Wednesday. Subject to change.

How much The park fee covers admission to both sectors on the same day (credit-card payment only).

Rainy-day blues Heavy rains cause the pools at Los Coyotes to lose their blue-green glow.

NATURE'S CHARM/SHUTTERSTOCK

Volcanic Power on View

At **Parque Nacional Rincón de La Vieja**, near Curubandé de Liberia, take a walk around Las Pailas sector to get a glimpse of the furious energy that is roiling just beneath the surface of the earth. The hiking trail **Sendero Las Pailas** is only 3.5km, but it bubbles with multihued fumaroles, tepid springs and steaming, flatulent mud pots, as well as a young and feisty *volcancito* (small volcano). You can't go to the crater, but this trail gives you a pretty good idea of what's going on up there. The park opens at 8am. Arrive early to beat the tour buses coming up from the coast.

If you want more, you might spend the better part of a day in the national park, as there are two additional trails (9km to 10km each) leading to scenic but unswimmable waterfalls.

JOSHUA TEN BRINK/SHUTTERSTOCK

The Lookout

For a perfect end to a perfect day, head to **El Mirador** (The Lookout) in Cañas Dulces for traditional food and spectacular views over the Guanacaste lowlands. The westward–facing panorama is grand at anytime, but sunsets are glorious. Cañas Dulces is about 11km west of Curubandé.

Top left Fumarole, Parque Nacional Rincón de La Vieja
Top right Hiking, Parque Nacional Rincón de La Vieja
Bottom left Crater, Parque Nacional Rincón de La Vieja

Soothing Soak

There's no better way to recover from a volcano hike, than a hot-spring soak. Let that same thermal power soothe your muscles and restore your energy. The most popular option is to stop at **Río Negro Hot Springs** on the way out of the park. This privately run endeavor offers nine pools in a scenic setting on the Río Negro. The thermally heated water is pumped into small, stone-built pools and cooled to varying temperatures, with access to the river to cool off. The facility provides towels, lockers and showers, but you'll want to bring water shoes for the river.

For a more rustic and all-natural experience, drive 30 minutes east to the **Santa María sector** of Parque Nacional Rincón de la Vieja. Here, a trail leads 3km through the 'enchanted forest,' past a lovely waterfall to sulfurous hot springs, or *aguas termales*. Surrounded by the tropical forest, you can soak in two rocky pools – crafted and heated

Poza Los Coyotes

While away an afternoon – or longer – in the true-blue waters of the Río Blanco. About 17km from the national park, near the town of Curubandé, you'll find a series of picture-perfect, sapphire-colored swimming holes, known as **Poza Los Coyotes**. Take your time and explore. Follow the well-marked trails to swim in *las pocitas* (literally 'little puddles'), jump off the rocks, float through the namesake cave, and don't miss the mini waterfall. Different sized tubes are available for rent at the office – life jackets, too – so you can explore the cave and float lazily along the river at your leisure to a soundtrack of howler monkeys.

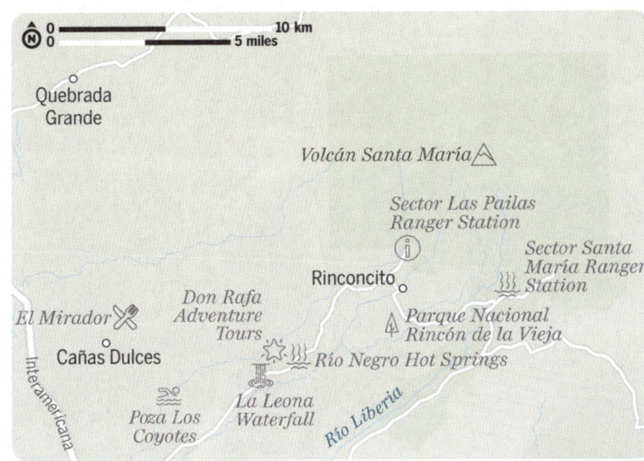

Left Río Negro Hot Springs
Below Turquoise-browed motmot

by Mother Earth – and cool off in the stream. Rain dilutes the pools, so you may have cooler temperatures, depending on when you go.

River Canyon Adventure

La Leona Waterfall is one in a series of waterfalls along the Río Blanco near Curubandé de Liberia. Although it's called 'White River,' it's actually heavenly blue, due to mineral deposits on the river bed. The exhilarating hike through the canyon features river crossings, rock climbing, cavern crawling and cliff jumping – if you so dare. You'll pass three waterfalls on the way, including one glorious cascade that is hidden inside a cavern. Book with **Un Tico y Una Gringa** or with **Don Rafa Adventure Tours**.

FAR LEFT: HEMIS/ALAMY
LEFT: ALEXEY STIOP/SHUTTERSTOCK

28 Forest Green & RIVER BLUE

SWIMMING | HIKING | WILDLIFE

From the dreamy blue waters of the namesake river to the deep greens of the surrounding forests, the Río Celeste region shimmers with vibrant, colorful life. Spend a day hiking and swimming amid the technicolor landscape, and stay for the night to see what lurks in the blackness.

JEROEN MIKKERS/SHUTTERSTOCK

How To

Getting here/around You'll need a vehicle to reach the national park, as well as Tapir Valley.

Muddy waters Heavy rains may dilute the water of the Río Celeste and stir up mud – causing the river to lose its dreamy blue hue. It's worth asking your accommodations to call about the status of the water (or checking the park's Facebook page) before you set out.

XENIA_PHOTOGRAPHY/SHUTTERSTOCK

Celestial Falls

The **Parque Nacional Volcán Tenorio** is a cool, misty, magical place, covered by cloud forests and teeming with life. Soaring 1916m above the forest is the park's namesake volcano. Below, is the glorious Río Celeste, which winds its way through the park in a series of waterfalls and lagoons.

A hiking trail leads from the entrance, showing off some of the river's highlights. You'll pass the **Catarata de Río Celeste**, a milky-blue waterfall that cascades 30m down the rocks into a fantastically aquamarine pool. Stop at the ***mirador*** (lookout point) for grand views of Tenorio from the double-decker wooden platform. Further on is the spectacular **Pozo Azul** (Blue Lagoon). The trail loops around the lagoon until you arrive at the confluence of rivers known as **Los Teñideros**

CHRISPICTURES/SHUTTERSTOCK

Why is the River So Blue?

The ethereal color of the Río Celeste is an optical illusion, caused by certain volcanic minerals suspended in the water. The water acts as a prism and separates the color waves as usual. But the mineral particles reflect the blue waves, giving the water its azure appearance.

Top left Río Celeste
Top right Parque Nacional Volcán Tenorio
Bottom left Pozo Azul

(The Dyers). Here, two small rivers mix together to create the blueberry milk of Río Celeste. It's quite a display.

The out-and-back trail is about 5km round-trip, but some parts of the trail are steep (and most parts are muddy). You'll want your boots.

Pearly Blue Pools

Swimming is strictly forbidden everywhere in the national park. But the river's luscious blue is irresistible, and if you want to submerse yourself in these enticing waters, you have a few options. From the park entrance, drive about 1km east to the first bridge. Here, a rough trail leads down to the river's edge. Known as the **Río Celeste Free Pool**, this is a popular spot for a post-hike dip. The other option is right next door at **Cabinas Piuri**, where the Río Celeste flows by in a series of sweet and swimmable pools. Non-guests pay a small fee to access the river. The water is cool, refreshing and beguilingly blue.

Deets about Dantas

Its official name is Baird's tapir, or the Central American tapir, but locally it's known as a 'danta.'

- Distantly related to a horse and a rhino, this gentle giant is a herbivore that weighs in at a hefty 150kg to 300kg.
- Tapirs are mostly solitary, but they are monogamous with their mate.
- Their babies have the color and pattern of a fawn – reddish-brown with white stripes and spots.
- Tapirs have few natural predators, but they are endangered due to loss of habitat.

Black of Night & Light of Day

They say that 60% of tropical rainforest animals are nocturnal, so it's worth coming out after dark to take a look. (Of course, they are harder to see. That's the downside.) **Tapir Valley Nature Reserve** borders Volcán Tenorio national park. Book a night tour for a rare chance to see the elusive (and endangered) Baird's tapir, as well as frogs, snakes, kinkajous and other creatures of the night.

If you're more of a morning person, you can opt for the three-hour birdwatching tour at 6am. Among the rare avian species here are the ornate hawk eagle, the colorful cotinga and the bare-necked umbrella bird. Three different viewing platforms provide an ideal perspective over the forest, the wetlands and a hummingbird garden.

Far left Baird's tapir
Left Yellow Eyelash Viper
Top Kinkajou

29 Beach HOPPING

SWIM | SUN | SEA

West of La Cruz, there is a little corner of coastal Costa Rica that is mostly untouched by international tourism. Cruise around the edge of the Golfo de Santa Elena – from Cuajiniquil to El Jobo – to discover tiny fishing villages and idyllic beaches, all surrounded by forest and farmland and spectacular views across the gulf.

GIANFRANCO VIVI/SHUTTERSTOCK

How To

Getting here/around You'll need your own vehicle to explore this area.

When to go The weather is consistently dry and sunny from December to April, but there are fewer people from May to November.

Eating and drinking There are a few eateries in Cuajiniquil, but otherwise few facilities. Bring plenty of water, snacks and sunblock.

NATURE'S CHARM/SHUTTERSTOCK

Heading from south to north from Cuajiniquil:

Playa Escondida A sweet little beach with no sign. Just offshore, a tiny island decorates the seascape and invites exploration. If you're hoping to find a deserted beach, this could be the one.

Playa Junquillal Part of the eponymous wildlife refuge, this gorgeous crescent of sand embraces a calm, quiet bay that's perfect for swimming. It's a popular spot for Tico families and iguanas. For your money, you'll get plenty of picnic tables, as well as bathrooms and showers. Two short trails (totaling 1.7km) hug the coast, traversing dry tropical forest. They lead to a marine bird lookout in one direction and to the mangroves in the other.

Punta Manzanillo The tiny beach south of El Jobo is not for swimming, but it's worth a stop to see colorful fishing boats bobbing at their lines and local fisherfolk hauling and cleaning their catch.

Playa las Pilas Off the road to Rajada, a rough road leads 500m south to this secret spot. Striated cliffs flank the rocky beach, which is otherwise surrounded by forest. It's a stunner.

Playa Rajada Lined with tree-shaded picnic tables, this long, narrow beach curves around its own bay, creating a perfect, placid swimming area. At the southern end, the outgoing tide leaves a lagoon of jumping fish and scurrying crabs. You can also sneak over to the tiny hidden **Playa Rajadita**.

Top left Playa Rajada
Bottom left Playa Junquillal

Wind & Water

Want to ride the wind? This remote northwestern corner of Costa Rica is the country's kitesurfing capital, where euphoric riders sail across Bahía Salinas, which stretches all the way to Nicaragua. From November to May, the wind howls at 20 to 40 knots, and the surrounding hills reliably funnel it into the bay. **Playa Copal** – as wide and wild as they come – is the perfect place to catch it and go for a ride. **Kiteboarding Costa Rica** offers accommodations on the beach, as well as equipment and instruction as needed. Hang on tight!

Where History Happens

WHAT WENT DOWN AT SANTA ROSA

Now a national park, Santa Rosa in Guanacaste was a focal point for Costa Rican history in the 19th and 20th centuries. Originally a farm, a replica of the old hacienda known as La Casona still stands as a testament to the history that unfolded here.

Top left La Casona
Top center Juan Rafael Mora Porras
Top right El Avión

CARL DEABREU PHOTOGRAPHY/SHUTTERSTOCK

Manifest Destiny Derailed

In the mid-19th century, the mercenary William Walker and his ragtag army attempted to conquer Central America, in an ill-advised effort to fulfill the 'manifest destiny' of the US. His initial foray into Mexico was a bust, but in 1855 he seized control of Nicaragua, taking advantage of the civil war raging there. Costa Rica went on high alert.

In February 1856, Costa Rican president Juan Rafael Mora Porras declared war on Nicaragua and recruited a volunteer army of some 9000 civilians to defend the northern border. The troops marched north from San José, while Walker's 'filibuster' army – composed mainly of European soldiers – came south to head them off. The Costa Rican patriots surprised the filibuster army at Santa Rosa, winning the battle in a record-breaking 14 minutes.

A month later, the Costa Rican fighters penetrated Nicaraguan territory and dealt another blow to Walker's men at the Second Battle of Rivas, where Juan Santamaría became a national hero (p59).

Nonetheless, Walker declared himself president of Nicaragua and the so-called Filibuster War continued for another year. But the Central American military coalition – led by Costa Rica – finally drove him out in May 1857 (and he was later executed in Honduras).

Cold War in the Hot Tropics

The 20th century also saw Yankee meddling in Central American affairs – in the very place where Costa Rica had so ably defended its independence 123 years earlier. In 1979 the rebellious Sandinistas toppled the American-backed Somoza

THE PICTURE ART COLLECTION/ALAMY

TIM FLEMING/ALAMY

dictatorship in Nicaragua. Alarmed by the Sandinistas' Soviet and Cuban ties, fervently anticommunist US president Ronald Reagan moved to support the Contra rebels who were inciting civil war in Nicaragua. The organizational details of the counter revolution were delegated to Oliver North, a junior officer working out of the White House basement. He dubbed the campaign 'Project Democracy.'

Under intense US pressure, Costa Rica was dragged in. The Contras set up camp in northern Costa Rica, from where they staged guerrilla raids. Clandestine CIA operatives and US military advisors assisted the effort. By the mid-1980s, they had built a secret airstrip in the jungle near Playa Portrero Grande (part of Parque Nacional Santa Rosa) to fly weapons and supplies into Nicaragua.

> Santa Rosa was a focal point for Costa Rican history in the 19th and 20th centuries. La Casona still stands as a testament to the history that unfolded.

In 1986 Óscar Arias Sánchez won the Costa Rican presidential election. A coffee baron and intellectual reformer, Arias had run on a platform of regional peace. Once in office, he affirmed his commitment to a negotiated resolution and reasserted Costa Rican national independence. He vowed to uphold his country's pledge of neutrality and to vanquish the Contras from its territory.

In a public ceremony, Costa Rican schoolchildren planted trees on top of the CIA's secret airfield. President Arias became the driving force in uniting Central America around a peace plan, which ended the Nicaraguan war and earned him the Nobel Peace Prize in 1987.

Remnants of History

President Arias's Nobel Peace Prize is the most noteworthy outcome of the US–Contra affair (and lasting peace, of course). But the Ticos – and the tourists – got a few other good things out of it.

Ollie's Point Nowadays, Playa Portrero Grande is a popular surfing beach. And the wave – a long, glorious right point break – is named for none other than Oliver North.

El Avión An old US cargo plane – retired from its gun-running days – is the centerpiece of a restaurant in Manuel Antonio. Best known as 'the Contra bar' (p207).

Listings

BEST OF THE REST

Wildlife-Watching

Arenal Oasis

Awesome place for a night walk in La Fortuna, with 35 species of frogs as well as other nocturnal creatures.

Bogarin Trail

Birdwatching and sloth spotting on a short, flat trail, just outside of La Fortuna. If you have your heart set on seeing a sloth, you should definitely spring for the guide.

Frog's Heaven

Here – in Las Horquetas – reside the most colorful frog species, including the red-eyed tree frog. Make a reservation for a tour to spot not only frogs, but bats, sloths and more.

La Selva Biological Station

A celebrated research station and wildlife reserve south of Puerto Viejo de Sarapiquí. Guided hikes will introduce you to some of the hundreds of species of resident birds, mammals and insects.

Monkey Park

White-faced capuchin monkeys are often sighted here, as well as frogs, anteaters and other rainforest friends. Located about 19km east of La Fortuna. Insect repellent is essential.

Monteverde Cloud Forest Reserve

The original cloud-forest reserve, founded by Quakers in 1972.

Santuario Ecológico Monteverde

A smallish sanctuary amid premontane forest and farmland. Hike on untrodden trails to spot coatis and birds, and to cool off beneath a 30m waterfall.

Tirimbina Rainforest Center

Situated 2km from La Virgen, this is a working environmental research and education center, with 9km of trails, a cacao plantation and a range of interesting wildlife tours.

Animal Encounters & Gardens

Butterfly Conservatory

The highlight of this facility in El Castillo is the enclosed habitats, fluttering with dozens of species of butterflies. But there are also botanical gardens, hiking trails and wonderful volcano views.

Monteverde Butterfly Gardens

In Monteverde, four gardens represent different habitats – altogether home to some 40 species of butterflies (and plenty of other insects). Witness the whole fascinating life cycle.

Bat Jungle

A small but super-informative exhibit – home to almost 100 free-flying bats. Learn all about echolocation, bat-wing aerodynamics and other amazing flying-mammal facts.

Postman butterfly

Jardín de Orquídeas

Shady trails wind past more than 500 types of orchids at the Orchid Garden in Santa Elena. See some rare species and learn how to keep your orchids at home beautiful and blooming.

 Hot Springs

Tabacón Hot Springs

The only hot-springs resort in La Fortuna that is built around Río Choillin, the actual free-flowing nature-made river that is warmed by the volcano (in addition to its human-made pools).

Springs Resort & Spa

The biggest hot-springs facility in La Fortuna, with 25 thermal pools of varying temperatures, a couple of swim-up bars and more.

Río Perdido

A high-end resort in Bagaces, with luxurious (but very sulphur-smelling) riverside pools, heated by Volcán Miravalles.

Las Hornillas

A unique family-owned place in Miravalles that includes a walkway through fumaroles and bubbling mud pots, in addition to the volcano-heated pools and mud bath.

Canyon de la Vieja

On the banks of the Río Colorado, this lodge has a series of thermal pools, plus a full-service spa and a glorious river swimming area.

 Lakes & Waterways

Arenal Kayaks

Explore the Laguna de Arenal from the seat of a kayak, with plenty of wildlife-watching and swimming stops along the way.

Green Rivers

The ever-amiable couple Kevín and Evelyn Martínez offer a wide variety of rafting and kayaking tours, from family-friendly floats to adrenaline-pumping rapid rides.

DON COUCH/ALAMY

Tabacón Hot Springs

Aventuras del Sarapiquí

Located right on the river in Chilamate, this outfit offers land, air and water adventures. In addition to white-water rafting, there's canoeing, horseback riding and a canopy tour on-site.

Sarapiquí Outdoor Center

Owner David Duarte is a local paddling authority in La Virgen. In addition to rafting excursions, SOC offers kayak rental and lessons.

 Canopy Tours

100% Aventura

This operation in Santa Elena boasts the longest zipline in Latin America, as well as a Tarzan swing, a 15m rappel, two Superman ziplines and a network of suspension bridges.

Arenal Mundo Aventura

This all-in-one adventure park has one of the best canopy tours in La Fortuna, as well as a waterfall rappelling and horseback riding adventure.

Mistico Hanging Bridges

Explore the rainforest and canopy at a peaceful pace, via six suspended bridges and 10 traditional bridges, along a single 3km trail near Laguna de Arenal.

Monteverde Extremo

This place has a canopy ride that allows you to fly Superman-style through the air, the highest and most adrenaline-addled Tarzan swing in the area, and a bungee jump from 150m. One way or another, you will scream.

Sky Adventures

All zipline and hanging-bridges tours include a gondola ride up to the top of the course. Locations in Santa Elena and El Castillo (near Arenal).

Learn Something New

Costa Rica Cooking

Learn to make *empanadas* (turnovers stuffed with meat or cheese), ceviche or other Costa Rican classics – then enjoy the fruits of your labor. In La Fortuna.

CPI Spanish School

Monteverde Spanish School offering language courses and lodging with local families for all levels, as well as more specialized courses.

Casados, Ceviche y Más

La Ventanita $

Fabulously tasty *chifrijo* (rice and beans in a bowl with fried pork pieces), as well as burritos, tacos and *batidos* (fruit shakes) in El Castillo. All tables have an incredible view of Arenal.

Jalapas $$

Perched high above La Fortuna, this excellent restaurant offers modern interpretations of traditional food, served in a spectacular setting. Choose between volcano views to the south and panoramic vistas of the lowlands in the north.

El Chante Verde $

Bright and inviting, this place is on the road to the waterfalls near La Fortuna. The menu is full of fresh salads and bowls, well-stuffed sandwiches and refreshing fruit drinks.

El Cacao $

Sadly, there is no chocolate on the menu at El Cacao, located at Best Chocolate in Chilamate. But there are tasty traditional dishes and intriguing pizzas, including the house special Pizza Theobrome (food of the gods), with chicken, shrimp and bacon.

La Cueva de Marisco $$

This unassuming place in Puerto Viejo de Sarapiquí cooks up seafood just right, offering grilled fish and scrumptious ceviche.

Hummingbird Café $

A delightful lunch spot in Bijagua de Upala, surrounded by birds, frogs and flowers. The menu is short and sweet: veggie burgers and fish tacos are highlights.

La Choza del Maíz $

A local favorite in Bijagua, this simple *soda* (small local restaurant) features the region's favorite ingredient: corn. Excellent place to try *chorreadas* (corn pancakes) or fill up on a *casado* (set meal).

Stella's Monteverde $$

Choose from healthy breakfast bowls, delicious sandwiches, sensational salads, just-baked quiche and more. Dine on the back patio among the birds.

SERGII KOVAL/SHUTTERSTOCK

Chifrijo

Restaurante Arrecife $$

Your perfect pitstop after a day of beach hopping. This breezy place is tucked away in the tiny village of Cuajiniquil. Look for fresh seafood and fruity cocktails, with or without the alcohol.

Bon Appétit $$$

When you have a hankering for Italian food (and wine), head to this delightful upscale eatery in Santa Elena. Handmade pasta and grilled meats are good for body and soul on a chilly evening in the cloud forest.

Brews & Booze

Mercadito Arenal $$

In 'downtown' La Fortuna, this little food court has places serving sushi, tacos and pizza. The talented bartenders at the Mixology Bar keep everything (and everybody) well lubricated.

Restaurante Celajes $$

Have a sunset drink on the terrace at the Hotel Belmar in Monteverde, featuring seasonal cocktails, craft beer and sweeping views to the Pacific. *Bocas* (appetizers) served daily from 4:30pm to 5:30pm.

Monteverde Brewing Co $$

Drink fresh beer and eat burgers in the cloud forest. This newish place in Santa Elena makes six types of beer, including a rich, delicious coffee stout and a hoppy, fruity IPA.

Café Monteverde $$

This delightful cafe in Santa Elena is connected to a fantastic community-run, sustainable coffee farm and education center. Drinking coffee is a given; you might as well help save the planet while you're at it!

Numu Brewing Co $$

A cool craft brewery in an industrial complex opposite the Liberia airport. Very limited snacks on offer, but the beer is the real deal. Can't beat a Numu Lager on a hot day.

Naked Indian $$

Tasty food, strong drinks and live music on Friday nights. This is an outdoor affair with a casual atmosphere. Menu highlights include the Tomahawk steak and lobster Thermidor. Come hungry.

Jungle Love $$

Craft cocktails with expansive views of Arenal volcano and lake. A cozy sunset from a tropical bar; reservations recommended.

Souvenir Shopping

Monteverde Natural Cosmetics

Their all-natural, eco-conscious products smell delicious – think cinnamon and organic coffee soap.

CASEM

This nonprofit artisan cooperative is dedicated to improving the lives of local women artists.

Monteverde Art House

This hub of creativity includes a wonderful boutique selling locally made products, as well as a coffee shop, gardens and an outdoor amphitheater.

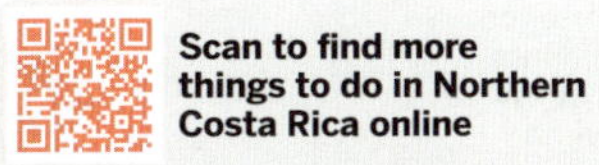

PENÍNSULA DE NICOYA

BEACHES | RAINFOREST | PARTIES

Experience Península de Nicoya online

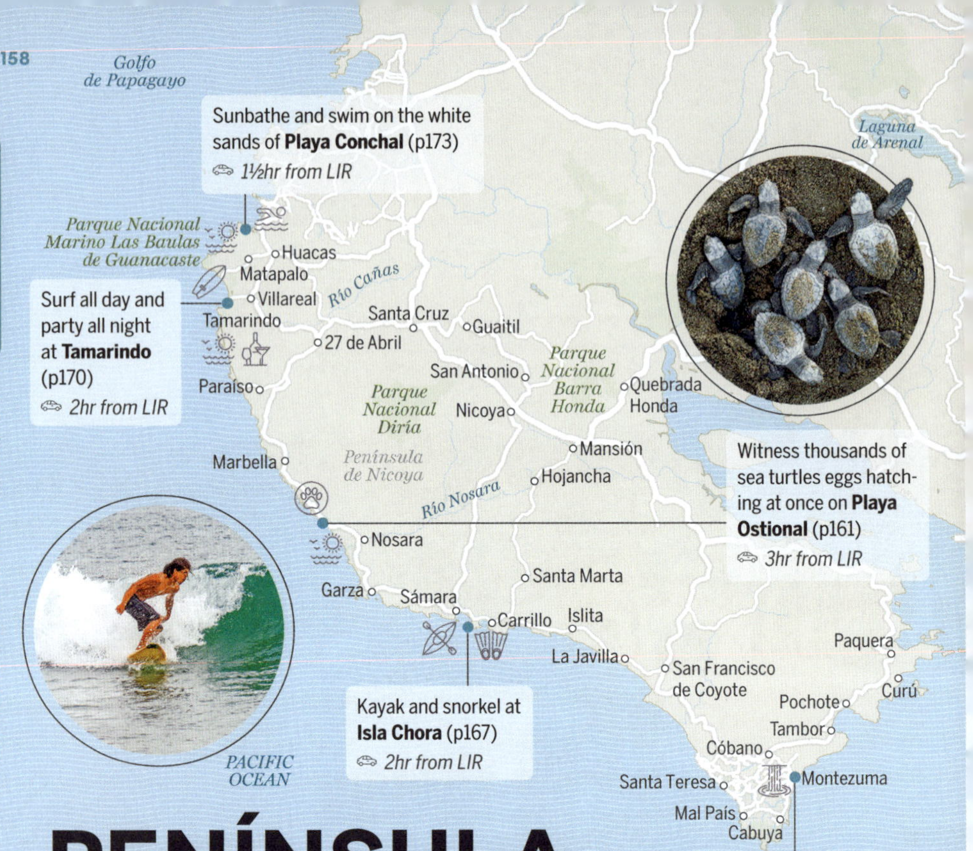
Golfo de Papagayo
Sunbathe and swim on the white sands of **Playa Conchal** (p173)
1½hr from LIR
Laguna de Arenal
Parque Nacional Marino Las Baulas de Guanacaste
Huacas
Matapalo
Villareal
Río Cañas
Surf all day and party all night at **Tamarindo** (p170)
2hr from LIR
Tamarindo
Santa Cruz
Guaitil
27 de Abril
San Antonio
Parque Nacional Barra Honda
Quebrada Honda
Paraíso
Parque Nacional Diría
Nicoya
Mansión
Marbella
Península de Nicoya
Hojancha
Río Nosara
Witness thousands of sea turtles eggs hatching at once on **Playa Ostional** (p161)
3hr from LIR
Nosara
Santa Marta
Garza
Sámara
Carrillo
Islita
La Javilla
Paquera
San Francisco de Coyote
Curú
Pochote
Kayak and snorkel at **Isla Chora** (p167)
2hr from LIR
Tambor
Cóbano
PACIFIC OCEAN
Santa Teresa
Montezuma
Mal País
Cabuya
Swim at waterfalls and jump on a Tarzan swing at **Montezuma** (p165)
4hr from LIR

PENÍNSULA DE NICOYA

Trip Builder

Surf culture with new-age hipster and hippie vibes. The beaches here boast some of the country's toughest currents and most brilliant sunsets. Celebrities, expats and backpackers come to connect with nature and the *pura vida* party scene.

PREVIOUS SPREAD: KOBBY DAGAN/SHUTTERSTOCK.
FROM LEFT: DARRYL BROOKS/SHUTTERSTOCK, MARIO WONG PASTOR/SHUTTERSTOCK

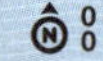

0 40 km
0 20 miles

Practicalities

Daniel Oduber Quirós International Airport, Liberia (LIR) Also known as Guanacaste Airport, this smaller international airport is convenient for visiting the Península de Nicoya. Shuttle buses run to the main beach towns.

CONNECT

LIR airport has free wi-fi as do most hotels and restaurants. Buy a Costa Rican SIM card to best maintain phone service.

MONEY

Booking a hotel that has breakfast included in the nightly price helps to save money. Meals are expensive in popular beach towns.

WHERE TO STAY

Town/ Village	Pros/Cons
Montezuma	New-age enclave known for its epic waterfalls.
Tamarindo	Surf spot and party town catering to tourists and expats.
Nosara	Easygoing energy attracting wellness-focused travelers.
Santa Teresa	Surfers, influencers and backpackers flock here.

GETTING AROUND

Car Renting a 4WD is necessary to navigate rough or unpaved roads and river crossings.

Bus and shuttle Private shuttles run from LIR airport to hotels in coastal towns, including Tamarindo, Nosara, Playas del Coco and Sámara. Public buses run from Liberia to various popular coastal points. They're cheaper but take longer.

TOP: VLADISLAV NOSEEK/SHUTTERSTOCK
BOTTOM: PILIPPHOTO/SHUTTERSTOCK

EATING & DRINKING

For a memorable sunset dinner on one of Nosara's magical beaches, make a reservation at La Luna. This Mediterranean restaurant is a departure from typical Costa Rican or seaside cuisine but its food is made with local ingredients and lots of love.

Always get a *batido* (fruit shake) or *agua fresca* made from fresh fruits like *sandía* (watermelon) or *piña* (pineapple). Try whatever is in season.

Best *casado* (set meal)
Rosi's Soda Tica (p180)

Must-try *ceviche*
La Cevichería (p180)

JAN–APR
Peak season, crowds, higher prices, hot, sunny, minimal rain

MAY–AUG
Rainy season begins, sunny mornings, afternoon storms

SEP–OCT
Rainiest months, roads may flood, excursions may get canceled

NOV–DEC
Less rain, holiday season begins

30 TURTLE Tours

ANIMALS | NATURE | ADVENTURE

At beaches up and down the peninsula, you can witness the fascinating reproductive rituals of various species of sea turtles. These diligent creatures return to their own natal beaches, dragging themselves across the sand to dig their nests and deposit their eggs, before making their way back to the sea. It's an incredible spectacle of nature's complexity and grandeur.

KRYSSIA CAMPOS/GETTY IMAGES

How To

Getting here Some turtle tours provide transportation from nearby towns.

When to go Peak *arribada* (nesting) season in Ostional is May through December, especially September through December. Sea-turtle nesting season at Las Baulas is from October to February, with tours taking place after sunset.

Guides Travelers are prohibited from going onto the nesting beaches during nesting season without a guide.

FRANCESCO PUNTIROLI/ALAMY

Olive ridley turtles Between July and December, olive ridley turtles *(tortugas loras)* make the arduous journey from the deep sea to **Playa Ostional** in **Refugio Nacional de Vida Silvestre Ostional**. This mass nesting event is called the *arribada* (arrival), with hundreds of turtles depositing their eggs in the sand, then trekking back into the sea. Tours take place in the evening or in the early morning. Reserve online via the **Asociación de Guías Locales de Ostional** Facebook page, or in person at their office in **Ostional**.

Leatherback turtles Located near Tamarindo, **Parque Nacional Marino Las Baulas** is home to the famous *baulas* (leatherback turtles), which nest and hatch here. This is the largest species of sea turtle, sometimes growing up to 2m long and weighing more than 450kg. During turtle nesting season, park rangers and guides take visitors on turtle conservation tours to see these gentle giants digging their nests and laying their eggs. Book at the ranger station or at the **Asociación de Guías Locales de Tamarindo** in Tamarindo.

Sea turtles The **Refugio Nacional de Vida Silvestre Romelia**, near Montezuma, is a sea turtle conservation and rescue center where you can volunteer to protect vulnerable baby turtles. The refuge runs a hatchery, where the eggs are shielded from both human and animal predators. Tasks include beach cleanups, tagging sea turtles and collecting eggs.

Top and bottom left Olive ridley sea turtles, Playa Ostional

Rules for Turtle-Watching

Sea-turtle-watching is generally a passive activity, but by being on the beach, you're part of the environment and have a part to play. If you're going to watch the sea turtles nest and hatch, wear black. The mother turtles swim along the coast searching for the safest beaches to lay their eggs, and if they see bright lights and colors, they won't nest at that location. Don't use your camera flash either because the turtles are sensitive to light. The best approach is to lay low, be an observer and don't touch the turtles or get in the way.

31 Bright NIGHTS

NATURE | RIVERS | KAYAKS

Floating in a sea of sparkling neon blue is an experience you can only have in a few places on the planet, and Bahía Ballena off Playa Pochote is one of the best in Costa Rica. Swim, snorkel or kayak in the glowing waters to experience the incredible biochemical phenomenon of bioluminescence up close.

How To

Getting here/around If staying in Montezuma or Santa Teresa, many tours offer transportation to departure points. Brave travelers with 4WD vehicles and solid cell service can drive on their own to meet their tour guides.

When to go New moons are the best times for these night tours because there's no moon lighting up the sky. Skip September and October when rains cause flooding and dangerous conditions.

Tours Most take between 90 minutes and two hours.

What is it? This bio magic is caused by the presence of single-celled organism called dinoflagellates. When the plankton is disturbed, it produces a chemical reaction that creates light energy. In large quantities, it causes the water to light up in an eerie but beautiful iridescent glow.

Sparkle swim Once your guide finds a good patch of bioluminescence, they will stop the boat and briefly demonstrate how it works by dumping a pail of glittering water aboard and pointing out the tiny fleck of teal inside. Then, you have the opportunity to jump in and ignite the bioluminescence yourself by paddling, diving, or simply treading water in a flurry of the sparkling ocean.

Above Bioluminescence kayak tour, Península de Nicoya

Beware The wonders of nature do come with a small price tag: the bioluminescence can be home to tiny sea insects that sometimes sting. The sting is startling but not dangerous, and the pain is momentary.

How to do it? Agencies in Montezuma and Santa Teresa offer bioluminescence tours, as does **Don Trino Camping** in Playa Pochote. Tours from Santa Teresa and Montezuma generally make a stop in either Playa Tambor or Playa Pochote before heading out into the bay.

Be Kind to the Bioluminescence

Disturb plankton-filled waters, and you'll see a blossom of blue swirling from the depths. It doesn't harm or interfere with the plankton when you swim with them, but you can take some precautions to ensure that your spangled swimming experience is both enchanting and plankton-friendly. Mainly, don't put on sunscreen, perfume, lotion or makeup before you go under. Some of these products can negatively impact the ecosystem, and it's best to avoid all of them, just in case. Also, don't be surprised if you return with a souvenir or two. People have reported seeing flashes of light from seawater-soaked swimsuits.

32 Wild, Wonderful MONTEZUMA

WATERFALLS | HIKING | BEACHES

Overlooking the Golfo de Nicoya near the peninsula's southern tip, Montezuma is a jungle-clad village with a bohemian soul. Beyond its boutique-lined streets are irresistible adventures, including swimmable waterfalls and deserted beaches. Take a quick boat ride across the gulf for a day (or more) of wild adventure.

TRAVELVIEW/SHUTTERSTOCK

How to

Getting here Water taxis zip between Montezuma and Jacó in about one hour. Zuma Tours is a good option.

When to go Like in the rest of the country, the best weather is from December to April. Green-season travelers will enjoy few crowds, if you can tolerate rain showers in the afternoon.

Water shoes The hike to Montezuma Waterfalls is not easy terrain! Wear good hiking sandals or water shoes with a good grip.

MAREMAGNUM/GETTY IMAGES

Left Montezuma Waterfalls
Below Ziplining, Montezuma

Montezuma Waterfalls South of town, a river trail winds up to an idyllic collection of **cascades**: each of the three *cataratas* falls into a deep glassy pool. The journey itself is steep, narrow and studded with rocks and vines. (Good hiking shoes are a must.) But it's worth the effort when your reach the terrific trifecta of swimmable waterfalls. Note that there's a fee to access the upper falls, which are on private property. If you prefer to fly above the falls, you can do so with the **Sun Trail Tours** canopy tour, which has nine ziplines across 13 platforms offering a bird's-eye view of the mighty falls.

Playa Cocolito Pristine and pale-pink **Playa Cocolito** is notoriously remote and covetously gorgeous. It's famous for its sky-high waterfall, **El Chorro**, which plunges dramatically and directly into the sea (reportedly one of only seven such falls in the world). It takes about 90 minutes to walk here along the **Sendero Sueño Verde**, accessible behind the Mercado de Artesanos. Alternatively, **Montezuma Tours** offers horseback-riding tours here.

Reserva Natural Absoluta Cabo Blanco Just south of Montezuma, **Reserva Natural Absoluta Cabo Blanco** was established in 1963 as Costa Rica's first nature reserve. **Sueco Trall** is a challenging hike with some steep ascents through dense rainforests, but it ends at a stunning white-sand beach, perfect for cooling off after a 5km hike.

Absolute Nature Reserve

The reserve at Cabo Blanco was established by a Danish-Swedish couple, Karen Mogensen and Olof Nicolás Wessberg, who settled in Montezuma in the 1950s and were among the first conservationists in Costa Rica. The couple was instrumental in convincing the government to establish a national park system, and they are buried in the **Reserva Absoluta Nicolás Wessberg**, the site of their original homestead.

Cabo Blanco is called an 'absolute' nature reserve because visitors were originally not permitted (prior to the late 1980s). The name hasn't changed, even though a limited number of trails are now open to visitors. The reserve remains closed on Monday and Tuesday to minimize environmental impact.

33 Island ESCAPES

DIVING | SNORKELING | KAYAKING

Even if you're not a surfer, there are many ways to have aquatic adventures on Península de Nicoya. Paddle a kayak or ride a boat out to the offshore islands to lounge on deserted beaches and snorkel or dive in clear Pacific waters.

JOAN VENDRELL/SHUTTERSTOCK

How To

Getting here You can paddle out to Isla Chora independently from Sámara, but the other islands are accessible only by guided tour.

When to go Underwater visibility is generally best during dry season (December through April) when there is little rainfall. That said, Islas Murciélagos is only accessible during the rainy season due to high winds at other times.

Dolphins Look for dolphins on the way to and from Isla Tortuga. They often like to play and jump next to tour boats.

MARC GUITARD/GETTY IMAGES

Top left Isla Tortuga
Bottom left Isla Chora

Isla Tortuga An island teeming with sea and land life, covered in gorgeous flowers and foliage, and ringed with snowy white beaches – this is Isla Tortuga, just 45 minutes by boat from Santa Teresa. Fine, clear waters make this a prime spot for snorkeling and diving. Snorkelers can spot graceful orange- and sapphire-colored angelfish, lime-green parrotfish, and stingrays, while divers can explore a volcanic reef and a shipwreck, frequented by white-tip reef sharks.

Isla Chora The pale, salmon-tinged sands of Isla Chora, just off the coast of Sámara, are a spectacular place to spend a lazy, beachy afternoon. The blissful sun-loafing is even more enjoyable because you have to work a bit for it. It takes 30 to 45 minutes to kayak to Isla Chora across a thin stretch of open ocean. Once ashore, you can snorkel in the shallows or take a leisurely hike around the island, spotting sizable iguanas and raccoons along the way.

Islas Murciélagos The so-called **Bat Islands** are 48km off the coast of Playas del Coco, across the Golfo de Papagayo. Take a relaxing boat ride across the bay to snorkel or scuba-dive with sea turtles, octopuses and nurse sharks. Scuba divers will see an underwater world shaped by volcanic activity. There are a variety of small beaches around the gulf where your captain can stop for a beach snack or *cerveza* (beer).

Turtle Island's Animal Life

There's a wealth of animal life on and around Isla Tortuga, but the name doesn't come from the green turtles that swim in these waters. Instead, the island is named after its shape. From the air, Isla Tortuga looks like a giant turtle, with its head extended and all four legs splayed out. If you squint and use your imagination, you can totally see it!

All manner of wonderful creatures populate this region, including peccaries (small boars), monkeys, peacocks, macaws and armadillos. You can see some of these animals right on the beach, take an Ecological Tour or explore the terrain yourself.

34 Surf's UP

SURFING | SWIMMING | BEACHES

Surfers have a smorgasbord of breaks and beaches to choose from throughout Península de Nicoya. Each of these surf-centric coastal towns has a distinct vibe, offering waves for every sort of traveler. Expert surfers congregate in beach towns across the coast to show off their skills and teach tourists.

CHRISTIAN ASLUND/GETTY IMAGES

How To

Getting around The roads around many of these coastal towns are unpaved, so a 4WD is a necessity.

When to go The rainy season (April to November) sees the biggest surf on the Península de Nicoya. That said, some of the best surfing beaches may be inaccessible because of flooding.

Surf camps All-inclusive surf camps are popular options for beginner surfers. Multiday packages usually include lessons, accommodations and meals.

NATURE'S CHARM/SHUTTERSTOCK

Nosara

Nosara has a multitude of perfect beaches for surfers of all levels. It may not have the same amount of traffic as other surf towns on the peninsula, but surfers like Nosara because the waves are consistent. **Playa Guiones** is known to be beginner-friendly and most surf schools are set up here. **Playa Nosara**, which has both a beach break and a reef break, is where more experienced surfers go for powerful waves.

Safari Surf and **Surf Simply** are excellent all-inclusive camps in Nosara. Alternatively, you can just rent a board from a local surf shop like **Juan Surfo's** or **Coconut Harry's** and go it alone.

Expert Surfers Only

Advanced surfers near Tamarindo head south to **Playa Langosta**. It's a more secluded beach known for consistent, challenging waves that test even veteran surfers. The most experienced surfers near Santa Teresa head to **Punta Barrigona** in Mal País, especially when the Pacific Ocean is active.

JOSHUA TEN BRINK/SHUTTERSTOCK

Top left Playa Hermosa (p171)
Top right Playa Langosta
Bottom left Mal País (p171)

Sámara

Sámara's beaches are known more for swimming than surfing. Absolute beginners – that is, people who've never been on a surfboard – will be comfortable here as the water is shallow, the waves are small and the bottom is sandy. This is where you learn the basics like practicing how to stand up on a surfboard and riding the white water to shore. A reef along the coast protects the bay from major waves, making it ideal for first-timers, other surfing newbies, and families with small children and elders.

C&C Surf School and **Pato's Surf School** are great choices if you want to give it a try.

Tamarindo

Tamarindo draws domestic and international travelers who want to surf hard and party harder. It's a great choice for beginner surfers because there are tons of breaks offering endless waves, and thus chances to practice.

Surf Like a Girl

A ranked Costa Rican surfer, Veronica Quiros, wanted to provide women a safe space to learn to surf. So she founded **Tica Surf**, a Santa Teresa surf school for women, by women. She and her team of all-female surf instructors offer lessons to women who are just getting started or who are looking for expert advice from one of Costa Rica's most celebrated surfers. The surf shop also carries Quiros' clothing line, including comfortable, functional, brightly colored and unique bikinis, shorts and surf gear for women. Their clothes are well made, quick-drying and designed to stay on, even in the rowdiest surf.

The waves break gently and the shore is all sand, which makes for soft landings.

There's a host of surf camps and surf schools, some favorites include **Iguana Surf**, **Costa Rica Surf Institute**, **Carlos' Surf School** and **Tidal Wave Surf & Travel**.

One drawback of Tamarindo's geography is that the waves are tide-dependent, so you may spend most of your day waiting for them to show up.

Santa Teresa

Sexy surfers, digital nomads and aspiring healers have found a home in Santa Teresa, one of the most beloved beaches on Península de Nicoya. The currents that make most of the beaches terrible for swimming make them incredible for surfers. **Playa Hermosa** is best for beginners and **Playa Santa Teresa** is where most surf camps are located. Hardcore surfers hit nearby **Mal País** and **Playa Carmen** for serious swells.

Rent a board or take a lesson from **Kina Surf Shop** or **Pura Vida Adventures**.

Left Surfer, Playa Santa Teresa
Below Tamarindo

FROM LEFT: IMAGEBROKER.COM/ALAMY, FOTOS593/SHUTTERSTOCK

35 Secret BEACHES

SWIMMING | SUNBATHING | SCENERY

Península de Nicoya has seemingly infinite beautiful beach options for all sorts of travelers. One could spend weeks driving along the coast, exploring a different beach town and stretch of Pacific Coast each day. While surfing gets most of the attention, this coast is also perfect for lounging under palm trees or taking in the sun.

CAROLINEBRANDT/SHUTTERSTOCK

How to

Getting around Having a rental car with a 4WD will allow you to beach-hop and explore the diverse beaches along the coast. Many roads are unpaved and taxi service is minimal and expensive.

When to go Visit from January through April for the sunniest days with the least rain. Beat the crowds in November or between May and August.

JOSHUA TEN BRINK/SHUTTERSTOCK

Playa Conchal

A standout beach on the northern part of the peninsula, Playa Conchal gets its name from the tiny snow-white seashells that make up the beach (*concha* means 'shell'). This unique feature combined with crystal blue waters put Playa Conchal consistently at the top of many 'most beautiful beaches' lists. There are a few larger luxury hotels set back from the beach, but the shore is public, and it attracts a congenial mix of Tico families and international visitors. (We admit, it's not really a secret, and it does get crowded on weekends.) Vendors ply the beach with food and drinks, but there are no other facilities here.

To reach Playa Conchal, walk about 20 minutes south from Brasilito. There is no road access.

GOOFYFOOTTAKA/SHUTTERSTOCK

Beach Safety

The biggest danger to travelers in Costa Rica is riptides: strong currents that pull swimmers out to sea. If you get caught in a riptide, don't try to swim against it – it's a no-win. Ride the current until it dissipates enough that you can swim parallel to the shore, then swim back in where there's no riptide.

Top left & right Playa Conchal
Bottom left Playa Junquillal (p174)

Playa Junquillal

About 30km south of Tamarindo, Playa Junquillal is a stunning, 2km-wide gray-sand wilderness beach. At the southern end is the vast Río Nandamojo estuary, and in the north, a scenic bluff overlooks the beach. In between are nearly deserted sands and a sea swirling with fierce rip currents. It can be dangerous for swimming, but the coastline lends itself to long, leisurely walks. And there are numerous coves for exploring and pools for frolicking during low tide. Junquillal sunsets are phenomenal, featuring blinding golds, molten oranges and shocking pinks.

Playa Rosada

At low tide, you can walk south from Playa Guiones in Nosara to reach this picture-perfect, pink-tinged beach, aptly named Playa Rosada. You might just have the place to yourself. If you're feeling ambitious (and if you're wearing decent hiking shoes),

Nature's Hot Tubs

About 20 minutes south of hot, dusty Santa Teresa lies an alternate universe, Mal País, dominated by rocky beach and unruly surf. As the tide recedes from this barren coastline, it reveals volcanic rock formations, with tide pools swirling in their nooks and crannies. These are the **Malpaís tide pools** (aka Mar Azul tide pools). Some are deep enough for soaking – or even swimming – while others are shallow enough to spy on the small fish and other creatures that were abandoned by the outgoing tide. (Be careful of sea urchins!) When the tides are timed correctly, this is an ultra-romantic sunset spot.

Left Malpaís tide pools
Below Playa Carillo

follow the 4km Playa Rosada loop, a moderately challenging jaunt through the forest and beach. You'll see the whole of Playa Rosada and plenty of wildlife, such as iguanas and shore birds.

Just be sure to pay attention to the tide charts (and the time), because Playa Rosada becomes inaccessible from the mainland once the tide rolls in.

Playa Carillo

About 5km south of Sámara, palm-fringed Playa Carrillo curves in a perfect crescent around the eponymous bay. It's a prime spot to hang up a hammock, read a book and soak in the tranquil vibes. The waters are warm, calm and swimmable, and it's flanked by two coral reefs, where you can see plenty of tropical fish in the clear water. Vendors sell beachy treats like ice-cold *pipas* (coconut water) to the Tico families lounging on the sand, while fishing boats trawl for roosterfish and mahi-mahi in the bright blue waters. Be sure to stay for the sunset, as the pink- and orange-tinged sky looks epic from this vast, flat *playa*.

FROM LEFT: TWO WEEKS IN COSTA RICA, HEATHER BARRETT/SHUTTERSTOCK

Protecting Costa Rica's Sea Turtles

GUARDING SEA TURTLES FROM OURSELVES

Sea turtles are the superstars of Península de Nicoya. The coast is home to thousands of endangered turtles who nest and hatch their eggs on the shores all year long. Conservation efforts are intertwined with Costa Rica's ecotourism initiatives and tourists play an important role in preserving the delicate environment.

Top left Leatherback turtle
Top center Turtle nesting, Playa Ostional
Top right Collecting olive ridley sea turtle eggs

STEPHANIE ROUSSEAU/SHUTTERSTOCK

One of the biggest draws to visiting Costa Rica is its captivating natural environment. Tourists quickly understand that humans are only a miniscule piece of the ecosystem because nature here is confronting and immersive. Most of the country's popular destinations require visitors to connect with the flora, fauna and weather. It's part of what makes Costa Rica magical.

Península de Nicoya is one of those locations where you have to slow down and recognize how nature is moving all around you. It's especially evident when it comes to sea turtles, a fixture along this coastline. Because endangered leatherback turtles nest here, and olive ridleys come in their thousands, Península de Nicoya has become a leader in global turtle conservation and ecotourism.

Leatherback turtles, typically found in Parque Nacional Marino Las Baulas, are the largest species of sea turtles, while olive ridleys, who take over Playa Ostional, are the smallest. One theory speculates that olive ridleys decide to hatch en masse to give themselves a better chance of surviving predators – a 'safety in numbers' plan of action. Even so, scientists have noted that both of these populations are dwindling over time, and the leatherback, in particular, is facing a serious threat of extinction. Both species are threatened by the poaching and selling of their eggs. These eggs are delicacies and are considered in many communities to have aphrodisiac powers. Another culprit for low survival rates is turtles getting caught up in commercial fishing nets or choking on plastic ocean pollution.

JARIB/SHUTTERSTOCK

XINHUA NEWS AGENCY/GETTY IMAGES

The role that conservation efforts will continue to have in sea turtle prospects cannot be downplayed. Volunteer opportunities have become more plentiful to help local conservationists conduct research on nesting ecology, population numbers, hatching success and the ratio of female to male turtles. Organizations are also committed to protecting turtle habitats. Most volunteers visiting from other countries stay a week or two. They help with a variety of tasks, including nighttime beach patrol, beach clean-ups and making signs. Some two-week volunteer programs are more in-depth, teaching visitors how to measure massive leatherbacks, and to tag and collect their eggs. Volunteers who support with data collection and monitor the beaches help ensure that the scientists' work can continue. Often volunteers will live at local homestays near the beach for the duration of their assignment. As with any volunteering opportunity, it's important that you research the credentials of any organization before signing up.

Península de Nicoya is one of those locations where you have to slow down and recognize how nature is moving all around you.

Because so many tourists are drawn to Costa Rica's remarkable natural environment, it's important that everyone does their part even if not volunteering. For example, pick up trash on the beaches, even if it's not yours. And make sure you know the local hatching season so that you're not stepping on turtle eggs during a sunset stroll.

Hatching Facts

Ostional is the only beach where poaching eggs is legal. The government allows locals to harvest eggs during the first three nights of an *arribada* (mass egg laying) because eggs laid on the first night often get destroyed by turtles on following nights.

During the two weeks that represent the middle of the egg's incubation period, the sand temperature in the nest determines the sex of the turtles that are hatched. If the sand temperature is above 30°C (86°F), the turtles will be female. If the temperature is below 27°C (81°F), the turtles will be male. In-between temperatures result in a mix.

SEEK OUT These Sights

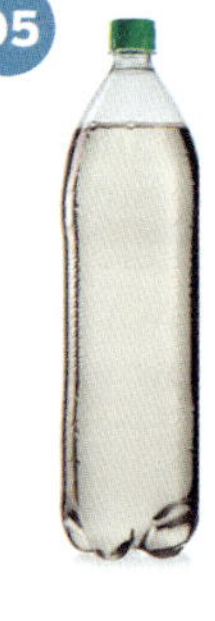

01 Leatherback Sea Turtles
The largest species of sea turtle nests and hatches on Península de Nicoya.

02 Surfboard
The allure of surfing permeates every beach along Península de Nicoya. Anyone can be surfer for a day.

03 Olive Ridley Sea Turtles
Thousands of these tiny turtles spend days nesting and hatching on the shores.

04 ATV
All-terrain vehicles might look apocalyptic, but they're a convenient way to navigate dusty, dry-season roads in the southern Península de Nicoya.

05 Coyol
A common sight at roadside stands along the highways. Those recycled plastic soda bottles are full of homemade fermented liquor made from coyol palm tree sap.

06 White-Faced Monkeys
These adorable monkeys travel in packs and will steal your food. After years of tourists feeding them in exchange for photos, they will ransack your bag if you leave it unattended.

07 Yoga

Nosara and Santa Teresa attract budding instructors and health-conscious yoga enthusiasts on wellness retreats.

08 Coral

Gorgeous and colorful coral reefs offer epic snorkeling and scuba sights for underwater explorers.

09 Waterfalls

While Montezuma is the main attraction, there are plenty of smaller hidden waterfalls for swimming or wading.

10 Bikinis

Bikini shops are ubiquitous. Local designers create styles specifically for surfing while others are made solely for lounging and looking cute.

11 Kayaks

The transportation of choice for bioluminescent night tours, meandering through mangroves and accessing remote snorkeling adventures.

01 DORLING KINDERSLEY/GETTY IMAGES, **02** LJUPCO SMOKOVSKI/SHUTTERSTOCK, **03** NATTAWUD GROODNGOEN/SHUTTERSTOCK, **04** PHOTOSTAR72/SHUTTERSTOCK, **05** MARIYANA M/SHUTTERSTOCK, **06** LEONP/SHUTTERSTOCK, **07** ARTFAMILY/SHUTTERSTOCK, **08** JAG_CZ/SHUTTERSTOCK, **09** MATT ELLIOTT/SHUTTERSTOCK, **10** ANNA KLEPATCKAYA/SHUTTERSTOCK, **11** PIXEL-SHOT/SHUTTERSTOCK

Listings

BEST OF THE REST

Learn to Surf

Witch's Rock Surf Camp

Witch's Rock in Tamarindo caters to complete surfing newbies, as well as intermediate and advanced surfers who want to explore the more intense waves across Guanacaste.

Hostel La Posada

This seven-day surf camp in Santa Teresa combines five surf lessons with three yoga classes and professional sports massage. The hostel has private rooms with private bathrooms, and dormitory-style rooms.

Safari Surf

The Safari Surf school in Nosara offers one-week all-inclusive stays with daily surf and yoga classes. The camp is led by a professional surfer and the suites have wi-fi, air-con and other amenities.

Peaks N Swells Surf Camp

This kid-friendly surf camp in Montezuma is geared towards families who want to learn how to surf together. Only three families are on-site at once, which gives individualized attention.

Mamawata's Women's Surf Retreat

This women-only surf camp in Nosara offers all-inclusive one-week retreats for solo travelers or small groups. The three retreats have different styles, but are all designed for maximum relaxation.

Sodas & Seafood

Pacifico Azul $$$

Get your fresh seafood fix at this restaurant on Playa Guiones in Nosara. The chefs offer family recipes cooked with local ingredients. Vegetarian and gluten-free options are available.

Soda Teresita $

Traditional *soda* (small local restaurant) in Playas del Coco open for early birds, with seaside views and big portions of *gallo pinto* (rice and beans) and lunchtime *casados* (set meals).

La Cevichería $$

This busy yet unassuming restaurant on the main road through Santa Teresa sells *ceviche* in all the ways. Try Peruvian with *aje chile* sauce, or the Tropical with mango and ginger.

Ylang Ylang $$$

Seafood and sushi dominate the menu at this beautiful beachside restaurant in Montezuma. Wide selection of meals to accommodate all tastes and dietary needs.

Rosi's Soda Tica $

Delicious and affordable hearty *casados* are served up at this Nosara *soda*, which attracts locals and visitors. Located near Playa Guiones.

Shambala Beachfront Restaurant $$

Excellent cocktails and artisan pizza, *ceviche* and pasta, with a gorgeous view of Playa Santa Teresa.

Roots Bakery $$

Choose from an array of tasty baked treats to appease your sweet tooth. Pick up breakfast, cinnamon rolls and organic coffee on your way to Playa Sámara.

Sweet Sleeps

Boho Lodge Montezuma

This remote ecolodge located 5km from the Montezuma Waterfalls has four air-conditioned units with kitchen and patios, as well as an outdoor pool and solid wi-fi.

Green Sanctuary Hotel

This family-owned and -operated boutique hotel is Costa Rica's first to be built entirely of shipping containers. Yogis frequent this sustainably designed space located in Nosara.

Beach Designs

Papaya Con Leche

Stop by Papaya con Leche, a sleek boutique in Tamarindo with locally designed women's wear for day and night. It specializes in custom-fit swimsuits and in-house handcrafted shoes.

Tica Surf

Get a bikini designed for surfing. Since 2004, Tica owner and designer Veronica Quiros has been outfitting women surfers in Santa Teresa so they can focus on their sport and not their suit.

EK Art Jewelry

This store in Tamarindo is owned by a married couple of silversmiths, who sell gorgeous jewelry inspired by the natural sights of Costa Rica. One of a kind, wearable art.

Feria Orgánica

This local farmers market takes places in Montezuma every Saturday from 10am to 2pm. Get fresh produce, baked goods, handmade soap and even jewelry and fine art.

Bri'ah Art Gallery

Get a keepsake piece made by local artists at this gallery of modern art in Mal País. It also offers painting parties for families and ones with wine for adults.

Take a Tour

Carrillo Tours

For nature adventures near Playa Sámara, book a tour with Carillo Tours. It is Costa Rican–owned and offers shuttles, sea/mangrove kayak tours, horseback riding, and visits to natural reserves.

Xplore Costa Rica

Xplore Costa Rica leads various nature tours throughout the Tamarindo area. Travelers can choose from ziplining, river rafting, sunset catamaran tours and various adventures.

Ecological Association Paquera, Lepanto & Cóbano (Asepaleco)

This conservation group runs tours of the Karen Mogensen Reserve, which is a privately owned sanctuary for local wildlife species and to protect the rivers and natural springs.

Nicoya Surf & SUP

Sign up with these local experts for surf lessons or SUP (stand-up paddleboarding) in Santa Teresa and Montezuma. Beginners and intermediates will enjoy some of the region's best waves.

Zuma Tours

Zuma Tours has been in business for 30 years in the Montezuma and Santa Teresa area. It offers various tours on land and sea, including scuba diving, sportfishing and ATVing.

Scan to find more things to do in Península de Nicoya online

CENTRAL PACIFIC COAST

BEACHES | MARINE SPORTS | NATIONAL PARKS

Experience the Central Pacific Coast online

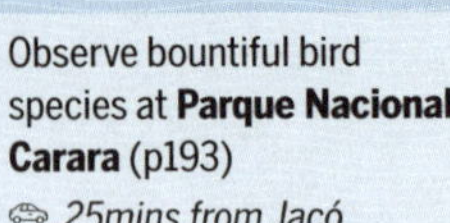

Observe bountiful bird species at **Parque Nacional Carara** (p193)
25mins from Jacó

Step up your surfing skills in **Playa Jacó** (p202)
2hrs from San José

Cheer on the brave surfers competing weekly in **Playa Hermosa** (p171)
15mins from Jacó

Cruise along the coast of **Bahía Biesanz** on a catamaran (p191)
30mins from Manuel Antonio

CENTRAL PACIFIC COAST

Trip Builder

The central Pacific coast is one of Costa Rica's biggest tourist destinations because of its proximity to San José and its abundance of mind-blowing beaches and ecotourism adventures. Visitors can relax, party, dive and hike through stunning nature scenes.

PREVIOUS SPREAD: JAKUB MACULEWICZ/SHUTTERSTOCK
CLOCKWISE FROM LEFT: GASTON PICCINETTI/SHUTTERSTOCK, MIKOLAJ OSTASZEWSKI/GETTY IMAGES, CLAUDE HUOT/SHUTTERSTOCK

Practicalities

DMITRIYBURLAKOV/GETTY IMAGES

ARRIVING

Juan Santamaría International Airport, San José (SJO) Most travelers will rent a car from SJO to drive to the Pacific coastal towns, or take a private shuttle to their hotel.

Quepos La Managua Airport (XQP) This small airport only serves domestic travelers, especially those visiting Manuel Antonio. A flight from SJO to Quepos takes 25 minutes.

Public buses Routes to various coastal cities including Jacó, Quepos and Manuel Antonio.

HOW MUCH FOR A

***Guaro* sour**
US$3

Craft beer
US$4

Smoothie
US$6

WHEN TO GO

JAN–APR
Peak season; dry season is sunny with little rain.

MAY–AUG
Less crowded; rainy season begins; sunny mornings, afternoon storms.

SEP–OCT
Rainiest months and end of rainy season; flooding possible; some businesses close.

NOV–DEC
Holiday season begins; storms subside.

GETTING AROUND

Car Rentals give travelers more freedom to explore. A 4WD is ideal for unpaved roads en route to waterfalls, rainforest hikes and other eco-adventures.

Taxi Uber is available in Jacó, Quepos and Manuel Antonio. Most hotels or home-shares have local taxi drivers for hire. Renting a taxi and driver for the day is an option, particularly for tours.

Bus Public buses are a cheaper option from San José, but are less comfortable and stop a lot. Once on the central Pacific coast, buses are a cost-effective way to visit beach towns that are close to each other.

EATING & DRINKING

The central Pacific coast offers a variety of typical Tico flavors. No breakfast in Costa Rica is complete without *gallo pinto* (pictured top right), the quintessential national dish of white rice and black beans. In honor of this region's party vibes, try all the *guaro* concoctions your stomach can stand. *Guaro,* made of sugarcane, is the national liquor; Cacique is the national brand. Chili *guaro* shots and *guaro* sours (picture bottom right) are most popular.

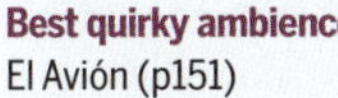

Best quirky ambience
El Avión (p151)

Must-try microbrews
Puddlefish Brewery (p206)

TOP: BRYCE JACKSON/SHUTTERSTOCK, BOTTOM: BRENT HOFACKER/SHUTTERSTOCK

CONNECT & FIND YOUR WAY

Connect Wi-fi is generally available at most hotels, restaurants and home-sharing properties. Cell service is solid in tourist-friendly areas along the coast. Cellular service may be unreliable or scattered on secluded roads where there's limited wi-fi access.

Navigation If planning to explore remote beaches or mountain areas, it's best to download maps before leaving wi-fi areas.

WHERE TO STAY

This region boasts a wide variety of beautiful coastal towns. Choose from locales near grand national parks or laid-back beach communities.

Town/Village	Pros/Cons
Jacó	A plethora of activities and beaches close to the airport. Big party scene.
Manuel Antonio	Lush ecolodges and resorts. LGBTIQ+ friendly vibes. Can get crowded.
Dominical	A popular surfer destination known for its waves. Quirky beach town.
Uvita	Best spot for whale-watching. Far from the airport.

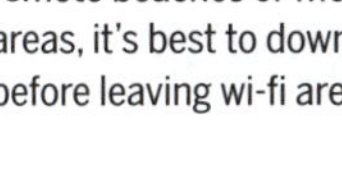

STAY AWARE

Jacó is a party town where many travelers come to indulge in drugs and sex tourism. Solo travelers should stay aware of their surroundings.

MONEY

ATMs are readily available and easily accessible in major tourist areas such as Jacó. Avoid paying credit-card transaction fees and taxes by paying for meals, groceries and souvenirs in cash.

36 ECO Adventures

TOURS | VIEWS | ADVENTURE SPORTS

Costa Rica's booming ecotourism sector means there are countless ways to connect with the country's vibrant natural environment. (At some adventure parks, you can try them all in one place!) Fly through the jungle on a zipline, parasail above the rainforest or ride horses along the beach at sunset. There are enough high-octane activities and low-key experiences to appeal to every sort of traveler.

PHOTO COURTESY VISTA LOS SUEÑOS ADVENTURE PARK, JACÓ - COSTA RICA, VLSCR.COM

How To

Getting around Many nature-focused tours offer transport from your accommodations and include it in the cost of the tour. Renting a vehicle allows for more opportunities to explore the region. Public buses run regularly along the coast and to more inland towns, but may require changing buses in Quepos.

When to go Rain can affect the safety of many outdoor activities, so it's best to visit in the dry season (December through April). It's also more crowded with international tourists.

RANCHO LA MERCED

Top left Vista Los Sueños Adventure Park
Bottom left Rancho La Merced

Vista Los Sueños Adventure Park Near Jacó, this place serves up family-friendly excursions. It offers an extensive playground and is also known for the safety, quality and maintenance of its cables and equipment. For those that want to stay on solid ground, Vista Los Sueños offers chocolate tours as well as horseback-riding tours that explore waterfalls and wildlife. You can spend a full day there doing a combination of tours; there's a delicious restaurant with Tico cuisine.

Zion Paragliding Paragliding is not for the faint of heart, but it awards fearless adventurers with a literal bird's-eye view of the Pacific coast. In Dominical, Zion is a paragliding school that provides tandem experiences as well as classes for those intent on learning how to fly. The tour takes brave visitors up to Cerro Escalares where you and your expert paragliding guide will take off (ie run off the mountain). The flight time is 15 to 20 minutes and offers astonishing views of the jungle, birds and beach below, where you'll land. Photos cost extra.

Rancho La Merced If you're closer to Uvita, this ranch provides horseback-riding tours to nearby waterfalls during the day and to Playa Hermosa for sunset. Because Rancho La Merced is an actual working cattle ranch, there's also a unique Cowboy Experience, where you spend a few hours herding cattle, learning how to check cows and calves in the grass, and other typical daily ranch tasks.

El Miro

Go to **Miro Mountain** for the best Pacific coast views in Jacó. It's located in the southern part of Jacó. Once you climb the mountain path, there's a lookout with grand views of the coast. To the left, you'll see an abandoned hotel in the distance. As you descend, you can stop at the building to see walls covered in animal murals. Further down, you'll see numerous types of trees, as well as monkeys, scarlet macaws, toucans, wild turkeys and sloths. There's also a variety of small animals, such as spiders and leaf-cutter ants.

Insight by **Wilson Viviano**, hostel owner in Jacó

37 Underwater WORLDS

DIVING | SNORKELING | MARINE LIFE

Nurture your inner mermaid in the enchanting waters of the central Pacific coast. The region boasts some of the country's best scuba-diving locales plus top-notch snorkeling in out-of-way coastal coves, many of which are protected by national marine parks. Water-sports enthusiasts can also explore the seas, with stand-up paddleboarding, banana boats and catamaran cruises all available.

OGPHOTO/GETTY IMAGES

How To

Getting around Most tour operators in this area include transportation in their prices. If you're staying in one area and plan to do several tours, you probably won't need a rental car. Public buses make stops along Ruta 34, but you'll need a taxi or other transport from the bus stop to your lodging.

When to go Dry season is ideal for enjoying all of the water adventures. Rainy season means more cancelled excursions.

Tip Visit *sinac.go.cr* before visiting national parks to book tickets and confirm hours.

JORGE A. RUSSELL/SHUTTERSTOCK

Top left Parque Nacional Marino Ballena
Bottom left Adapted stand-up paddleboarding (SUP) class, Playa Herradura

Parque Nacional Marino Ballena The massive **marine park** near Uvita is famous for its migrating whales, but it's also a great place to see smaller marine creatures. Dive shops like **Costa Rica Dive & Surf** offer snorkel and dive trips in the vicinity, including Whale Rock, a rock formation with thriving coral reefs and impressive marine life.

Parque Nacional Manuel Antonio Snorkelers can experience excellent visibility and biodiversity off the coast of **Manuel Antonio**. You can bring your own gear and snorkel from the beach. Alternatively, a guided snorkel-kayak tour allows you to paddle into deeper, fish-infested waters. Book with **Manuel Antonio Kayak Tour** or **Iguana Tours**, both in Quepos.

Bahía Biesanz Many aquatic tours come to this gorgeous **bay**, where the water is clear and still, providing ideal conditions for snorkeling, kayaking and paddleboarding. Catamaran cruises offer stunning views of the coastline and plenty of camaraderie as you sail along the glimmering bay. **Sunset Sails** is a popular option.

Playa Herradura If looking at pretty fish doesn't do it for you, maybe you want to *catch* mighty fish – like blue marlin and yellowfin tuna. You've come to the right place. The central Pacific coast is a year-round sportfishing destination. Charter a boat with **Pelagic Pursuits** or **Allin Sport Fishing**, both located at Los Sueños Marina near Jacó.

River Adventures

Inland waterways also offer opportunities for adventure! Just 20km south of Manuel Antonio, the **Río Savegre** has Class II and III rapids that are ideal for first-time white-water rafters, families or easy-adventure enthusiasts. You'll spend about four hours riding the river through wild rainforest, with pit stops at hidden waterfalls and swimming holes. Alternatively, head to the **Río Naranjo** on the border of Parque Nacional Manuel Antonio, where Class III and IV rapids challenge experienced white-water paddlers from June to November. Book trips with **H2O Adventures** or **Amigos del Río**.

38 Wilding OUT

NATIONAL PARKS | WILDLIFE | HIKING

A visit to Costa Rica isn't complete without seeing its official national animal: a smiling sloth. National parks established by the government and private reserves safeguard one of the country's most precious resources: its flora and fauna. These parks offer the opportunity to encounter Costa Rica's other resident creatures too, such as crocodiles, monkeys, macaws, iguanas and toucans.

GIANFRANCO VIVI/SHUTTERSTOCK

How To

Getting around You'll need a car for all of the excursions listed, and a 4WD to visit Los Campesinos Ecolodge.

When to go Outside September and October (when flooding may cancel outdoor activities), any time of year is fine. The driest and sunniest weather is from December through April.

Fun fact A group of crocs is called a 'bask' of crocodiles. You'll understand why when you see them soaking up the sun.

ARTUSH/SHUTTERSTOCK

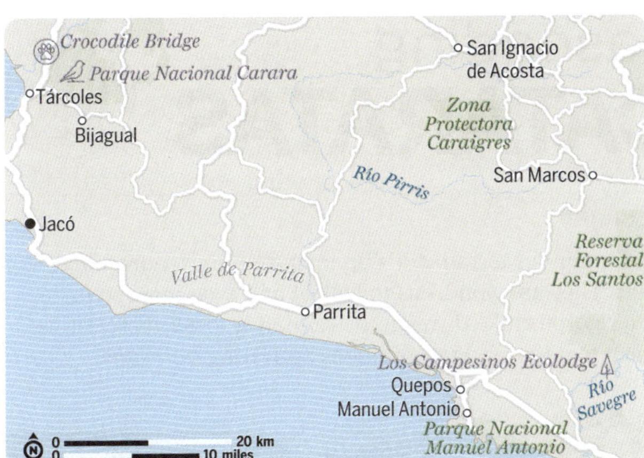

Bird haven About 25 minutes north of Jacó, **Parque Nacional Carara** covers 51 sq km of land protecting the Río Tárcoles basin. Birdwatchers love this national park for its unique overlap of tropical dry rainforest and tropical rainforest. Plants native to both ecosystems grow here, attracting countless species of insects and thus copious amounts of hungry birds. Among the many short trails (1km to 2km) winding through the forest, there's a **Sendero Universal**, a trail for visitors with a disability. Not only is it smoothly paved for wheelchairs, it also has signage in Braille and statues of the local birds.

Crocodile Bridge Just north of Carara, the Costanera Sur Hwy (Ruta 34) crosses the Río Tárcoles, a well-known croc hangout. Take a walk across the **bridge** to see the bask of crocodiles lounging in the river below. These are American crocodiles and they are huge – sometimes 4m long!

Community tourism In the small village of Quebrada Arroyo, a group of local families decided they wanted to share their piece of paradise with the world. Together they created **Los Campesinos Ecolodge**, a rural site with jungle trails, waterfalls, natural pools and hanging bridges, including a 127m suspension bridge. Trails are mostly easy and wildlife is abundant. Roads are rough, so a 4WD is recommended.

Top left Crocodile Bridge
Bottom left Yellow-throated toucan

Huetar History

When the Spanish conquistadors arrived in present-day Costa Rica, the most organized society and powerful people was the Huetar nation. At that time, the Western Huetar Kingdom spanned the Central Valley and Pacific coast, stretching from the Río Virilla to the ocean along the Tárcoles river basin. The kingdom was ruled by King Garabito, considered the most important indigenous ruler at that time. There is evidence that the language of the Huetar people was known by all of Costa Rica's indigenous groups – another indication of their power and influence.

39 Cascading CATARATAS

WATERFALLS | SWIMMING | HIKING

Heavy rainfall plus mountainous terrain adds up to one glorious, refreshing and gorgeous thing: waterfalls. They are wondrous to look at and even more so to swim under, especially after a rigorous hike through the rainforest to get there. Drive into the hills behind Dominical to discover a few of these captivating *cataratas*.

SESTOVIC/GETTY IMAGES

How To

Getting around A 4WD ensures you can handle any river crossings or other unpaved and unpredictable terrain.

When to go More rain means robust waterfalls. Too much rain means flooded roads and canceled excursions. September and October, the rainiest months, are worst for waterfall hikes. December is great – it's the beginning of dry season, yet the rivers are still full from rainy season.

Gear Wear water shoes with good grip, and consider bringing a dry bag.

COLIN D. YOUNG/SHUTTERSTOCK

Top left Nauyaca Waterfalls
Bottom left Catarata Manantial de Agua Viva

Multitiered magic Among the country's most majestic waterfall experiences, **Nauyaca Waterfalls** include two sets of falls: the upper falls, with a 54m straight drop; and the stunning lower falls, which drop 26m over multiple tiers. The lower falls terminate in a luscious deep blue pool. This water wonderland has two entrances. The original Nauyaca Waterfalls entrance is a 20-minute drive from Dominical. From here, it's a 6km hike or horseback ride (or 4WD ride) through lush rainforest to the cascading beauty. Alternatively, 30 minutes down the road on the other side of the falls is the newer **Nauyaca Waterfall Nature Park** *(nauyacawaterfall.com)*, which offers easier 4WD access and more services.

Cliff jumping Sitting pretty on family-owned land, **Eco-Chontales Waterfall** requires less effort for a big reward. It's a relatively easy hike to reach this 46m stunner. Swim under the falls, slide down a natural water slide, and dare to jump off an 8m cliff into the water. There are on-site cabins and a restaurant.

Waterfall cave **Diamante Waterfall** requires a challenging hike, but there's plenty to see along the way, including cloud forest, an organic garden and multiple waterfalls and pools. The centerpiece is spectacular 183m twin cascades, which conceal a large cavern in the facade behind them. The cave is open for exploration, and waterfall rappelling is an optional add-on.

Waterfall Wonderland

The hills surrounding Jacó are home to some impressive waterfalls – the trickiest part is choosing which one to visit. A popular option is the **Catarata Manantial de Agua Viva** (aka Bijagual Waterfall), which is one of the country's highest. The steep, 3km hike to its base requires sure-footing, solid shoes and a bit of stamina. But it's worth the effort for its natural swimming holes and lush rainforest setting. A more wallet-friendly experience, the smaller **Catarata El Salto Gamalotillo** has a great swimming hole. The lesser-known **Catarata El Encanto** is popular for canyoning and rappelling, in addition to fresh-water swimming.

40 Small but SUBLIME

ADVENTURE | WILDLIFE | HIKING

Parque Nacional Manuel Antonio is one of the country's smallest national parks, but still its most popular, thanks to the sheer diversity of wild beauty packed into its small space. Encounter monkeys, sloths and toucans as you explore the tropical rainforest and pristine beaches.

SIMON DANNHAUER/SHUTTERSTOCK

How To

Getting here Buses run regularly from San José and Quepos to Manuel Antonio. There's no official parking area for the national park, but private parking areas near the entrance charge about US$10 per day.

When to go The earlier the better! The park opens from 7am to 3pm; it's closed on Tuesdays.

Tickets Reserve in advance for your timed entry into the **park** *(serviciosenlinea.sinac.go.cr)*. ID is required to enter.

IMAGEBROKER.COM/SHUTTERSTOCK

Hike Through the Rainforest

The park has 11 trails of varying lengths and difficulty levels. Near the entrance, **Sendero El Perezoso** is a raised (wheelchair-accessible) walkway that traverses the mangroves, leading to additional trails and beaches. Keep your eyes peeled for the tiny red crabs scurrying around here. Another accessible trail is **El Manglar**, a 726m path that has interpretive and Braille signage.

Branching off from Perezoso, **Sendero La Catarata** leads to a small waterfall. It's a worthwhile destination during the rainy season, but from January to March it's barely a trickle.

Formerly an island, **Punta Catedral** is the park's photogenic peninsula, covered

Park History

Parque Nacional Manuel Antonio was born out of community efforts. In the late 1960s, the area was slated for a coastal development project, but local residents protested and advocated for its preservation. The government designated 1685 acres as protected land in 1972, and expanded it in 1984.

WIRESTOCK CREATORS/SHUTTERSTOCK

Top left Playa Manuel Antonio (p199)
Top right Rainbow crab
Bottom left Red-backed squirrel monkey

in dense vegetation. It's connected to the mainland by a natural bridge, or *tómbolo*. The 1.4km **Sendero Punta Catedral** crosses the *tómbolo* then makes a loop around the peninsula, with a few lookout points with expansive sea views. Keep an eye out for migrating humpback whales.

Sendero El Mirador is a more challenging 1.3km trail through primary forest. The namesake *mirador*, or lookout, is worth the effort: you can enjoy a stunning seascape of Playa Puerto Escondido and Punta Serrucho beyond.

Hit the Beach

Swimming is allowed at all of the beaches within Parque Nacional Manuel Antonio, with on-site showers and dressing rooms. Note that soap and shampoo are forbidden.

Two beaches flank the *tómbolo*, the natural bridge that leads out to Punta Catedral. On the northwest side is **Playa Espadilla**

Flora & Fauna of Manuel Antonio

Parque Nacional Manuel Antonio is home to nearly 350 plant species, 184 species of birds and 109 species of mammals. Highlights are two- and three-toed sloths, white-faced capuchin monkeys and scarlet macaws. You'll also want to keep your eyes peeled for howler monkeys, titi monkeys, coatis, agoutis, toucans and white-tailed deer. You don't need a guide to visit the park, but a knowledgeable naturalist guide (carrying a high-powered telescope) will enhance your wildlife-spotting experience. Book in advance or just pick up a licensed guide near the park entrance.

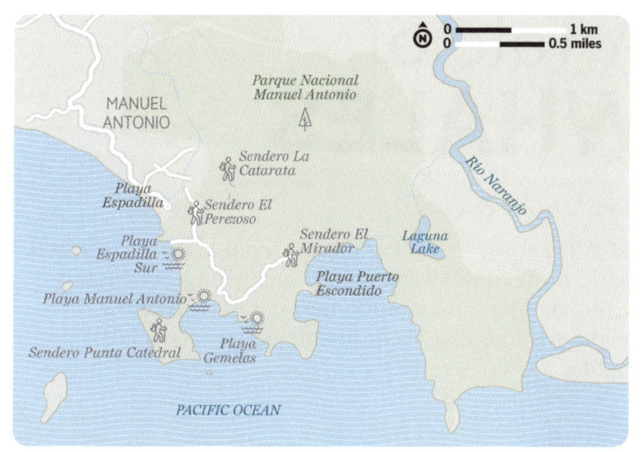

Sur, a gorgeous stretch of sand backed by lush tropical forest. Beware of swimming here, as currents can be dangerous. On the southeast side, **Playa Manuel Antonio** is the park's best swimming beach. There are tide pools and corals offshore, making it good for snorkeling. At the western end of the beach, you can see a semi-circle of rocks, known as **La Trampa**, which was created by indigenous peoples as a trap for sea turtles and fish. Playa Manuel Antonio is also one of the surest spots for sighting monkeys, who play in the trees behind the beach.

A dedicated trail leads to **Playa Gemelas**, a small but spectacular beach composed of two grey rocky coves, surrounded by jungle. Crowds are lighter here, especially in the morning. Watch where you walk, as iguanas like to sunbathe in the sand.

Left White tailed deer, Parque Nacional Manuel Antonio
Below Parque Nacional Manuel Antonio

FROM LEFT: RODRIGO T. ANDREOTTI/SHUTTERSTOCK, JAVIER FERNÁNDEZ SÁNCHEZ/GETTY IMAGES

41 A Tale of WHALES

BEACHES | WHALE-WATCHING | LOCAL CULTURE

Located on the coast adjacent to Uvita, Parque Nacional Marino Ballena is Costa Rica's first marine park, protecting 55 sq km of beach, mangrove estuary, lowland rainforest and marine habitats. Its name comes not only from the humpback whales that breed here, but also from the distinctive shape of Punta Uvita, a sandbar that resembles a whale's tail.

AGA PRZYBYLSKA/SHUTTERSTOCK

How to

Getting here/around
The main park entrance at Bahía Ballena is just west of Uvita. From the entrance it's a 20-minute walk to the Whale's Tail.

When to go
Whale-watching season is from December to March and July to October.

Tip Walk along the Whale's Tail at low tide, when the shore and rock formations are exposed.

GIANFRANCO VIVI/SHUTTERSTOCK

Whale's Tail The park's distinctive feature is the sandbar that emerges at low tide in the shape of a whale's tail. The **Whale's Tail** (or *Tómbolo*) is an interesting walk. Tide pools form in the rocks, teeming with life – bring your mask and snorkel to get a closer look. To really appreciate the shape of the peninsula, drive into the hills behind Uvita to see it from above.

Whale-watching The Costa Ballena, aka the Whale Coast, isn't just a name. Thousands of humpback whales migrate to this part of the Costa Rican coastline, stopping in the area's temperate, food-rich waters to breed and rear their young. There are two whale-watching seasons: from late December to early March, humpbacks arrive from northern California and Washington state; from mid-July to October, the southern hemisphere humpbacks migrate up from Antarctica. In season, you can see whales from the shore, or take a boat tour with **Bahía Aventuras** or **Ballena Tour**, both based in Uvita.

Celebrations Every September, at the height of the humpback-whale migration, the local community celebrates these gentle giants at the **Festival de Ballenas y Delfines**. The town of Uvita hosts a community fair with traditional dances, art displays, live music, food, vendors and more; tour operators provide programming to promote conservation efforts in the region. Bonus: discounted whale-watching tours.

Left False killer whales
Below Whale's Tail, Parque Nacional Marino Ballena

Marine Life

The Parque Nacional Marino Ballena protects 55 sq km of marine area, principally located around the breeding and nursery grounds for the visiting humpback whales. However, the massive marine mammals aren't the only ones that benefit from the conservation zone. False orcas and pilot whales are often also present, along with spotted, beluga and bottlenose dolphins, olive ridley turtles, Pacific sea turtles and more. Offshore, the **Islas Tres Hermanas** are three rocky islets that are an important site for nesting seabirds.

42 SURFING Safari

POINT BREAKS | BEACH BREAKS | RIVER-MOUTH BREAKS

Whether you are a surfing aficionado or a curious beginner, Costa Rica's central Pacific coast has a wave for you – plus surf towns, party scenes and plenty of good vibes. Drive along this stretch of the coastline to sample some of the country's best breaks.

GASTON PICCINETTI/SHUTTERSTOCK

Trip Notes

Getting around Public buses and private shuttles run up and down this coast, stopping at Jacó, Dominical and Uvita.

When to go Skilled surfers might prefer the massive waves during rainy season, but this coastline is surfable year-round.

Surf schools Jacó, Dominical and Uvita are all home to excellent surf schools, where you can get started or hone your skills.

Serious about Surfing

Playa Hermosa (pictured) has long been the site of surfing events, thanks to community support and the wave's incredible consistency. **Vida Hermosa** restaurant hosts a weekly surf competition on Saturday afternoons to provide a stage for local groms and pros looking for sponsors. For the best show, check it during the springtime south swell season.

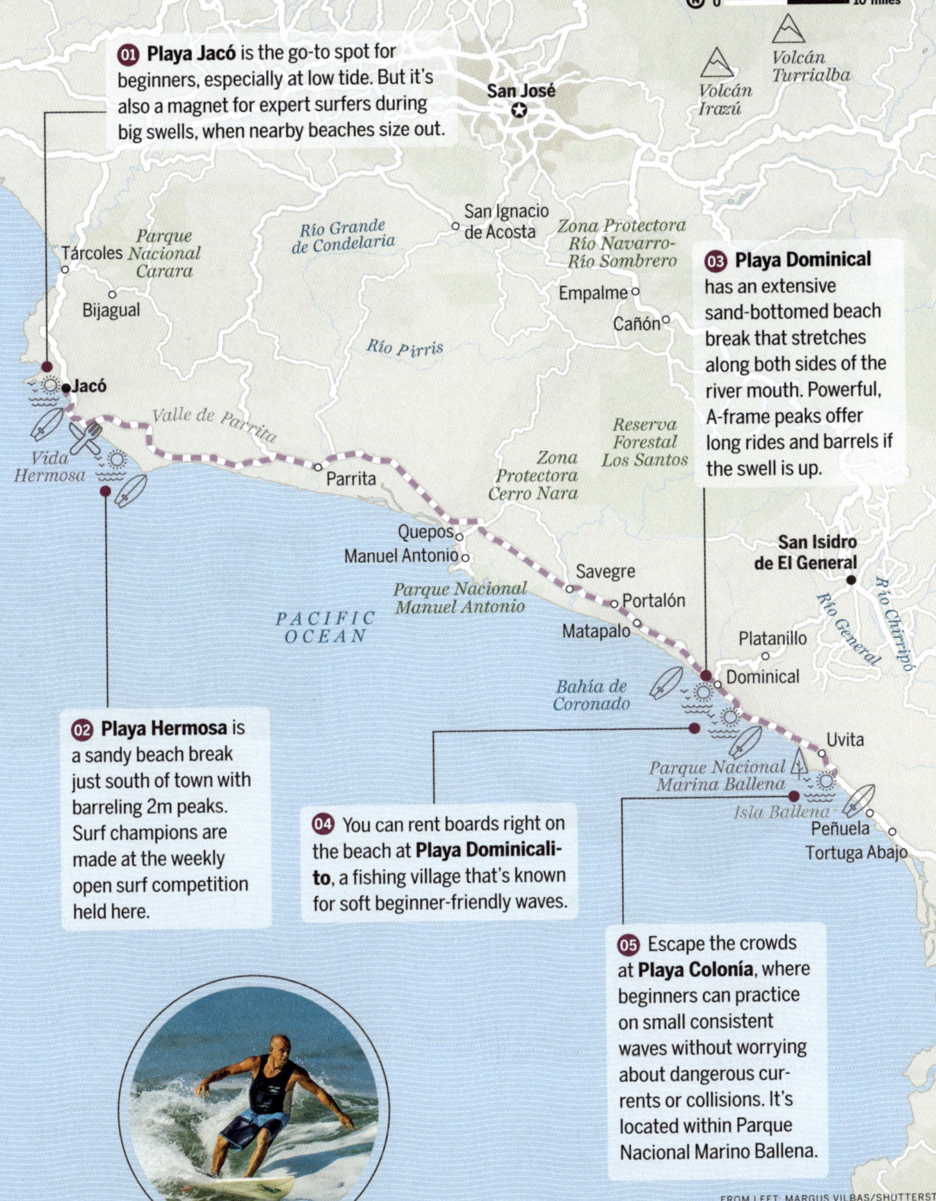

FROM LEFT: MARGUS VILBAS/SHUTTERSTOCK

THINGS THAT
Make You Go Ahhh...

01 Crocodiles
The stars of the world-renowned 'Crocodile Bridge' (p193), where tourists come to watch them swim and hunt in the Río Tarcoles.

02 Humpback Whales
These majestic mammals breed along the Pacific coast. See them from mid-December though mid-April; brave rainy season to see them from July through November.

03 Ziplines
Flying above the jungle is one of the region's most beloved and adrenaline-pumping adventure excursions.

04 Howler Monkeys
The loud monkeys that wake you up early in the morning. Their howls and bellows were used in the movie, *Jurassic Park*.

05 Waterfalls
One of the most common sights and excursions in the area for swimming, hikes, picnics and photos. Always breathtaking.

06 The Whale's Tail

The whale-tail-shaped shore in Parque Nacional Marino Ballena at Uvita (p200) is the home of humpback whales.

07 Leaf Cutter Ants

The hardest working insects in the jungle. They work steadily, carrying leaf bits back and forth across the rainforest.

08 SUP

If surfing is too intense, stand-up paddleboards are an alternative way to enjoy time on the rivers and calm, coastal waters.

09 Fer-De-Lance Snakes

One of the most dangerous snakes in Costa Rica. It's venomous and aggressive, and lives in the rainforest.

10 Chili Guaro

You'll undoubtedly be offered this shot of Cacique, hot sauce and lime juice, which is a standard at every bar. It's sweet, spicy and strong.

01 PHOTOONGRAPHY/SHUTTERSTOCK, **02** ARTWIZARD/SHUTTERSTOCK, **03** EVOCATION IMAGES/SHUTTERSTOCK, **04** NATURE'S CHARM/SHUTTERSTOCK, **05** VENKO/SHUTTERSTOCK, **06** CL-MEDIEN/SHUTTERSTOCK, **07** ERIC ISSELEE/SHUTTERSTOCK, **08** PIXEL-SHOT/SHUTTERSTOCK, **09** GOODFOCUSED/SHUTTERSTOCK, **10** LUISGS1103/SHUTTERSTOCK, MADDYZ/SHUTTERSTOCK, JOINTSTAR/SHUTTERSTOCK

Listings

BEST OF THE REST

After Dark

Puddlefish Brewery $$

Hang out in Jacó at PuddleFish's outdoor beer garden and sample brews made on-site. Stay for the live music most nights of the week.

Republik Lounge $$

Part nightclub, part hookah lounge. Ultimate Jacó pool-party spot, with VIP tables, multiple rooms and varying DJs.

Jacó Bar $

A Jacó institution with live music and DJs, cold craft pints and decent cocktails. This spot gets rowdier as the night goes on.

Ronny's Place $$

Insane views of two pristine bays and jungle on all sides, plus a long list of cocktails and imported beers. It's worth a detour for a drink and a tasty meal.

Cuba Libre $$

Second-floor terrace grill with excellent views over the marina in Quepos. Go for the creative cocktails, speedy service and mouthwatering ceviche.

Rum Bar $

Drop in to this spot if you're looking for live music and tasty cocktails in Dominical. A great place to watch sports and play pool, foosball and darts.

Mosaic Wine & Sushi Bar $$$

The extensive wine list and craft cocktails are a standout at this restaurant and bar in Uvita. Uses local ingredients. Awesome sushi menu.

Adventure Experts

Kayak Jacó

A reliable tour operator for snorkeling, kayaking and stand-up paddleboarding adventures in Playa Agujas. Sixteen years of experience guiding tours.

Jade Tours

One of the best tour operators for Parque Nacional Manuel Antonio and mangrove tours of Isla Damas. Knowledgeable, friendly and experienced guides.

Dolphin Tours

With 20 years of experience in responsible sea tourism, this company operates whale-watching boat tours from Uvita. It takes safety and sustainability seriously.

Adventure Tours Costa Rica

Over a decade of experience managing tours in Jacó. It specializes in nature adventures like 4WD tours, white-water rafting and monkey tours.

Canopy Safari

Based in Quepos, this is the oldest established canopy tour in the region. Besides ziplining, it includes rappelling lines, a suspension bridge and a wildlife sanctuary.

Bahía Aventuras

For 20 years, this tour company has been committed to sustainable marine tourism in Uvita. It offers snorkeling and scuba-diving excursions as well as whale-watching.

Pineapple Tours

Specializing in kayaking and SUP in Dominical. No experience needed to enjoy the mangrove tours.

Tico Tastes

Restaurante Rústico $

This local soda serving Costa Rican cuisine is known for hearty portions buffet-style at an affordable price. Laid-back vibes and consistent quality.

Indómitos Café & Bar $

Copious healthy options for vegetarians and vegans in Uvita. Start your day with a superfruit smoothie or healthy craft concoction.

El Avión $$

This restored 1980s gun-running airplane was converted to a restaurant and cocktail bar near Manuel Antonio. Try the cocktails and check out the cockpit views.

Gabriella's Steakhouse $$$

This open-air restaurant sits on the marina in Quepos. It's the perfect place to catch the sunset and feast on a delicious seafood dinner.

Tiki Bar $$$

Enjoy the vivid Pacific sunsets over seafood and cocktails at this hotel restaurant on Playa Jacó.

La Choza de Alejo $$

Authentic Mexican food on the Pacific coast. A surprising gem in Uvita with yummy fresh-fruit margaritas and good portions that bring back repeat customers.

Emilio's Cafe $$

Sweeping mountain views and some of the freshest seafood in Manuel Antonio. Enjoy friendly service, live music and immersive wildlife.

Cafe Mono Congo $$

Health-conscious eaters, vegetarians and vegans will rejoice at this breakfast and lunch eatery in Dominical along the Río Barú. Fresh and flavorful options abound for meat-lovers too.

CHARLIEMILLERKB/GETTY IMAGES

Mangroves, Parque Nacional Manuel Antonio

Arts & Eats

Dantica Gallery

The gallery located in the Jacó Walk Shopping Center sells art and home goods made by talented Tico artisans. Perfect for souvenir shopping for yourself and loved ones.

Villa Vanilla

Stock up on organic spices after a tour of a working organic biodynamic spice farm near Manuel Antonio. Bring home vanilla extract, Ceylon cinnamon and chocolates made on-site.

Mariposita Gift Shop and Gallery

This humble locally owned gift shop in Quepos is a wonderful place to purchase typical Costa Rican souvenirs and art created by local artisans. An assortment of wooden crafts and gorgeous paintings.

Scan to find more things to do in the Central Pacific Coast online

SOUTHERN COSTA RICA & PENÍNSULA DE OSA
ECOTOURISM | RAINFOREST | WILDLIFE
Experience Southern Costa Rica & Península de Osa online

Watch quetzals in the highlands of **Providencia de Dota** (p212)
2hrs from San José

Summit **Cerro Chirripó**, Costa Rica's highest peak (p214)
2hrs from Providencia

See pre-Columbian spheres at **Sitio Arqueológico Finca 6** (p219)
2hrs from Cerro Chirripó

Dive deep and explore coral reefs at **Isla del Caño** (p218)
45mins from Bahía Drake

Hike La Leona coastal trail at **Parque Nacional Corcovado** (p224)
2hrs from Puerto Jiménez

SOUTHERN COSTA RICA & PENÍNSULA DE OSA

Trip Builder

This region boasts unmatched biodiversity and some of the most unique ecotourism and cultural tourism experiences in the country. Amid the highlands, cloud forests, indigenous communities and pristine rainforests, travelers can have extraordinary adventures that are distinctly Costa Rican.

PREVIOUS SPREAD: CAMPPHOTO/GETTY IMAGES, MARIO WONG PASTOR/SHUTTERSTOCK

Practicalities

ARRIVING

Juan Santamaria International Airport (SJO) From the airport in Alajuela, it's a two-hour drive to Providencia de Dota. Bahía Drake and Puerto Jiménez have domestic airports with several flights a day from SJO.

CONNECT

Wi-fi is minimal and cell service spotty in Providencia de Dota and Terraba. Download navigation apps before you leave wi-fi areas.

MONEY

Larger towns along Ruta 2 such as San Isidro de General and Buenos Aires have ATMs. Puerto Jiménez has two ATMs.

WHERE TO STAY

Town/ Village	Pros/Cons
Providencia de Dota	Peaceful village tucked away in the highlands. Rural and communal.
San Gerardo de Rivas	Perfect for cloud-forest hikes and birdwatching.
Puerto Jiménez	Centrally located for various ecotourism and rural activities. Has an airport and ATMs.

GETTING AROUND

Car and bus Driving via car or bus is the only way to navigate southern Costa Rica's highlands and cloud forests. Rental cars are available at the Puerto Jiménez airport and allow access to areas not directly reachable by bus.

Boat You can reach Bahía Drake via motorboat through Rio Sierpe. Bahía Drake is walkable and many excursions are by boat.

TOP: ERIK COX PHOTOGRAPHY/SHUTTERSTOCK
BOTTOM: JAVIER RAMIREZ/ALAMY

EATING & DRINKING

Providencia and the Los Santos region are renowned for their coffee (pictured top left). Visit Coopedota, a local coffee cooperative based in Santa María, for a plantation tour and tasting. Visitors to Península de Osa should try the ink-colored *piangua ceviche* (pictured bottom left). This local specialty is made from a mollusk that lives in the Pacific's mangroves.

Best health food
Kapi Kapi (p234)

Must-try seafood
Soda Marbella (p234)

JAN–APR
Peak summer; it's dry season and thus busiest.

MAY–AUG
Mix of rain and sun; possible flooding in June.

SEP & OCT
Rainiest season; flooding likely; some businesses close.

NOV & DEC
Summer begins; busy season.

43 HIGH IN Providencia de Dota

QUETZALS | RIVERS | COFFEE

Visit Costa Rica's highlands to spot the resplendent quetzal and to sample the country's best coffee, to breathe crisp, fresh air and to swim in Costa Rica's cleanest river. This distinct mountain region is a corridor for tapirs, pumas and birds traveling coast to coast. Providencia de Dota is a departure from expected rainforest experiences.

TANGUY DE SAINT-CYR/SHUTTERSTOCK

How To

Getting around A car is necessary due to the winding and mostly unpaved mountain roads. A 4WD is essential during rainy season, but is a good idea year-round.

When to go Dry season (January to April) is the best time to go to avoid flooding. The minimal fog and clouds means unobstructed views of the lush valleys and mountains, oceans in the distance and a brilliant night sky.

JANNA ZINZI/LONELY PLANET

Birdlife Visit **Parque Nacional Los Quetzales** or the village of San Gerardo de Dota for a chance to see the resplendent quetzal, the mystical, colorful bird known as 'Gods of the Wind' by the Maya. Quetzals congregate in this area because their favorite food is plentiful – the fruit of the *aguacatillo* tree (a kind of wild avocado). Sunrise hikes in the park or on private farms are the most advantageous ways to glimpse these vibrant birds. Alternatively, stop for coffee or lunch at **Miriam's Quetzals** in San Gerardo de Dota to see who is visiting the feeder on her back terrace.

Rivers and waterfalls Four rivers flow through Providencia de Dota creating numerous opportunities to see (and swim in) waterfalls. For a relaxed experience, pack a picnic for **Catarata El Salitre**, a small double waterfall that isn't swimmable but is quite mesmerizing. Or take a brisk dip at **Catarata El Pocerón**, a popular swimming hole close to the main road. Also beautiful is the **Río Savegre Waterfall**, but the trail conditions are neglected – only expert hikers should attempt to reach the main waterfall.

Coffee Don't leave without sampling the locally grown and harvested coffee from the Coopedota cooperative. You might also take an educational tour of Santa María and the Coopedota *finca* (farm) to learn about the growing and roasting processes. **Coopedota** unites local coffee-farming families to ensure everyone is paid fairly for their cultivation.

Top left Resplendent quetzal
Bottom left Catarata El Pocerón

Be Part of the Family

Visiting Providencia not only supports local families and projects, but also is a way for us to share our culture and community. We love making cultural connections with visitors and new people because it's difficult for us to travel and get to know other countries. The families in our community are *pura vida* and truly know the rich natural beauty that surrounds us.

Insight by **David Retana**, extreme biker and local tour guide. *@retanadav1d*

44 Hiking in the CLOUDS

MOUNTAINS | HIKING | CLOUD FOREST

San Gerardo de Rivas is home to Costa Rica's highest peak, Cerro Chirripó, which stands tall amid the stunning Cordillera de Talamanca mountain range. This quaint town attracts hikers excited to summit Cerro Chirripó, as well as nature enthusiasts seeking cloud forest and birdwatching adventures. Afterward, relax in thermal pools with epic mountain views.

MAX ILLY/EYEEM/GETTY IMAGES

How To

Getting around Driving is the best way to explore this mountain town and the surrounding sights.

When to go January through April (dry season) is best for ensuring dry hikes and clear skies to take in the grand views.

Viewpoints Be cautious driving here on the Interamericana (Ruta 2), especially around Cerro de la Muerte (Death Mountain), which is known for its dangerous curves, blind spots and monumental views of the Talamanca Mountains.

ALISA_CH/SHUTTERSTOCK

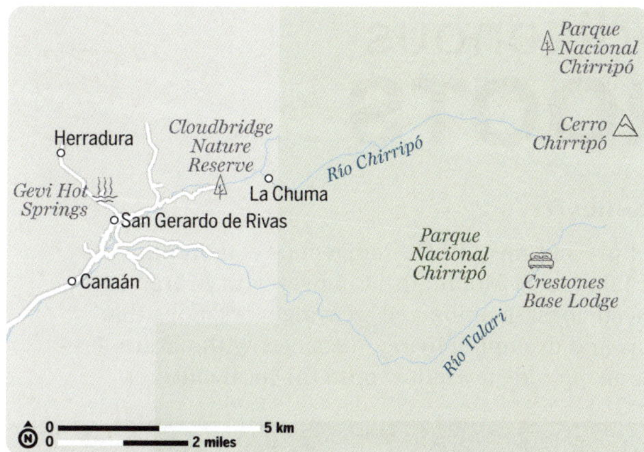

Top left Cerro Chirripó
Bottom left Cloudbridge Nature Reserve

Cerro Chirripó Costa Rica's **highest peak** is a bucket-list experience for hiking aficionados. On a clear day, from the 3820m peak, you will have breathtaking views of both the Caribbean Sea and Pacific Ocean. But you will work for that view. It's a steep 36km hike round-trip through the **Parque Nacional Chirripó**. Only 52 permits per day are given for overnight hikers, making it a rare experience worth bragging about. Most people take two days for the hike, spending the night at a base camp 5km from the top, then reaching the summit the following morning in time for the sunrise. Book well in advance to procure your park permit and reserve your bed at **Crestones Base Lodge**.

Cloudbridge Nature Reserve The adjacent **Cloudbridge** is a 280-hectare privately owned nature reserve dedicated to conservation and reforestation of the cloud forest. Every type of hiker can enjoy this misty cloudscape: there are leisurely 600m trails with scenic waterfalls, as well as rugged 8km treks where you can train for your Chirripó summit.

Gevi Hot Springs The **Aguas Termales Gevi** are tailor-made to soothe hikers' sore muscles. Two thermal pools overlook the mountains and valleys, while local birds flutter in the garden's hibiscus bushes. The water temperature is warm rather than hot, which still feels rejuvenating but not dehydrating.

Overnight at Height

Stay for two nights instead of one to have more time to explore Cerro Chirripó. If you summit one day and then descend the next, you miss out on some unique trails around the peak and the base camp, and it can feel rushed. It's a long and strenuous hike to base camp and then to summit, so it's worth giving yourself an extra day to enjoy the views and hike some of the less-populated trails before heading back down the mountain.

Insight by **David Elizando**, owner of Hotel de Montaña el Pelicano and longtime guide for Cerro Chirripo. *@hotelpelicano*

45 Indigenous ROOTS

HISTORY | INDIGENOUS | COMMUNITY

Costa Rica's past and present meet in the indigenous communities of Térraba, situated amid the Talamanca Mountains. Connect with Brörán and Boruca families through cacao, mask-making and weaving workshops that carry on ancestral traditions and exemplify living in concert with nature. Pre-Columbian sites and museums provide a window onto the local culture.

AGEFOTOSTOCK/ALAMY

How To

Getting around Renting a car is the only way to fully explore this region since the communities are spread out and public transportation is minimal or nonexistent.

When to go December through April is dry season, guaranteeing sunny days, clearer nights and smoother travel along the serpentine mountain roads. Expect rain during May through November, possibly causing landslides and treacherous roads in September and October.

Workshops Book them via *lokaltravel.com*.

JUAN CARLOS MUNOZ/ALAM

Far left Boruca masks
Bottom left Carving Boruca masks

Cacao Visit **El Descanso Térraba** to learn about cacao from the Brörán people. You'll participate in the full cacao process, from picking the fruit to roasting and shelling the beans, and grinding the beans using a stone grinder as their ancestors once did. The payoff is a delicious warm chocolate beverage and a deeper understanding of its connection to indigenous culture.

Museum In the Boruca community, the small **Museo Comunitario Indígena de Boruca** gives insight into pre-colonial life through replicas of their living quarters and cooking tools. One of the pre-Columbian stone spheres is on display along with powerful art depicting their gods, goddesses and warriors. Visitors can also attend mask-making and weaving workshops led by local Boruca artisans. Watch these skilled craftspeople make intricate masks out of cedar depicting nature motifs and fierce warrior faces. This honors their ancestors who fought the Spanish conquistadors, and the masks are used for festivals in late December and early January re-enacting the bravery of their forefathers.

Weaving Workshops demonstrate the impressive complexity of weaving the various threads on an imposing loom, as well as seeing how the Boruca use various plants and natural materials, such as turmeric and *mata azul*, to dye their thread. Gorgeous colorful bags, wallets and table runners are for sale directly from women artisans or at the museum.

A Continuing Legacy

A lot of the conversation about indigenous people, our tribes and families talks about us as if we were completely annihilated or extinct. We are talked about in the past tense and our presence is erased. But we are here, building our communities and keeping our traditions alive. My family and I love to host travelers from all over the world to share our culture on the land of my great-grandparents. We hope more visitors to Costa Rica will come learn about our rich history and how we are continuing the legacy of our ancestors.

■ Insight by **Jeffrey Villanueva**, Brörán community leader and owner of El Descanso Térraba. *facebook.com/eldescansoterraba*

46 Under the SEA

DIVING | SNORKELING | MARINE LIFE

Península de Osa attracts snorkelers and scuba divers for its crystal waters and impressive underwater views. Isla del Caño, near Bahía Drake, is a marine biological reserve teeming with coral, turtles and tropical fish, while Golfo Dulce, near Puerto Jiménez, is one of four tropical fjords on the planet. Dolphin and whale sightings are common and absolutely awe-inspiring.

ANDAMANSE/GETTY IMAGES

How To

Getting here/around Driving between Bahía Drake (Drake Bay) and Puerto Jiménez takes about 1½ hours on bumpy, dirt roads. A 4WD is ideal. Both places have airports and are a 20-minute flight apart. Take the motorboat ferry to Bahía Drake from Sierpe for a seafaring adventure.

When to go Peak diving season is January through June when underwater visibility is best. During rainy season, the water will likely be murky, limiting visibility.

DAVE HAMILTON/GETTY IMAGES

Isla del Caño Snorkelers and scuba divers flock to Bahía Drake to dive at **Isla del Caño**, a world-renowned marine reserve with excellent visibility during diving season. It's common to swim among whale sharks, bull sharks, octopuses, sea turtles, rays and dozens of species of fish. Divers visit **La Cueva del Tiburón** (Shark Cave) and a shipwreck known as **El Sharko** – so, yes, lots of sharks. Book your trip with **Drake Bay Diving** or **Costa Rica Adventure Divers**, both located in Bahía Drake.

The 300-hectare island holds centuries of Costa Rica's indigenous history. It was a burial ground for the Chiriquis people and contains pre-Columbian stone spheres like the ones found in Sierpe at the **Sitio Arqueológico Finca 6**. Unfortunately, tourists have not been permitted to visit the island since 2020, and it's unclear when it will re-open.

Golfo Dulce On the other side of the peninsula, Golfo Dulce is a rare phenomenon – a tropical fjord. It's a snorkeling and wildlife-watching utopia, teeming with pods of dolphins and bales of sea turtles. Golfo Dulce is also a sanctuary for various shark species and a breeding ground for humpback whales. **Osa Wild** and **Aventuras Tropicales**, both in Puerto Jiménez, offer snorkeling and kayaking tours in this marine wonderland.

Top left Isla del Caño
Bottom left Pantropical spotted dolphins, Golfo Dulce

Packing Pro Tips

Be prepared for this tropical rainforest climate by protecting yourself from the sun and the bugs. Make sure you have reef-safe sunscreen, a long-sleeved shirt, sunglasses and a hat that covers your face and neck. Have water shoes for Golfo Dulce adventures, and don't forget water to drink!

Insight by **Yessenia**, tour guide and owner of Zompopas Tours, Playa Blanca, Península de Osa. *@zompopas_trails_costa_rica*

Whales, Waterfalls & WILDLIFE

WHALE-WATCHING | WATERFALLS | NIGHT TOURS

Bahía Drake (pictured below) offers a plethora of opportunities to experience the region's biodiversity. Explore this remote bay and the surrounding areas via these nature adventures, which showcase the splendor of the Península de Osa.

STEFAN NEUMANN/ SHUTTERSTOCK

Trip Notes

Getting here/around Skip driving a rental car here and take the ferry via Sierpe. Bahía Drake (Drake Bay) township is walkable and many excursions provide transportation.

When to go Although dry season (December through April) offers the best weather, it's the most crowded time. Consider visiting in May, July and November. You may get some rain, but it won't last all day, and there will be fewer tourists.

Footwear Bring sturdy hiking boots and waterproof sandals!

Night Moves

Living on the Península de Osa means that just beyond the next mud puddle or tropical tree, there's a chance to slip into whole new worlds of wonder – bundles that creep, crawl and fly by night. So pack a headlamp. Exploring the forest at night will reveal creatures never seen by day.

Insight by **Tracie Stice**, 'The Bug Lady,' biologist and night tour guide in Bahía Drake. *@drake.sachatamia*

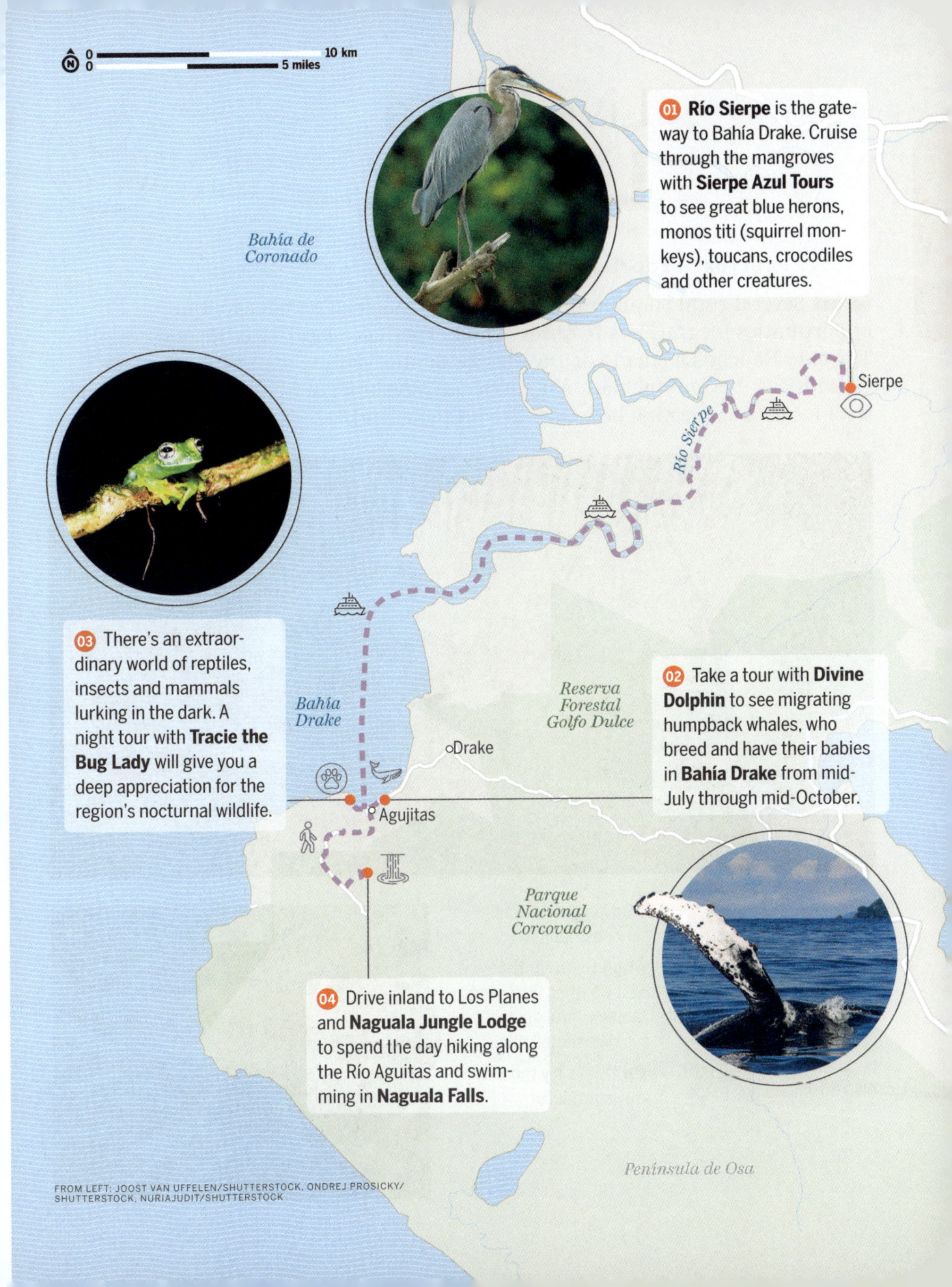

0 10 km
0 5 miles

Bahía de Coronado

01 Río Sierpe is the gateway to Bahía Drake. Cruise through the mangroves with **Sierpe Azul Tours** to see great blue herons, monos titi (squirrel monkeys), toucans, crocodiles and other creatures.

Sierpe

Río Sierpe

03 There's an extraordinary world of reptiles, insects and mammals lurking in the dark. A night tour with **Tracie the Bug Lady** will give you a deep appreciation for the region's nocturnal wildlife.

Bahía Drake

Reserva Forestal Golfo Dulce

Drake

Agujitas

02 Take a tour with **Divine Dolphin** to see migrating humpback whales, who breed and have their babies in **Bahía Drake** from mid-July through mid-October.

Parque Nacional Corcovado

04 Drive inland to Los Planes and **Naguala Jungle Lodge** to spend the day hiking along the Río Aguitas and swimming in **Naguala Falls**.

Península de Osa

FROM LEFT: JOOST VAN UFFELEN/SHUTTERSTOCK, ONDREJ PROSICKY/SHUTTERSTOCK, NURIAJUDIT/SHUTTERSTOCK

48 Live Like a LOCAL

NATURE | CULTURE | ECOTOURISM

Several rural communities in the Península de Osa offer unique opportunities for travelers to observe and experience local Tico life and culture. Travel to Rancho Quemado or Dos Brazos de Río Tigre to experience the true Costa Rica – beyond the national parks and adventure activities – by connecting with locals and learning how they live off their land.

TIM FLEMING/ALAMY

How To

Getting here/around Renting a car is the best way to approach these rural regions. As always, get a car with 4WD to cope with unpaved roads. Also download any maps in advance since cell service is limited.

When to go For the best weather, visit from January through April to avoid torrential rains.

Tip Always try the locally grown produce!

JEAN-BAPTISTE TOUSSAINT/SHUTTERSTOCK

Rural living In the small village of **Rancho Quemado**, about 45 minutes from Bahía Drake, residents have opened up their homes to show tourists what daily life is like outside the beaches and national parks. Travelers can learn about native plants, fish or birds in a local *laguna*, or take a cooking class.

Gold mining A highlight is coming to **Finca Las Minas** to try your hand at mining for gold in a local creek. The owner, Don Juan Cubrillo, shares the history of gold mining and its significance to the region, as well as information about his indigenous heritage. He then guides you to the nearby river where you witness and experience panning for gold in the iron-rich ochre soil. Afterwards, his wife Rosa serves a delicious and hearty home-cooked meal from their outdoor kitchen, using local ingredients.

Eco adventures About a 45-minute drive from Puerto Jiménez, **Dos Brazos de Río Tigre** is another former mining center, which now has hiking trails, hidden waterfalls and ecolodges. Here is the entrance to the **El Tigre** sector of Parque Nacional Corcovado, where local experts offer tours for birdwatching and medicinal plants. The local conservation association, **Acodobrarti**, also offers gold-panning experiences, including an overnight hiking tour to the former mining community at **Piedras Blancas**.

Top left Península de Osa
Bottom left Scarlet macaw

Doz Brazos de Rio Tigre

Dos Brazos is a small and tranquil rural community. It does not get crowded so you can really enjoy nature and get to know the people. You can bathe and swim in the river, and drink the water. It comes from the mountain, more delicious than bottled water! Tourism is a growing industry for us and we have so much knowledge to share about the rich history of this land and especially the plants.

Insight by **Esther Coronado**, president of Acodobrarti, Corcovado el Tigre, a local conservation organization. *@corcovadoeltigre*

49 Welcome to the JUNGLE

HIKING | WILDLIFE | NATURE

Famously containing 2.5% of the world's biodiversity, Parque Nacional Corcovado is bursting with life. Whether visiting for a morning hike or a multiday trek, travelers are immersed in the coastal rainforest, surrounded by all of its sounds and scents and flora and fauna.

MARGUS VILBAS PHOTOGRAPHY/SHUTTERSTOCK

How To

Getting here/around Take a taxi or *colectivo* from Puerto Jiménez to Carate. From there, it's a 3.5km hike to La Leona ranger station. Tour boats go to La Sirena or San Pedrillo stations.

When to go Visiting between December and April ensures dry trails and ample animal sightings. Avoid September and October when heavy rains can cause flooding and road closures.

Guided tours You must have a licensed guide to enter Corcovado, even for a day hike. Book with Osa Wild or La Picolina Tours.

SPACAJ/SHUTTERSTOCK

Day Trips

Many visitors take day trips to the **San Pedrillo** sector from Bahía Drake (by boat) or to the **La Leona** sector from Puerto Jiménez (by *colectivo* and on foot).

The most popular trip is traveling to **La Sirena** by boat (from either town). The bumpy boat ride is a treat, as whales and dolphins are often spotted on the way. Be prepared for a 'wet landing' on the beach at Corcovado: you'll jump out of the boat into calf-deep water and walk up to the beach to enter the park.

The trails around La Sirena are the top spot in Corcovado (if not in all of Costa Rica) for spotting wildlife, including some truly rare species. But the trails around La Sirena get

MARGUS VILBAS PHOTOGRAPHY/SHUTTERSTOCK

Corcovado Dos & Don'ts

- **Do** book a tour. Visitors must have a licensed guide.
- **Don't** bring food into the park.
- **Do** bring plenty of water in refillable bottles.
- **Don't** feed, touch or harass the animals.
- **Do** take out everything you bring in.

Top left Parque Nacional Corcovado
Top right Trogon
Bottom left La Sirena ranger station

undeniably overcrowded, especially since the recent increase on the number of day-trippers allowed to visit.

Choose Your Own Adventure

Travelers in search of a more immersive experience can stay overnight in the park. **La Sirena** ranger station has dormitory-style lodging with clean shared bathrooms, a dining hall, and a small shop with souvenirs, coffee and first-aid items. An overnight stay allows travelers to access trails in the early morning and late afternoon, when animals are more active and there are fewer people in the park.

Two-day itineraries might start with a 24km hike from **Los Patos** station, on the northern edge of the park (near the village of La Tarde), to La Sirena station. This challenging route traverses dense primary and secondary forest and is accessible during the dry season only. On the second night, the hike out might follow the 20km route from La Sirena to **Carate/**

Immerse Yourself in Nature

If you want to visit Parque Nacional Corcovado, the best experience is an overnight tour, which can be two days/one night or three days/two nights. Other excellent options that are less-saturated with tourists are day tours of La Leona sector, or **El Tigre** sector, which is managed by the local community. I would put the option of Sirena from Drake Bay or Puerto Jiménez last, especially in high season, because it is too crowded and overwhelming. The magic of Corcovado is lost with so many people on the same trail.

Insight by **Ifigenia Garita Canet**, tropical biologist and Founder of Osa Wild. *@osawild*

Left Spider monkey, Parque Nacional Corcovado
Below Baird's tapir

La Leona. This route follows the coastline, with several river crossings, wild deserted beaches and forest trails. It is gorgeous, but hot. This entire route is sometimes done in reverse, starting at Carate/La Leona and ending at Los Patos. There are also a dozen trails to explore in the vicinity of La Sirena station, for travelers who care to spend an extra day and night in the park.

Rare Sights

Parque Nacional Corcovado is world-renowned for its biodiversity and you will be up close and personal with wildlife. One of the most famed animal residents is the tapir, a relatively rare herbivore mammal. They are most active in the morning or evening when they are gathering food, but a good tour guide will usually help you spot one sleeping in the bushes after its meal. Noisy howler monkeys and their spider monkey cousins will swing above you; and wild turkeys, peccaries and coatis will cross your path. You may see crocodiles gliding through the Río Claro or hear the squawking scarlet macaws as they fly overhead.

FROM LEFT: ONDREJ PROSICKY/SHUTTERSTOCK, MARK_KOSTICH/SHUTTERSTOCK

50 Osa ADVENTURE

SURFING | ECOTOURISM | SLOTHS

Overlooking the glorious Golfo Dulce, the eastern part of the Península de Osa is a patchwork of hidden beaches, crystal coves, family farms and wildlife preserves. Explore this scenic coastline to discover exciting ecotourism adventures.

JEM2LIFE/ SHUTTERSTOCK

Trip Notes

Getting around Rent a car from the Puerto Jiménez airport to best explore various parts of the Península de Osa.

When to go December through April offers the best weather, but also the most crowds. Visit instead during the low season to avoid crowds. But avoid September and October when heavy rain could ruin your plans.

Travel time Give yourself ample time to travel and take in each destination.

Puerto Jiménez

Jiménez, as the locals affectionately call it, is the main hub of the Península de Osa. It serves as a great launching pad for exploration. Transportation around the Osa can be difficult and expensive. If you are comfortable driving on dirt roads, renting a 4WD vehicle will open up the entire peninsula for you.

Insight by **Eytan Elterman**, co-founder of Lokal Travel. *@lokaltravels*

FROM LEFT: JORGE A. RUSSELL/SHUTTERSTOCK, PARKOL/SHUTTERSTOCK

Preserve & Protect

CARING FOR THE LANDS WE VISIT

Costa Rica is a global leader in conservation and ecotourism due to its extraordinary biodiversity. Even as much of the land is protected, the allure of experiencing these natural resources attracts tourists from all over the world. How can travelers engage with Costa Rica's distinct climate while honoring and respecting the land?

Top left Scarlet macaw
Top center Tree-climbing crab
Top right Iguana

DANIEL LAMBORN/SHUTTERSTOCK

Costs & Benefits

Much of Costa Rica's allure lies in its unmatched natural environment. It's a major selling point for its tourism marketing, as ecotourism is a burgeoning national industry. However, with the increasing popularity of Costa Rica's nature adventures, mass tourism puts these environments at risk. This is felt acutely in Península de Osa, which *National Geographic* named 'the most biologically intense place on Earth,' and where multinational hotel corporations with political backing are looking to expand.

The southern region and Península de Osa encompass a vast range of climates, from mountain highlands to cloud forests to tropical rainforests and beaches. The landscape is lush, the water fresh and the air crisp. Local experts in each of these areas have noted the delicate balance between encouraging tourism and preserving the habitat. Tourism boosts the local economy and is a means to share culture and educate visitors about the land. Yet many of these remote places don't have the infrastructure to sustain the increasing visitor numbers. This can drain natural resources and negatively impact the local families who have built these communities for generations.

San Gerardo de Rivas, for example, has gained popularity for international expats looking for retirement or investment properties. The increase in construction affects the cloud-forest microclimate while also raising prices for longtime Tico residents. Another issue is that Parque Nacional Corcovado is becoming a top destination, but the infrastructure in Bahía Drake isn't designed to accommodate large numbers of tourists. Thus electrical

DANIEL LAMBORN/SHUTTERSTOCK

JON NICHOLLS PHOTOGRAPHY/SHUTTERSTOCK

blackouts are common. Also, more visitors in the park means more disturbance to the animals and foot traffic on the trails. Although permits are required to visit, Costa Rica hasn't been tracking the number of visitors to monitor the impact. Because Parque Nacional Corcovado houses 2.5% of the world's biodiversity, it's critical that efforts to mitigate the effects of increased tourism are made.

Climate change is also an undeniable factor and locals talk about it as a grave threat to the country's unique ecosystems. But when compounded with mass tourism, the environmental impact is even greater. Mass tourism necessitates more highways, hotels and disturbing of the land. Higher temperatures and overdeveloped land definitely shift already fragile conditions.

> The landscape is lush, the water fresh and the air crisp. Yet many of these remote places don't have the infrastructure to sustain the increasing visitor numbers.

Conscious Travelers

As conscious travelers, we can be intentional in how we show up. There are simple things we can do such as bringing reusable water bottles to eliminate single-use plastic bottles and picking up your (and others') trash when on the beach. We can also patronize hotels and restaurants owned by Ticos and/or that use sustainable practices. Lastly, book tours with operators who support local guides and ecotourism excursions that honor the pure splendor of Costa Rica.

Sustainable Tourism

In response to the ballooning tourist economy, Costa Rica's tourism board created a Certification for Sustainable Tourism (CST) to evaluate hotels and lodging operators' use of sustainable practices. It's not a perfect measuring stick since it's a voluntary program, but it encourages tourism businesses to consider their impact on their surrounding natural environment and the local community, and how they engage their visitors in conservation efforts. The country's tourism board incentivizes businesses to step up their sustainability practices by offering promotional opportunities and a branded logo that lets consumers know they are making an ecofriendly choice.

SIGHTS
of the South

01

02

04

01 Dolphins
These marine mammals are ubiquitous, swimming in schools throughout Golfo Dulce and Bahía Drake.

02 Macaws
Scarlet macaws are endangered animals, but are ubiquitous on Península de Osa. They mate for life and always fly in pairs.

03 Coffee Beans
The Santa María region near Providencia de Dota is where Costa Rica's best coffee is grown.

04 Boruca Mask
Indigenous Boruca artists hand-carve and paint these masks to represent their cultural pride and their fight against colonialism.

05 Trap Door Spider
You only see these nocturnal creatures if you know where to look. They camouflage themselves on mossy surfaces.

06 Mono Titi (Squirrel Monkey)

The smallest of all of Costa Rica's monkeys travel in large groups and are found along the central and south Pacific coast.

07 Resplendent Quetzal

This colorful bird revered by the Maya people is found in highland forests, including the Dota region.

08 Cacao Fruit

This plant is sacred to indigenous communities, and visitors can taste it in all forms: beverage, beans and bars.

09 Whales

These massive mammals are a common sight as they migrate up and down the Pacific coast all year long.

10 Diquís Spheres

These mysterious stone spheres date back to the pre-Columbian indigenous societies that lived throughout the region.

01 NEIRFY/SHUTTERSTOCK, **02** SANIT FUANGNAKHON/SHUTTERSTOCK, **03** NATTIKA/SHUTTERSTOCK, **04** SABENA JANE BLACKBIRD/ALAMY, **05** TIMOTHY COTA/GETTY IMAGES, **06** ROSA JAY/SHUTTERSTOCK, **07** RAJH.PHOTOGRAPHY/SHUTTERSTOCK, **08** VALENTYN VOLKO/SHUTTERSTOCK, **09** JONAS GRUHLKE/SHUTTERSTOCK, **10** XENIA_PHOTOGRAPHY/SHUTTERSTOCK

Listings

BEST OF THE REST

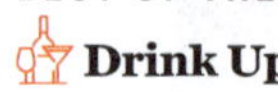

Drink Up

DinerCraft Bar and Restaurant $$$

Stop by the bar in Bahía Drake's Hotel Margarita for fresh fruit margaritas and craft cocktails. Stay for an exquisite seafood dinner.

Playa Blanca Beach Bar $

Sip on a cold Pilsen with local Ticos and other tourists as you take in the gorgeous Golfo Dulce scenery.

Batsu Gastropub $$

Taste some Costa Rica craft beers and cocktails made with fresh ingredients at this family-friendly pub and restaurant near Parque Nacional Chirripó.

For the Foodies

Kapi Kapi $$

Start your day in San Gerardo de Rivas with creative concoctions of fresh fruit, herbs and other locally sourced ingredients. Extensive dinner menu for health-conscious travelers.

Marea Alta $

Visitors and locals in Bahía Drake enjoy delicious food and a great soundtrack. Try the squash ceviche or hefty *casados* (set meals).

Flacos Bar $

This popular place in Térraba town specializes in seafood and scrumptious burgers.

Soda Marbella $$

You know it's good because the locals are here. This is the go-to spot in Puerto Jiménez for seafood, especially ceviche.

Kalaluna Bistró $$$

Enjoy a flavorful fusion of Mediterranean and Latin American cuisine at this gourmet restaurant along the coast of Bahía Drake.

Iguana Lodge $$$

Dine beachside overlooking Playa Platanares in Puerto Jiménez. Taste the lemony super slaw among various other salad and fresh fish options.

Soda Leila $

A great pit stop after a day of snorkeling and swimming in Playa Blanca. Some of the best *casados* in the area.

Truchero Los Cocolisos $$

Catch your own fish at this trout farm and restaurant in San Gerardo de Rivas. Fun for families and groups who want to try trout prepared in different ways.

Drake's Kitchen $$

Can't go wrong with seafood and ceviche at this riverside family-run restaurant in Bahía Drake. It also has lodging available.

Buena Esperanza (Martina's Bar) $$

If you get hungry on your way to or from Parque Nacional Corcovado, stop at this delightful open-air restaurant near Matapalo. Don't leave without trying the locally made ice cream.

Robino's Foodies $

Hip little place on the main square in San Gerardo de Rivas. Take a seat on the balcony overlooking the forest and fill up on pizza and comfort foods.

Soda Jiménez Colectivo $

Tico home cooking for breakfast, lunch and dinner in Puerto Jimenez. Affordable and filling *casados*, nachos and *empanadas* (turnovers stuffed with meat and cheese) are crowd pleasers.

Mar Luna Lodge $$$

A hidden gem near Cabo Matapalo with artisanal pizzas with a house-made crust, and refreshing cocktails to enjoy poolside.

 Gifts Galore

Puerto Jiménez Souvenir Shop

It's a one-stop shop for goods made by local artisans and farmers. Peruse jewelry, chocolate, bathing suits and more.

Museo Comunitario Indígena de Boruca

Support the indigenous Boruca artisans by purchasing woven wallets, bags and home goods, as well as Boruca masks.

 Adventure Time

Extreme Bike Trails

For the hard-core bikers, join Senderos Providencia on harrowing dirt trails through the Talamanca Mountains of Providencia de Dota.

Psycho Tours

Not your typical tours. Play in nature near Matapalo with guided activities like tree climbing and waterfall rappelling.

Osa Wild

The hub for ecotourism experiences throughout Península de Osa. Based in Puerto Jiménez, Osa Wild can connect you to a variety of outdoor adventures with expert naturalist guides.

Lokal Travels

Comprehensive trip planning focused on ecotourism and rural tourism itineraries

JUAN CARLOS MUNOZ/ALAMY

Museo Comunitario Indígena de Boruca

that support local businesses, covering Providencia de Dota, San Gerardo de Rivas, Térraba and Península de Osa.

Sand, Swimming & Sunbathing

Playa San Josecito

This quiet, golden-sand beach outside Bahía Drake is perfect for sunbathing and relaxing. Beware of the strong currents when swimming.

Playa Colorada

One of the main beaches in Bahía Drake. There are many restaurants and shops along the shore, but try a ceviche *caldosa* from the family-owned food truck.

Playa Blanca

This beach along the Golfo Dulce is known as one of the cleanest beaches in Costa Rica. A jump-off point for snorkeling tours outside Puerto Jiménez.

Playa Platanares

Enjoy a lazy beach day at this local beach on the outskirts of Puerto Jiménez, with sweeping views of Golfo Dulce.

Scan to find more things to do in Southern Costa Rica & Península de Osa online

Practicalities

Right Santa Teresa (p171)

EASY STEPS FROM THE AIRPORT TO THE CITY CENTER

Most travelers visiting the country come through either of the two international airports: Juan Santamaría International Airport (SJO) or Guanacaste Airport (LIR) – also known as the Daniel Oduber Quirós International Airport – in Liberia, in Costa Rica's northwest. At SJO there are two terminals: the main terminal for international travel and the domestic terminal for short in-country flights.

AT THE AIRPORT

SIM CARDS
At SJO, there's a Claro SIM-card stand in baggage claim where you can purchase a prepaid Costa Rican SIM card. It's open daily from 5am to 9pm and later on weekends. There's nowhere to buy a SIM card at LIR, so go to a cellphone store or supermarket.

CURRENCY EXCHANGE
There are 24-hour Global Exchange counters in the lobby and boarding area and at baggage-claim carousels 3 and 5 at SJO. At LIR, there are Global Exchange exchange counters in the lobby, customs, baggage claim and by international departures.

GIANFRANCO VIVI/SHUTTERSTOCK

WI-FI There is free wi-fi at both SJO (Network Free SJO) and LIR (Network Liberia Airport Wifi).

ATMS At SJO, there are ATMs in the baggage-claim area and by departures. At LIR, there's an ATM in the arrivals hall.

CHARGING STATIONS Electrical outlets are plentiful throughout SJO and LIR.

CUSTOMS REGULATIONS
Travelers are allowed to bring 400 cigarettes or 50 cigars or 500g tobacco. Travelers over 18 can bring 3L of alcoholic beverages.

GETTING TO SAN JOSÉ CITY CENTER

UBER Generally more cost-effective than taxis, an Uber from SJO to the San José city center costs US$15 to US$20 and takes 30 to 50 minutes.

BUS Two companies, Tuasa and Station Wagon, offer bus service from SJO to downtown San José for ₡400 (payable in colones only). Both buses stop across from the arrivals terminal.

TRAIN The train is not that convenient because it requires a 2.5km taxi ride to the Alajuela railway station, from where it's a 50-minute train ride to San José. A one-way ticket costs ₡800.

SHUTTLES
Various travel companies offer direct shuttle buses (US$23 to US$35) from SJO to hotels in the city center, with advance arrangements.

DOMESTIC TERMINALS
If you fly into the domestic terminal at SJO, the ride-share pick-up location is a five-minute walk from the terminal's exit.

TAXIS These are available at the airport, but usually cost more than Uber.

OTHER POINTS OF ENTRY

If you're flying into Guanacaste Airport (LIR), the Liberia city center is a 10-minute drive east of the airport; however, most visitors head west to the beaches and towns on the Pacific coast. The airport is a one-hour drive from Tamarindo and two hours from Sámara. Most car-rental agencies offer free shuttles from the airport to their nearby car centers.

Alternatively, shared and private shuttle services are available to hotels in Tamarindo, Papagayo, Playas del Coco, Sámara and other popular beach locations. Book in advance and the shuttle will be waiting for you at the airport. A public bus to Liberia from the airport will cost about US$1.

Cruise-ship passengers enter at ports in Puntarenas on the Pacific coast and Limón City on the Caribbean coast. If you're traveling over land, there are border crossings with Nicaragua in the north (at Peñas Blancas) and with Panama in the south (at Pasa Canoas and Sixaola). To enter, you'll have to show proof of your ticket for an outbound flight within the period of your visa validity (90 or 180 days, depending on your country of origin).

TRANSPORT TIPS TO HELP YOU GET AROUND

For the most flexibility, renting a car allows travelers to go wherever they want, at their own pace. That said, it is possible to explore most of Costa Rica using public buses and private shuttles, with the occasional supplemental tour or taxi trip. Domestic flights are also useful for longer-distance destinations.

BUSES

Buses are a low-cost way to travel throughout the country. Private companies operate the buses depending on the region and thus bus condition varies. Know the name of the company you're traveling with because each company has its own bus stop.

BOAT

Many ferries are more like motorboats than barges. Tortuguero and Parismina are only accessible by boat; Bahía Drake is also often reached by boat. Car ferries ply the routes between Puerto Jiménez and Golfito, and between Puntarenas and Península de Nicoya.

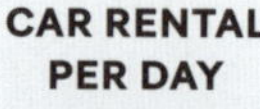

CAR RENTAL PER DAY

Sedan
US$15 to US$65

SUV
US$25 to US$75

Pick-up truck
from US$65

CAR RENTAL Make sure to rent a car that has 4WD, especially if you're traveling during rainy season (June through November) or planning to drive in more rural or remote areas. These vehicles tend to be listed as medium SUVs. It's a good rule of thumb to have a 4WD for most road trips in Costa Rica considering some roads may be unpaved or there may be stream and river crossings.

TOURIST SHUTTLES An alternative to public buses, tourist shuttle services are faster, more comfortable and more expensive. They offer online booking and door-to-door service in popular tourist destinations.

DOMESTIC FLIGHTS Domestic flights are a quick way to get to remote places. These propeller planes usually carry 20 to 25 people, which may be unnerving for those used to much larger planes. Enjoy the breathtaking views and avoiding long drives, bumpy roads and traffic.

DRIVING ESSENTIALS

Costa Rica drives on the right side of the road.

Two-lane highways are the norm.

The normal speed limit on the highway is 90km/h (56mph).

18

The legal driving age is 18, but to rent a car it's usually 21 to 23.

Important signs: **Ceda al paso** (Yield), **No hay paso** (Do not enter), **Cruce de fauna** (Animal crossing), **Puente Angosto** (Narrow bridge)

INSURANCE

When renting a car, you're legally required to pay for third-party liability insurance, so add an extra US$12 to US$20 a day to any online quotes. If your credit card provides collision insurance, you needn't take out that coverage with the rental agency; however, you may need to show proof. To avoid unexpected charges, skip the third-party booking engines and book your car directly with a rental agency.

ROAD CONDITIONS

When driving in the mountains, be on the alert for *derrumbes* (landslides), particularly during or after rain. Rainy season can also make unpaved roads and river crossings more treacherous.

AFTER DARK

Whenever possible, avoid driving after dark, as most roads and highways have no lighting so it's impossible to see potholes, wildlife and other possible hazards, not to mention signs and turnoffs.

KNOW YOUR CARBON FOOTPRINT

A domestic round-trip flight from SJO to Puerto Jiménez would emit 213kg of carbon dioxide per passenger. A SUV or van would emit 152kg for the same distance. There are a number of carbon calculators online. We use Resurgence at *resurgence.org/resources/carbon-calculator.*

ROAD DISTANCE CHART (KM)

	Cahuita	Jacó	La Fortuna	Limón City	Manuel Antonio	Manzanillo	Puerto Viejo	San José	Tamarindo
Jacó	300								
La Fortuna	255	150							
Limón City	45	255	215						
Manuel Antonio	320	70	220	265					
Manzanillo	30	330	285	75	340				
Puerto Viejo	20	320	270	60	320	15			
San José	200	100	130	160	140	235	220		
Tamarindo	460	235	210	415	300	490	485	260	
Uvita	350	125	275	310	65	385	370	220	360

SAFE TRAVEL

Costa Rica is a generally safe country for travelers. As with most destinations, use common sense to protect yourself from theft by securing your wallets and purses and not leaving your belongings unattended on the beach.

FAKE TAXIS There's a common scam targeting solo travelers waiting at bus stops. If you're at a bus stop, do not get into a 'taxi' that tells you the bus has already left or there's a strike, and offers to take you to the next stop. The driver will take you to an ATM to extort money.

SEX TOURISM Sex work is legal in Costa Rica, so it's a popular destination for sex tourism. San José and Jacó are particularly known for their abundance of sex workers. Women travelers, especially solo, should do research before booking hotels because some are known to cater specifically for sex tourism.

DRUGS Medical marijuana is legal, but recreational marijuana is illegal, even though you'll smell it everywhere. Drug possession for immediate personal use is decriminalized, but police may stop and search you, and it's up to their discretion what constitutes 'personal use.' Cocaine and hallucinogens are plentiful. Use at your own risk.

Riptides The biggest danger to tourists in Costa Rica is riptides – strong currents that pull a swimmer in different directions. If you are caught in a riptide, do not struggle against the current. Instead, swim parallel to shore (or float) until the riptide dissipates.

TRAIL SAFETY Never attempt to pet, handle or feed wildlife. When hiking in the forest, wear long pants and closed-toed shoes to protect against poisonous snakes that may be camouflaged in the grass.

DENGUE FEVER

This painful viral infection, transmitted by mosquitoes, will ruin your vacation. The best way to prevent dengue is using bug repellent, especially at sunset when mosquitoes are most active.

PLANT MEDICINE

Many travelers are interested in trying plant medicine like ayahuasca. These plants can have powerful effects on those who consume them, so do your research on who is administering the ceremony and their plan for health emergencies.

FAR RIGHT: ANDI EDWARDS/ALAMY
RIGHT: DAVID HAVEL/SHUTTERSTOCK

QUICK TIPS TO HELP YOU MANAGE YOUR MONEY

ATMS Banco Nacional and Banco de Costa Rica (BCR) are the most ubiquitous banks and ATMs. In San José, you'll find international banks like HSBC and Scotiabank. Most ATMs offer the option of Spanish or English, and the option of colones or dollars. Most cities and towns have ATMs; however, rural areas, even if tourist-friendly, may not. Always have cash on you.

CURRENCY
Costa Rica's national currency is colones. The colorful bills depict local animals including capuchin monkeys, sloths, hummingbirds and more.

CREDIT CARDS
Visa and Mastercard are accepted by most businesses around the country. Major hotel or rental-car chains may accept American Express. Always carry some cash.

CURRENCY

colones (₡)

HOW MUCH FOR A

Cup of coffee
US$1

Guaro sour
US$6

Casado
US$8-10

DOLLARS VS COLONES Although colones are the official currency, US dollars are widely accepted (and sometimes preferred) in Costa Rica. Dollars are acceptable for hotels and tours, but you'll want colones for local restaurants, markets and bus fares. Many ATMs dispense dollars as well as colones. Note that if you pay in dollars, you'll still get change in colones.

TIPPING Tipping in Costa Rica is optional. A tip is not expected, but if you receive excellent service, it is much appreciated by hard-working guides and servers.

EXTRA CHARGES
Value-added tax (13%) is added in stores, hotels and restaurants. Usually it's already factored into tour and excursion prices. Restaurants charge a 10% service tax, which may not be included in menu prices.

GREEN SEASON
Prices for flights and accommodations are cheaper outside the peak season (December to April). For the biggest savings, book your trip between August and November, when prices are often cut in half. Pack your rain gear.

SAVING COLONES To spend less while traveling in Costa Rica, do as the Ticos do. Travel by bus and stay in *cabinas* (cabins) or hostels. Eat at local markets and *sodas* (places that serves a counter lunch). Drink tap water – it's free (and safe). Skip expensive tours and choose activities you can do independently. Many beaches and hiking trails are free to access, while national parks and nature preserves have trail systems that are designed for independent exploration.

RESPONSIBLE TRAVEL

Tips to leave a lighter footprint, support local and have a positive impact on local communities.

ON THE ROAD

Cycle or walk when you can. Many popular tourist locations are walkable or have bikes available for rent to explore the surrounding areas.

Travel by tourist shuttle or tour groups instead of renting a car. Carpooling is better for the environment!

Bring a reusable cloth shopping bag to reduce your single-plastic use. Recycling is limited in many parts of the country.

Use reef-safe sunscreen when swimming, snorkeling or doing any water activities. Protect Costa Rica's beautiful and rare coral reefs, which are essential to global ocean health.

Leave it better than you found it. Volunteer with a local conservation group, or do an informal beach cleanup by picking up garbage on the sand whenever possible.

Turn off the lights, fans and air-con when you're out and about to reduce electricity usage.

JARNOGZ/GETTY IMAGES

GIVE BACK

Cloudbridge Nature Reserve *(cloudbridge.org/volunteering/volunteer-opportunities)* is dedicated to protecting the cloud forest in the Cordillera de Talamanca. While many biologists conduct research there, volunteers need no formal education or experience. Volunteers help in various ways: planting trees, greeting visitors and maintaining trails.

Sea Turtle Conservancy *(stcturtle.org/green-turtle-eco-volunteer-program)* offers a Turtle Eco-Volunteer Program for eight days during nesting season from June through November. Volunteers help count eggs, record data and measure turtles.

Proyecto Asís *(institutoasis.com)* is dedicated to the conservation of local wild animals. Individuals and families can volunteer by preparing food for the animals, cleaning the enclosures, repairing and building enclosures, and making environmental enrichment toys for the rescue animals.

DOS & DON'TS

- **Do** follow the strict 'carry in' – 'carry out' policy at national parks and many private reserves. Don't bring disposable packaging (including bottles) into national parks.
- **Don't** feed wild animals (especially the monkeys at national parks, who are habituated to being fed by tourists). Do make sure your bags are secured at parks and beaches.

LEAVE A SMALL FOOTPRINT

Ecofriendly lodging Many hotels have enacted sustainable practices, including using recycled construction materials, reforestation and utilizing natural springs for water. Look for the Certification for Sustainable Tourism (CST) logo when choosing accommodations. It acknowledges lodging operators who are minimizing their impact on the environment.

Farm life Sample fresh tropical produce, artisanal coffee and other local delicacies at farms and farmers markets. Many farms also offer tours where you can learn how to implement sustainable farming or gardening practices at home.

BARBARA ASH/SHUTTERSTOCK

SUPPORT LOCAL

Book excursions and courses with local tour operators to ensure your money goes directly to locals without agencies taking a big cut.

Explore private reserves to support local organizations and individuals who are doing their part to protect wild territory.

Take a hike on El Camino de Costa Rica (p93) to discover remote villages and indigenous communities that have rarely seen the tramp of tourists' feet.

CLIMATE CHANGE & TRAVEL

Lonely Planet urges all travellers to engage with their travel carbon footprint, which will mainly come from air travel. While there often isn't an alternative, travellers can look to minimise the number of flights they take, opt for newer aircrafts and use cleaner ground transportation, such as trains.

One proposed solution – purchasing carbon offsets – unfortunately does not cancel out the impact of individual flights. While most destinations will depend on air travel for the foreseeable future, for now, pursuing ground-based travel where possible is the best course of action.

The UN Carbon Offset Calculator shows how flying impacts a household's emissions:

The ICAO's carbon emissions calculator allows visitors to analyse the CO2 generated by point-to-point journeys:

RESOURCES

turismo-sostenible.co.cr
sinac.go.cr
ateccr.org
terraba.org

UNIQUE AND LOCAL WAYS TO STAY

As an international leader in ecotourism, Costa Rica has a plethora of ecolodges and sustainable lodging options. They range from luxurious high-end hotels to cozy, low-frills family cabins, with options for travelers across the spectrum. The through line is that many travelers want to be surrounded by, and connected to, the country's natural grandeur.

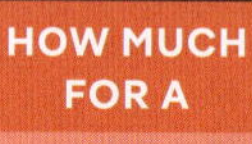

HOW MUCH FOR A

Hostel per night
US$25-45

Hotel per night
US$125-250

Ecolodge per night
US$200-400

NICK FOX/SHUTTERSTOCK

HOMESTAYS

Staying with a family is one of the best ways to learn about Costa Rica and its people. Many families in rural and remote areas have cabins on their property that they rent out to visitors. These often include home-cooked meals and specific excursions that reflect the culture and attractions of the area. At **El Descanso Térraba**, stay within a Brörán community in cabins on their family's ancestral land. In Rancho Quemado, enjoy warm hospitality and home-cooked meals offered by a local family at **Rancho Verde de Osa**.

SURF CAMPS

Make your surfing dreams come true at a surf-camp stay on Península de Nicoya or along the central Pacific coast. Numerous camps offer seven- to 10-day programs to teach beginners fundamentals, or to help expert surfers enhance their existing skills. These packages usually include accommodations, equipment, meals, local transportation and daily lessons.

SERGE GOUJON/SHUTTERSTOCK

CABINAS, CASITAS & CONTAINERS

Most accommodations in Costa Rica are smallish, family-owned lodgings, often in the form of cabins. Traditionally, *cabinas* are very basic and inexpensive rooms. But there are plenty of midrange and upscale lodgings with comfortable and stylish cabins, sometimes called *casitas* (little houses). In recent years, even shipping containers have been converted into attractive cabins.

MAQUENQUE LODGE

TREEHOUSES

Your inner child will be overjoyed to spend the night in an actual treehouse in the middle of the rainforest. The Maquenque Lodge (Boca Tapada) has treehouses 12m above the ground with unobstructed views. No buildings or other treehouses are in sight because it's a 10-minute hike from the main lodge. Rooms have everything you'd need, including hot water, coffee and tea maker, a minibar and a furnished terrace. They also include one screen wall so they're completely open to the sights and sounds of the forest. A full breakfast, a guided hike and canoeing on the nearby lagoon are all included in the price.

Located deep in the rainforest, 25m up in a Nispero tree, Nature Observatorio is another fantastic treehouse experience. (It may be in a different tree by the time you get here, since it moves every seven years.) Strap into a harness and ascend a rope like an arborist to reach this unique structure, built without a single nail. Surrounded by the rustles and chirps of the nocturnal jungle, you'll sleep in a hammock (or a bed, if you prefer), bathe in a rainwater shower, and receive meals in a basket via rope.

BOOKING

Book your lodging six months in advance for travel during the peak tourist season (December through March) when accommodations fill up quickly. The busiest times, particularly for coastal destinations, are the holiday season around Christmas and New Year, and Semana Santa (Easter Week) because of the influx of international tourists and domestic tourists from San José.

You can book Costa Rica accommodations on the major booking sites, but there are also some country-specific sites that focus on unique experiences:

Costa Rica Guides *(costaricaguides.com)* This vacation planning service can help organize hotels, transportation and tours all around the country.

Arenal Costa Rica *(arenal.net)* Choose from loads of lodgings in La Fortuna area, with filters like 'volcano views' and 'hot-spring hotels.'

Costa Rican Vacations *(vacationscostarica.com)* Local experts custom-design vacation around an appropriate theme like family, adventure or honeymoon.

Luxury Villas Costa Rica *(luxuryvillasincostarica.com)* Dozens of stunning properties, mostly located on the Península de Nicoya.

ALL-INCLUSIVE

All-inclusive options are available for those looking for a contained and easy vacation experience. Most all-inclusive hotels are located in Guanacaste or along the Pacific coast and many are adults only.

ESSENTIAL NUTS-AND-BOLTS

DRONES

Flying a drone is legal in Costa Rica, but foreign flyers must be registered with the Dirección General de Aviación Civil (DGAC).

4WD REQUIRED

A 4WD is required to navigate unpaved roads, river crossings and remote regions, especially during rainy season.

WI-FI

Wi-fi is common (and free) in hostels, hotels, cafes, restaurants and some public places.

FAST FACTS

Time Zone
CST (-6 GMT)

Country Code
+506

Electricity
110V/60Hz

GOOD TO KNOW

The legal drinking age is 18.

Visitors from most countries in Europe, North America and South America are allowed to stay in Costa Rica for a maximum of 180 days.

Costa Rica has no military.

Costa Rica uses the metric system.

The national language is Spanish, but in tourist destinations most people also speak English.

ACCESSIBLE TRAVEL

Under Costa Rican law it's mandatory for all public and private establishments to provide accessible services. However, implementation is dependent on the location, particularly with regard to transportation like taxis, buses or domestic flights. Check out the Costa Rica Accessible Tourism Network *(costaricaturismoaccesible.com)*.

Many national parks have accessible trails for people in wheelchairs or with limited mobility. Check in advance at the Sistema Nacional de Áreas de Conservación website (SINAC; *sinac.go.cr*).

Costa Rican Accessible Tourism Network *(costaricaturismoaccesible.com/donatapa/playa-accesible)* has created wheelchair-accessible paths and entrances for certain beaches across the country.

Hotels are more likely to be wheelchair-accessible than rental homes, which often have stairs or unpaved paths. Check with the hotel or rental-home owner before booking to ensure entrances and bathrooms are suited to those with disabilities.

Specialized tour companies offer trips for wheelchair users, including Il Viaggio Travel Costa Rica *(ilviaggiocr.com)* and Wheel the World *(wheeltheworld.com)*.

SMOKING

Smoking is banned in all public places, including restaurants, bars, casinos and public transportation.

STREET FOOD

Street food – often for sale at the beach or at roadside markets – is a great option for a cheap, quick and satisfying snack.

TAP WATER

Tap water is safe to drink almost everywhere in Costa Rica.

FAMILY TRAVEL

Airport aid Families with small children enjoy expedited service through immigration upon arrival at both international airports.

Discounts for kids Children under the age of 12 enjoy many discounts, including 25% off domestic airplane fares and reduced rates for museums, activities and lodgings.

Facilities Most restaurants have high chairs on hand, but changing tables are a rarity. Baby products like diapers and formula are widely available.

RESTAURANT MEALS

Meals in restaurants are a leisurely experience, even at lunchtime. Food is generally prepared from scratch at the time of the order, so it doesn't appear on the table right away. Allow plenty of time for your lunch break and you'll enjoy it much more.

TO FLUSH OR NOT TO FLUSH

Because of rudimentary plumbing and low water pressure, it is best to dispose of toilet paper (and feminine hygiene products) in the trash. Avoid flushing anything that doesn't come out of your body.

SERGIO A. SIMON/SHUTTERSTOCK

LGBTIQ+ TRAVELERS

Costa Rica is one of the most liberal countries in the region for LGBTIQ+ rights, legalizing gay marriage, allowing transgender people to change their gender on legal documents, and passing anti-discrimination laws codifying penalties for hate crimes.

Pride events take place in San José (Marcha de la Diversidad) and Manuel Antonio (Orgulio en la Playa) in June or July.

Manuel Antonio is a long-standing hot spot for gay travel, with dedicated hotels, tour agencies and spas. Follow *@gaymanuelantonio* for more info.

LANGUAGE

Spanish pronunciation is easy, as most sounds have equivalents in English. Also, Spanish spelling is phonetically consistent, meaning that there's a clear and consistent relationship between what you see in writing and how it's pronounced.

If you read our pronunciation guides as if they were English, you'll be understood. Note that *kh* is a throaty sound (like the '*ch*' in the Scottish loch), *v* and *b* are like a soft English '*v*' (between a '*v*' and a '*b*'), and *r* is strongly rolled. The stressed syllables are in italics in our pronunciation guides.

BASICS

Hello.	*Hola.*	*o*·la
Goodbye.	*Adiós.*	a·*dyos*
Yes.	*Sí.*	see
No.	*No.*	no
Please.	*Por favor.*	por fa·*vor*
Thank you.	*Gracias.*	*gra*·syas
Excuse me.	*Con permiso.*	kon per·*mee*·so
Sorry.	*Perdón.*	per·*don*

What's your name?

¿Cómo se llama usted?	*ko*·mo se *ya*·ma oo·*sted* (polite)
¿Cómo te llamas?	*ko*·mo te *ya*·mas (informal)

My name is ...

Me llamo ...	me *ya*·mo ...

Do you speak English?

¿Habla inglés?	*a*·bla een·*gles* (polite)
¿Hablas inglés?	*a*·blas een·*gles* (informal)

I don't understand.

Yo no entiendo.	yo no en·*tyen*·do

TIME & NUMBERS

What time is it?	*¿Qué hora es?*	ke *o*·ra es
It's (10) o'clock.	*Son (las diez).*	son (las dyes)
Half past (1).	*Es (la una) y media.*	es (la *oo*·na) ee *me*·dya
morning	*mañana*	ma·*nya*·na
afternoon	*tarde*	*tar*·de
evening	*noche*	*no*·che
yesterday	*ayer*	a·*yer*
today	*hoy*	oy
tomorrow	*mañana*	ma·*nya*·na

1	*uno*	*oo*·no	**6**	*seis*	seys
2	*dos*	dos	**7**	*siete*	*sye*·te
3	*tres*	tres	**8**	*ocho*	*o*·cho
4	*cuatro*	*kwa*·tro	**9**	*nueve*	*nwe*·ve
5	*cinco*	*seen*·ko	**10**	*diez*	dyes

EMERGENCIES

Help!	*¡Socorro!*	so·*ko*·ro
Go away!	*¡Váyase!*	*va*·ya·se
Call a ...!	*¡Llame a ...!*	*ya*·me a...
the police	*la policía*	la po·lee·*see*·a
a doctor	*un doctor*	oon dok·*tor*
I'm lost.	*Estoy perdido/a.*	es·*toy* per·*dee*·do/a (m/f)

Index

000 Map pages

F

G

H

P

Q

R

S

'I had to hold back tears when I saw a mama whale and her baby on the boat ride to Parque Nacional Corcovado (p224). It was so beautiful!'

JANNA ZINZI

'On my birthday, I woke up to a rare clear view of Volcán Arenal (pictured left; p119). Mother Nature's birthday present.'

MARA VORHEES

'Volcán Irazú (p63) holds a special place in my heart and each visit feels unique. It's always an adventure and the view feels, in every way, transcendent.'

ROBERT ISENBERG

'Hiking through the cloud forest in Providencia de Dota (p212) transported me to another world. I can still see the verdant greens in my mind's eye.'

JANNA ZINZI

'That time I got some uninvited guests at my jungle treehouse – a band of coatis (pictured right) escaping the rain.'

MARA VORHEES

TOP: MARICEL QUESADA/SHUTTERSTOCK
BOTTOM: BUCHPETZER/SHUTTERSTOCK

THIS BOOK

Commissioning Editor
Jen Ruiz

Production Editor
Jenni McCann

Cartographer
Val Kremenchutskaya

Image Editor
Gwen Cotter

Assisting editors
Imogen Bannister, Felicity Hughes, Helen Koehne, Brana Vladisavljevic

Cover researcher
Kat Marsh

Thanks
Ronan Abayawickrema, Sofie Andersen, Karen Hendeson, Alison Killilea, Robin Yule

lonely planet

NEW YORK CITY

John Garry

Scale cloud-piercing tower
panoramic views. Catch a ferry
topped harbor islands. Open d
grand buildings built for roy
respects at monuments hon
legends. Deck yourself out
from unique boutiques. S
global dining options. S
inside hidden speakea
excitement as curtai
show. Walk streets g
lights from skyscra

This is New Yor

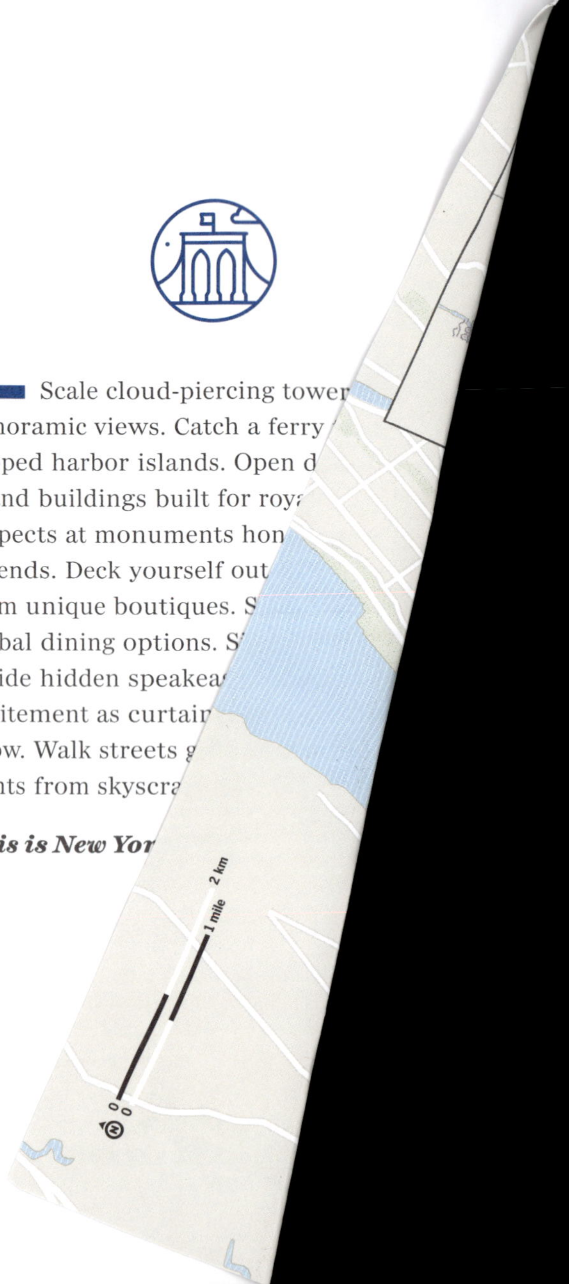

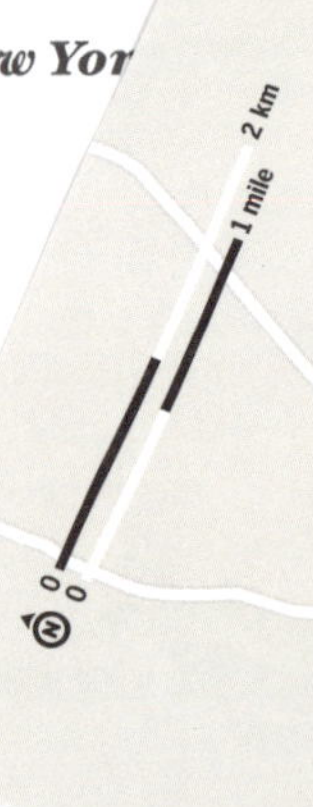